DATE DUE

Return Material Promptly

Create Your Own Love Story

The Art of Lasting Relationships

David W. McMillan, Ph.D.

BEYOND
WORDS
Publishing

Beyond Words Publishing, Inc.
20827 N.W. Cornell Road, Suite 500
Hillsboro, Oregon 97124-9808
503-531-8700
1-800-284-9673

Editor: Ann Bennett
Cover design: Principia Graphica
Typesetting: William H. Brunson, Typography Services
Printer: Publishers Press
Proofreader: Marvin Moore

Printed in the United States of America
Distributed to the book trade by Publishers Group West

Library of Congress Cataloging-in-Publication Data

McMillan, David W.
    Create your own love story : the art of lasting relationships / David W. McMillan.
        p.   cm.
    Includes bibliographical references.
    ISBN 1–885223–60–9
    1. Love.   2. Intimacy (Psychology)   3. Interpersonal relations.   I. Title.
    BF575.L8M23   1997
    158.2 — dc21   97-21979
                                                                      CIP

The corporate mission of Beyond Words Publishing, Inc.:
Inspire to Integrity

Contents

Foreword

Many find themselves embarked on a quest: to find a relationship that is alive and vibrant, based on commitment, trust, and understanding. In this search, couples often seek tools and information that will help them integrate passion, equality, integrity, and harmony into their relationships.

My own books and seminars have assisted many men and women on this quest to develop fulfilling personal connections. Vast numbers of us have participated in a quiet revolution in which male and female differences have been embraced with empathy and celebration rather than resolved through dominance: no longer do we expect either partner in a marriage to stifle or sacrifice that which makes him or her uniquely male or female.

I believe that David McMillan's new book complements my own work. Now that men and women face each other as equals who honor each other's differences, it is time for them to write their own love stories — stories that, like all art, are living creations that transcend time. Using a four-part paradigm — Spirit, Trust, Trade, and Art — McMillan empowers couples to create a love that is strong enough to survive external challenges yet nurturant enough to shelter each partner's spirit. Practical, optimistic, and wise, *Create Your Own Love Story* is an invaluable guide for couples on a quest for true love that triumphs over time.

John Gray, author of
Men Are from Mars, Women Are from Venus

Preface

It is a dreary Wednesday night in late November, the month in Nashville when rain seems a permanent condition. I sit at the kitchen table, waiting for my wife to come home and writing the reports to managed-care companies that will allow my patients to continue their work with me. Marietta's car sloshes up the driveway and turns into the garage. I hear the car door open and shut. Through the kitchen window I see her slowly climb the steps with her head down, her briefcase strapped over one shoulder and a large purse hanging heavily from the other. She wears no raincoat and carries no umbrella, indifferent to the rain. I take a towel from the kitchen drawer, and as she comes in the door, I carefully drape it over her head and rub away the rain from her hair as well as I can. "How was your day?" I ask.

"Just like any other day in family court," Marietta tells me. She drops her briefcase and purse on the floor and takes a chair at the kitchen table. "A man hit his wife so hard he broke her nose, all because she wouldn't let him talk to his son on the phone." She folds the damp towel and sets it on the table. "And a woman withdrew ten thousand dollars from a joint savings account and left town with the couple's five-year-old girl. How was your day?"

"Not much better," I confess. "One husband I saw today tested positive for AIDS. His wife knows he's sick, but he doesn't know how to tell her he has AIDS. I saw another man today who's depressed because his wife of twenty-five years left him and moved to Wyoming with a woman. It took him completely by surprise. He came home and found a note from his wife and half the furniture gone."

Marietta and I labor in the fields of marital discord, she as judge and I as therapist. We share similar stories nearly every day, stories that bewilder us at times and make us wonder whether marriage is an institution peculiarly subject to disorder and violence. Stories like these seriously challenge the notion that people are capable of embracing a set of rules or acquiring skills that will help their marriages endure and thrive.

Marriage used to be a much more stable institution than it is today. Those who study the subject point to social changes affecting the stability of modern marriages: the increase in premarital sex, availability of contraceptives, reduced legal and social stigmas against children born out of wedlock, increase in the number of working women, and changes in concepts of male and female roles. All these changes have contributed to the fragility of marriage as an institution. And its stability is affected, far more than in the past, by the love relationship between the partners.

In the past Mother and Father perhaps loved each other, or perhaps they did not. Whether they did or not was irrelevant. Society then separated the ideas of love and marriage. Today, for better or worse, most couples demand love in a relationship. If love leaves a couple in this culture, they will probably divorce. Families disintegrate. Children lose their father and sometimes their mother. Children from divorced homes become statistics proving how damaging divorce can be. These children are more likely to replicate divorce in their own marriages, drop out of school, become pregnant out of wedlock, become criminals, abuse others, drink, and do drugs than are the children of intact marriages.

Some experts argue that divorce as an epidemic is leveling off. The rate shot from 2.2 divorces per thousand Americans per year in 1960 to 5.3 per thousand in the latter seventies, and in 1993 it slid down to 4.6 per thousand. But it is difficult to take comfort in the fact that now 60 percent of marriages fail instead of 67 percent. Is this where we want to level off? At this rate more than one million American children endure parental divorce each year.

In the last forty years a great deal of research has gone into explaining why males and females have such a difficult time maintaining their love for each other. Many believe that the differences between males and females are so pronounced that their living together in a love relationship is almost impossible.

Contemporary research has helped us understand why people marry and why things so often go wrong. Much of it unfortunately tends to support the common belief that the excitement of courtship inevitably turns into the weariness and cynicism of married life. Many believe that men and women are ultimately incompatible and that love cannot long survive marriage. Is there any hope?

I believe there is. Marriage as an institution offers incalculable benefits for society as well as for individuals. Marriage is good for raising healthy children. It has the calming effect on young males essential for a stable society. It creates an intimate community of two people who can help each other and care for each other—and it may be the last best hope for individual happiness. Because our culture has connected marriage with love and passion, our challenge is to find a way to build strong marriages that nurture and contain love and passion.

This is no easy task. The difficulty lies not only in the work demanded of each partner but also in the fact that the road to a vital marriage is full of surprises. For example: Who would have thought that the remedy for disappearing sexual passion is not losing a few pounds, buying sexy lingerie, or learning clever lovemaking techniques but is actually found in a certain way of handling the truth? And who would have guessed that it is not necessary to deny the mercenary or "negotiating" aspect of marriage but on the contrary to affirm this aspect as part of a healthy relationship? These kinds of surprises require us to give up conventional ideas about marriage and deeply ingrained ideas about each other in order to build more satisfying relationships.

To date no one has offered a social research-based theory of what love is and explained how it works in ways offering couples practical tools they can use to mend, improve, and revitalize their relationships. What is love? How do we get it, nurture it, and sustain it? How can we best prepare people to find their way through the forest called marriage, where the path can quickly turn into a tangle of demands for time, energy, and attention, and into a thicket of concerns about money, sex, children, health, and death? Our culture needs answers to these questions.

Politicians are scrambling to be the first to say that government must step in to protect relationships and families. The Democrats have proposed a Families First Contract. The Republicans have proposed a Contract with America, ostensibly to protect the family. Some legislators are at work on making divorce more difficult by ending no-fault divorce as a legal option. All are responding to real and urgent problems that American families face today.

The problem of making love last, however, does not lend itself to political solutions. Preventive and therapeutic programs seem to offer more promise. One such program, developed by a ministerial alliance in Modesto, California, and Austin, Texas, requires couples who plan to marry to take part in serious premarital counseling and marriage training, and it claims impressive success. The outcome of programs like these encourages new optimism in marriage as an institution. Perhaps it is salvageable, open to reform and improvement. We can develop a new confidence in the idea that people can gain practical skills enabling them to nurture their marriages and make love last.

In *Create Your Own Love Story*, I embrace this optimism and confidence. Using practical knowledge gleaned from years of clinical experience and a belief in the power of stories as teaching parables, I have attempted to provide answers to many of today's questions about love and marriage.

Theories offer explanations. They demonstrate the relationships between causes and effects. They clear up mysteries. My theory of how love works grew out of my view of marriage as an intimate community. The principles applied to larger communities can also be applied to couples. My hope is that this book will provide a place where the reader can come for help, encouragement, and practical advice.

When I was a boy, I always longed for "something more." When I was six, I thought that once I got a bicycle, then everything would be OK. When I was eight, it was a baseball glove that I thought would make the difference in my life. When I was twelve, it was a football jacket. When I was fourteen, it was a driver's license. When I was sixteen, it was a car. When I was twenty-five, it was a Ph.D. But there was one thing that transcended all the others, and that was a promise I got from Walt Disney movies that once I met the right person and could get her to love me, I would live happily ever after.

After years of personal marital experience and in helping others with their marriages, I can safely say that finding love is not a destination. It is the beginning of a journey, a for-better-or-worse journey—and there are a lot of times when it feels like it's worse. A relationship requires work. It challenges us as much or more than it comforts us. This book is about that work, the work that comes after you've begun the happily-ever-after journey. You will discover that once you accept love as a process and not a product, the work becomes easy and the rewards plentiful.

Acknowledgments

My mentor, therapist, supervisor, and friend Bob Stepbach told me some years ago that life lacks an important dimension if your imagination is not somehow artfully engaged. Since I couldn't draw or carry a tune, writing was the only choice left for me. Bob's faith in me and my art gave me the confidence to take on this project.

David Yarian gave me four blank tablets for my forty-eighth birthday and told me to write a book. And so I did.

I wrote the first draft in two weeks. I shared it with my agent, Jan Keeling, who agreed to represent me if she could make editorial suggestions. The draft I gave Jan was like taking the reader for a ride on a bumpy, muddy road. She took the manuscript and made it into a paved highway. It took the eye of Cindy Black of Beyond Words Publishing to see the potential in the early draft that was presented to her, and it required her visionary guidance to conduct the book through its many authorial and editorial revisions. Along the way, J. Lee Bonnet, Susan Welch, Bob Newbrough, Brian Barger, Joseph Berger, Stacy Coleman, Susan Lewis, and Beverly Mahan took a crack at it. Lydia Howarth took my book and made it into an interstate highway ride for the reader. Ann Bennett gave the interstate six lanes. I am especially grateful to Gloria Schmittou, who went above and beyond the call of duty, typing draft after draft after draft as this book grew into what you're reading today. On behalf of the reader, I thank all of you for taking the bumps out and widening the road.

I would never have known what love is without my mother, Elizabeth McMillan (1911–1992), and my wife, Marietta Shipley. Thank you is not enough.

How to Use This Book

Each chapter in this book is devoted to a major element of the McMillan Relationship Theory. I describe the place of each element in the theory. Next I turn to stories drawn from my practice with couples. The stories demonstrate the importance of these elements in love relationships. In these stories you will witness people struggling, some more successfully than others, to come to terms with the requirements these elements impose on our relationships. Some are working to reaffirm the spirit that unites them, some to deepen the trust between them, some to improve the trades between them, and others to share the art that sustains their love. Many, of course, are attempting to remedy failings in more than one of these four basic areas.

Following each story I offer practical information, and some of the stories are followed by four-part relationship exercises. Partners wishing to strengthen and revitalize their bond may use this information and the exercises. Partners who have not decided to make a commitment to each other can use this book to help determine if they are indeed ready for a relationship. Learning the skills of empathetic listening and truth-telling will be of value to them for the rest of their lives, and it is not too soon to discuss their ideas about how power will be allocated and how trades will be made should they decide to become a couple. I have used the material in this book with some success with my patients contemplating marriage as well as with those committed to each other.

There are principles involved in loving. Some of us know these principles, or laws, instinctively because our parents modeled them as they loved us and the rest of their family and friends. Those of us who didn't inherit this wisdom from the love of our parents can find ways to learn it. The principles of love outlined in this book and represented in these stories can become part of your life through study and practice until you become a master at using love's laws.

• Using the Relationship Exercises

Throughout the book you will find a series of exercises to help you bring the information in this book to life in your own relationship. Some couples may wish to start with the first exercise and do each one as it occurs. Others may wish to vary the order. Even if you decide to leave out an occasional exercise, do not omit the first two exercises. These exercises are designed to develop the essential skills of truth-telling and empathetic listening. Truth-telling is the foundation for a successful relationship, and empathetic listening makes truth-telling possible. If you do not develop these skills, the other exercises will be meaningless. Each exercise is presented in four parts:

Visualizing

Prepare yourself for the work to come by visualizing. Leave the relationship for a while, and collect yourself. Sit alone, close your eyes, and be still. Let your imagination play with the topic at hand. As you let yourself dream and play, you will become closer to your authentic feelings. Let your thoughts roll through your mind as you talk honestly with yourself without fear of internal or external criticism.

Journal Writing

Now it is time to use journal writing as a vehicle of self-discovery. Do not be concerned about grammar or spelling! Let your written words flow onto the page. Nobody else needs to see this important work.

Talking with Yourself

Find two characters inside yourself, and let them have a dialogue. Return to your visualizing posture for this, or write this dialogue in your journal. Remember that you must divide yourself into two individuals so that you can "argue with yourself." Talk aloud, write your thoughts, or talk silently to yourself. Then you will be ready for the real dialogue with your partner.

Talking with Your Partner

By visualizing, collecting your thoughts in a journal, and starting an internal dialogue, you have understood yourself better and become aware of your own feelings and desires. These three steps prepare you for this final step, the partner dialogue. Remember that the rules of empathy apply to the partner conversation: *listen, pay attention, and reflect.* When you are privately visualizing, journal writing, and talking to yourself, you may be as outrageous (and critical of your partner) as you like. But there is no place for blaming, name-calling, or abusive language when you sit and talk with your partner. If this happens, one or both of you will throw up your defenses, truth-telling will be blocked, and doing the exercise will become a waste of time or a source of further injury.

What If Your Partner Isn't Willing to Participate?

Any time one person in a relationship becomes more self-aware and more competent, the relationship grows in power and resources; it has more than it did before. So even if one partner refuses to participate in the relationship work, the work done by the other partner will have value. Sometimes the "nonparticipating" partner will become aware that he or she can gain a lot from becoming an active participant. This work is something that serves both people, not just one.

The First Story

An Introduction to Love

♦ Abe and Sarah

Obviously the couple in my office loved each other. Both in their forties, they sat close together in the middle of the couch and held hands. Abe was a doctor. He had taken a midday break from his practice for our appointment. He was still wearing his white coat, his tie loosened. Sarah wore a small pearl cross pendant and a neat, loose-fitting skirt and jacket.

"We don't know what to do with him," Sarah said. She was speaking of their twenty-seven-year-old son. "He went to college for seven years. He flunked out of four colleges before he finally graduated with a history/drama major and then came home. He doesn't seem to be able to get a job, even though his father and I have done everything we can to help him."

Abe interrupted. "I used to do his math homework for him, but that didn't work because he couldn't do the problems on a test."

"We always bought him the best," Sarah said.

"Yes," Abe agreed. "The best bike, seven baseball gloves. He lost them all. A new Chevrolet Camaro. After he wrecked that, he went through three used Volvos. His car insurance is four thousand dollars a year."

As they talked about their son, Isaac, they were obviously tense. They appeared to know what had happened and seemed embarrassed as they sat with me, telling the tale of their son's lack of character. I changed the subject. "Tell me about yourselves. How old were you when Isaac was born?"

This subject seemed to release them from the awkwardness of their confessions. They looked warmly at each other in silence.

"We were very young, and circumstances weren't the best," Sarah began. Abe looked at her admiringly as he remembered with her. "I was eighteen and Abe was twenty-one. He was a junior in college, doing well, with a premed major and hopes of med school. He was home from college that summer, working at a grocery store. He had saved enough money to put down his part of the deposit on an apartment near the college so that he and some friends would have a place to live when they started school in late August. He was proud of this, almost as proud as he was of his 1957 blue-and-white Chevrolet with a 257 V-8.

"Abe's parents believed in education, but they also believed in hard work. They paid his college tuition and dormitory fees, but Abe had to work to pay for everything else.

"Then came a day when I had something I had to tell Abe, something that was going to change everything. I knew his shift at the grocery was over at three o'clock, so I waited until just before three to call him at the store. His boss answered the phone. I could barely speak. I muttered, 'Please tell Abe to come by my house on his way home. I need to talk to him.' I had never called Abe at work before. His boss politely took my message.

"It was hard waiting alone on the front porch to talk to Abe. I had already told my mother and father. Mother took to her bed crying, just as she had when my grandfather died. My father took me into his study and closed the doors. We didn't even sit. Both of us just stood there, and he said, 'I'm disappointed in you. I'll contribute to your education, just as I always have, but the rest is now up to you and Abe.' And he walked away, leaving me standing there looking at the books. For weeks afterward he spoke to me only with polite coldness.

"I felt very alone waiting for Abe. I was afraid to face him, afraid he would disappoint me. Finally he drove up in front of the house. I was sitting on the rocking chair on the front porch, leaning forward, not rocking, just waiting. When he opened the door and hopped out of the car, I was already running down the walk to him. After we kissed, I suggested that we go for a walk.

"My knees felt weak as we crossed the street to the park. I headed straight for the large swing that hung from the branch of a big oak tree. 'Push me in the swing,' I told him. I got in the swing, and he pushed. I was glad I couldn't see his face when I finally said, 'I'm pregnant.' He stopped pushing. He said nothing, and the swing slowed and finally stopped.

"'How do you feel about that?' I asked. I was still looking straight ahead. I didn't want to see his face.

"'Well,' he said, 'I don't know exactly *how* I feel.'

"'Why not?' I asked impatiently.

"'Look, Sarah,' he said. '*You* must have known or sus-pected for a while. *I* just found out.'

"When he said that, I began to sob. I let go of the ropes on the swing and covered my face. Abe grabbed the swing and stopped it from wobbling. 'I'm sorry,' I said. I kept saying I was sorry, crying and holding on to myself.

"Abe was kneeling in front of me, holding me and the swing. 'Don't be sorry,' he said. 'I'm scared, but I'm not sorry.'

"'I feel so ashamed,' I said.

"'I'm not,' he said. 'I'm not ashamed of loving you. I hope you're not ashamed of loving me.'

"'I'm not, but I'm ashamed that I will burden you.'

"'Yes, you will,' he said, 'and our child will burden us both—but obviously God thinks we can handle it.'

"'I'm sure we can,' I said. 'I'm not sure I can. My childhood is over,' I said.

"'Mine, too,' he said, and he looked sad for the first time. 'I'll have to tell Mother and Dad,' he said.

"'I've already told my parents. It wasn't fun.'

"'It won't be fun for me, either.'

"'You may have to drop out of school,' I pointed out.

"'I know,' he said, 'but I'll work.'

"'I can type one hundred words a minute,' I volunteered.

"'You'll have to work hard and I will, too,' he said. 'No more shooting baskets with my buddies or drinking until the sun comes up.'

"'No,' I agreed.

"We didn't say anything for a long time. Then he said again, 'I'm scared.'

"'I am too,' I said. And I tried to comfort him as we held each other.

"He put his hand on my stomach, lifted my face so that our eyes met, and with tears in his eyes and a great smile on his face, he said, 'You're having our baby.' Then we cried and held each other and time seemed to stand still.

"He passed the hardest test I think I could ever give him, and since then he has passed many more. I'll never forget those words: 'I'm scared, but I'm not sorry.'"

When Sarah finished talking, the two cried and hugged. Sarah and Abe had shared with me a part of their sacred secrets, a story of a time that called for courage to speak personal truths. Each had possessed enough self-awareness to know and express feelings about the other and about their relationship. Each had been able to summon the courage to tell the other the truth about these feelings. Each had even been able to tell the truth about the negative feelings, the fearful feelings, and each had found a way to do this without blaming the other or causing the other to feel ashamed.

I learned more about how Sarah and Abe had struggled together. They raised their son in the shadow of guilt and shame, which their parents helped to foster. They attempted to compensate for their guilt feelings by indulging their son.

When they came to me, it may have been too late for them to rescue their son from their overindulgence. But as they grounded themselves in one of their sacred secrets, they remembered who they were and celebrated their marriage again together.

Telling me about this sacred secret did not make me a part of the secret. Sharing such a secret is an emotional experience. A person who was not a part of the secret cannot know the secret. No matter how many facts you might relate to another person about a secret, telling the story cannot include that person in the real "knowing." Even after Abe and Sarah told me their story, I really didn't know what they knew about themselves and about each other. This was a knowledge that only they could share completely. It made them members of an exclusive community made up of only two people and a spirit: love.

There is one essential skill that the reader must have to use this book effectively. That skill is the ability to know what you feel. Before going further, you might wish to refer to Appendix A (p. 229) to read about a man who doesn't know how he feels and to see how this problem can be solved.

CHAPTER I

Spirit

The Theory

A Relationship's Passion

The spirit of a relationship involves mystery and wonder. We cannot predict or control it. Think about the initial start-and-stop behavior of couples as they are becoming physically connected. There is a similar kind of uncertainty and fickle spontaneity—of *Here I am*, then *No, I'm not*—involved in the development of a couple's spiritual relationship. Perhaps she becomes connected, and then the connection smothers her. She retreats. Then she yearns to return. She isn't certain how her lover will react. He, too, might be frightened. As she now moves toward him, he backs away. Or he might not care enough to be unsettled by the connection, or he might have the courage to stay for now. How the two get together is a mystery and a wonder to them both, something neither one fully understands or controls.

Spirit is much more than this mystery and wonder. No one knows for certain what causes the spark that ignites a couple's interest in each other. But certainly a relationship's spirit begins with a spark of affection that comes to life when there is a safe atmosphere for telling the truth. Later the spark develops into the spiritual atmosphere that surrounds a couple. The couple may experience the spirit as a third entity, as much a "being" as each of the two individuals making up the relationship.

When people say that love is difficult to define, they refer to the part of love sometimes called spirit, chemistry, passion, or fire. It is the something that brings a couple together, and it becomes the something that defines them together as a unit.

Identifying the source of the initial spark may be impossible, and the couple may think their connection magical when it begins to grow. But they can recognize the conditions that allow that initial spark to grow into the spirit. If

3

they recognize these conditions, they can nurture and maintain them. The conditions essential to the development of the spirit of a love relationship are *telling the truth, empathy, boundaries*, and *a sense of belonging.*

Truth-Telling Is Arousing

Partners sometimes try so hard to protect each other's tender feelings. Their protective defenses become cumbersome. They cannot connect, draw close, or touch each other emotionally because of these defenses. The object of truth-telling is to break down these defenses—to stop the protection and tell the truth.

But there is a catch. Before telling the truth to your partner, you must learn what "the truth" means. Then you must learn how to tell the truth in a way that minimizes the risk of destroying that very thing you want to create.

The truth we are talking about is not about the facts. It is about how you feel. We can always argue about the facts. But you, the speaker, are the authority on how you feel. You are the only one who can represent your emotions. The most powerful truth is how you feel about the other person in the present, the "right-now-as-we-speak" moment.

I call these expressions *sacred secrets*. Such self-disclosures are exciting and dangerous. When you first meet someone, you follow a socially expected script. Whether you call this a line or polite conversation, it means you do not express your real feelings—perhaps a nearly overwhelming desire to touch the other person, or an immediate feeling of trusting the other person, or a fear of rejection. When you follow a script, everyone knows what to do and what to say. But when you tell what you really feel, you change the script, and no one is certain what will occur.

When you speak a sacred secret, the truth is out. You cannot contain it, and you cannot predict or control the outcome. When you tell the sacred secret, you can't predict how your partner will feel or what your partner will say, and you don't know how you will feel once you've heard the response. This is the wonder and mystery of the spirit of love.

In fact, this is the answer to the question, "How can we keep passion in our relationship?" The early stages of most couples' relationships contain a fair amount of sexual passion. With the passage of time and neglect, the passion all too often disappears. "How to keep love alive" is a hot topic in women's magazines, and advice may include preparing sexual surprises, buying slinky nightgowns, and other such tips. But these intriguing suggestions are not the real answer. *The way to keep passion and excitement in a relationship is to learn how to tell each other important truths.* When you throw away the script, you face the challenge to respond to the unpredictable. This need to be creative and aware keeps the excitement and passion in a relationship.

In the final story in this book, I help the two partners speak their truths to each other. After they air the truth, I ask the two if they now feel more sexually interested in each other. This question is not a joke. Telling the truth in a safe atmosphere results in all kinds of excitement.

When a couple tells sacred secrets, it is as if they are rafting down the Colorado, just the two of them. The river carries them, and they must ride, because there is no exit until the raft reaches the takeout point. These sacred secrets can capsize the boat. The truth can kill an individual spirit. A great deal is at stake. But once out of the rapids, if the couple has told the truth and revealed secrets and survived, they have cleansed their relationship and it has a chance to become whole, stronger, and more exciting.

Listening Connects

For a couple to be able to tell each other their sacred secrets, they must be safe together. Being safe together means that each partner must have the capacity for empathy and compassion. *Empathy is the desire and the ability to understand one's partner compassionately.* It is the second essential element in building love's spirit.

Acceptance is the most important component of empathy. Acceptance means that one partner can speak her truth and that the other partner will acknowledge it as her truth without trying to convince her of his own. The listener works to accept what the speaker feels as a statement about the speaker and not as a statement about the listener.

It is even possible for the listener to absorb with empathy ugly words and expressions the blaming person speaks. This does not mean that empathy justifies or forgives abuse, but only that empathy offers help in understanding the source of abuse. The skilled empathetic listener understands that blaming, name-calling, and bitterness are statements of the speaker's anger that come from the speaker's hurt and fear. Such statements say far more about the speaker than about the one spoken to.

For the listener, giving empathy takes strength and skill. It requires listening, reflecting, and acknowledging, all done without blaming. If truth-telling is the fire fueling the spirit or passion of a relationship, empathy is the fireplace containing the fire and protecting the relationship from a blaze that can destroy and injure everything in its path.[1]

Boundaries Lead to Freedom

Another requirement for building love's spirit is creating boundaries. Boundaries mark the emotional safety zone that permits a couple to tell each other their sacred secrets. Boundaries include physical walls, time boundaries that set aside and protect the couple's time together, conversation boundaries that create limits to what one can say, and personal-space boundaries that define how one can be touched. Boundaries protect the relationship from romantic competitors and, perhaps more important, from well-meaning friends, family, and children.

The paradox in this principle is that boundaries, which at first appear restrictive, actually are a means of creating *more* freedom and excitement in a relationship. Without the emotional safety that is provided by relationship boundaries, couples cannot relax enough to share their personal truths.

Just as it is difficult to love and value a person who does not love and value himself or herself, it is difficult for parents, children, and friends to respect a love relationship that does not create its own boundaries. Children especially have no interest in supporting their parents' intimate life. They don't even want to know about it. Neither do friends or parents. No one cares about your sex life but you and your partner, and it is up to both of you to create the boundaries that protect your intimate moments.

A couple must make time to be alone together, take time to talk without interruptions, and "get away" now and then. Sometimes a couple can spend a weekend away from the family or hire a babysitter during the day when both still have energy to pay attention to each other and to be adults alone together. Couples who cannot afford relief of this kind can go to another room and shut the door for a while or ask a friend to keep the children.

Boundaries that set off time and place are important, but more may be required to prevent others from intruding on a relationship. If you and your partner plan a romantic weekend away but spend the whole time talking about the children, you have not formed effective boundaries. Set up the boundaries—then, within them, give your attention fully to your spouse.[2]

Have Faith, Make Room, Know and Love Your Partner

The last element required to nurture love's spirit is *a sense of belonging*. A feeling of belonging together is essential when a couple lives together. In a love relationship, each party must feel that he or she belongs beside the other. One witnesses this spirit when one member of the couple approaches the other in a crowd and somehow space is made for the approaching mate. The atmosphere changes, and the two people create a warmth or energy that wasn't there before. The approaching party has obviously been made welcome.

One part of a sense of belonging has to do with a partner's expectation. If we believe we belong and that our presence is welcome and desired, this expectation of belonging can create part of our sense of belonging.[3] Another part is what we do to make our partner feel welcome. This might mean small gestures such as saving for our partner a place beside us or introducing our partner to our friends. The third part of a sense of belonging is acceptance.[4] Acceptance implies a knowing, a knowing that comes from truth-telling and sharing sacred secrets. Acceptance means that a person is known—the good and the bad—and loved. To know and love is the greatest gift we can give to one another.

Boundaries, empathy, and telling the truth also contribute to a sense of belonging, and all are essential components of love's spirit.

Stories

Telling the Truth

◆ Ernest and Cynthia

Ernest and Cynthia came to see me at three o'clock. When Cynthia made the appointment, she asked for a two-hour block of time because her husband, Ernest, wanted to get to work right away. If he didn't see results fast, she said, he would refuse to continue with therapy.

Ernest was an imposing man, six foot five inches, two hundred fifty pounds, and fifty-eight years old. He was dressed in his lawyer's blue pinstripe suit with braces. Cynthia was tall and thin. She wore a sophisticated gold suit and moved like a model. She was forty-one years old. They had been married for four years. When I asked, "How may I help you?" Cynthia responded.

"I don't know what has happened," she said. "Once we had a passionate relationship. When I met Ernest, I was married to another man. My first husband was no longer interested in me, but Ernest was. Now I feel as if I am married to my first husband."

"Are you talking about sex?" I asked.

"What else!" were Ernest's first words.

"I don't know what happened," Cynthia continued. "I have asked Ernest about it, and he won't say anything to me."

"Ernest, will you say how you feel about Cynthia and what has inhibited your sexual interest?" I asked.

"I don't have anything to say." There was a long silence.

Finally, I said, "Therapy can help people if they tell the truth about how they feel."

"I have nothing to say," Ernest said.

"So what are you doing here?" I asked.

"OK!" Ernest blurted. "You want the truth about how I feel. I'll give you the truth. I'm sick of her flat chest." He pointed at Cynthia's chest and glared at her. "She's a stick. I want a real woman, a woman with breasts."

I was stunned. This was not exactly what I meant by telling the truth, but Ernest may have believed that truth-telling was what he was doing. I didn't know what to say, but Cynthia did.

"You used to like my body, Ernest. You liked it a lot. You told me you couldn't get enough of me. I don't think my breasts are the problem. It's your impotence...."

"Yeah, look at your anorectic body. I am disgusted by it. Your body would make anyone impotent. Who would want to make love to that?"

"Would you like me to find out? I didn't have much trouble the last time I had a husband who ignored me for four months."

"Is that a threat?"

"If this keeps up, it's a promise."

I finally found my voice. "*This is not the truth.*"

"What do you mean it's not the truth?" Ernest challenged. "It's my truth. Is it getting too hot for you, Doc?"

"Yes," I said, "and *that's* the truth. Now, when I say it's getting too hot for me, I am not accusing you, blaming you, or talking about you. I am saying that this intense anger frightens me. It is difficult for me to work in this atmosphere. Now, Ernest, without blaming Cynthia or talking about her, tell *your* truth. Tell me what happened the last time you and Cynthia had sex. The truth."

Ernest was quiet for a moment before he spoke. "I had just finished a murder case," he said. "I don't think my client was guilty, but I lost. He got the chair. Cynthia was trying to distract me by seducing me. It didn't work. That never happens. That was the first time ever that it didn't work. It doesn't happen to me. It can't happen to me.

I don't lose a capital case, and I don't fail to perform. That is unacceptable."

"You sound angry," I said.

"You're damn right I'm angry." Ernest took a deep breath. "I guess I'm not really angry at Cynthia." He looked at her. "I'm angry at myself. I'm angry that I'm getting old and that I feel it. That's the truth."

"Yes it is," I said.

A truth that never blames is important to lovers. It is not about someone else. The truth is always about us. It is about how we feel. It exposes us. It makes us vulnerable. It is risky.

Ernest was not bothered by Cynthia's flat chest until "it didn't work." The fact that "it didn't work" was unacceptable to him. He used Cynthia and her chest as his scapegoat. Ernest was afraid, and he couldn't face his fear, so he resorted to blaming, which is never the truth.

If you cannot trust your partner, telling him or her the truth is dangerous. Ernest was not sure he could trust Cynthia to accept his truth and to handle it with kindness. But he at last found the courage to tell his truth. His telling the truth gave his relationship with Cynthia a new chance, an opportunity for renewal.

Probably Ernest could not have told his truth without the help of an "honest broker" third party, a therapist in this instance. If a couple tries to tell the truth and finds that their truth-telling injures instead of heals, this couple needs to consult a professional—probably a therapist who treats marriages and families—who can listen and help them feel safe enough to tell their truth.

▼

▼ How to Begin Telling the Truth to Each Other

Decide together if you need help from a third party such as a therapist. If you do, make an appointment. After both of you have seen the therapist, decide if you feel comfortable talking with that particular one. Truth-telling will occur only in an environment where both partners feel relatively safe. If you do feel safe, go back. If you don't, find another therapist and try again.

1. Truth-telling means describing ourselves and our experiences.

2. Truth-telling does not mean assigning blame. The world is not divided into the guilty and the innocent. Each of us fits into both categories.

3. Remember that name-calling is not truth-telling. We can't characterize someone's essence by using a label. We can describe an incident in concrete terms and say how we feel, but calling a person a name is not the way toward the truth. It is simply a way of expressing how hurt and afraid we are.

4. It is never the truth that another person does something that "makes" us feel a certain way. We respond with feelings to what a person does, but we choose which emotion we will feel and how we will express that emotion. People do not make us feel bad. Describing how we feel about what they do is the truth. For example, we might say, "When you do _____, I feel _____," not "You make me feel _____."

5. Telling the truth involves many media, and we must use the medium of touch. The way we touch each other communicates, and touching each other is a way of telling each other the truth. It's important to communicate through words *and* through touch, as physical intimacy is essential to a relationship.

The most powerful truth is how one person feels about the other in the present moment. It is usually not appropriate to speak this powerful truth until trust has been established by first speaking less powerful and risky truths.

▲

• Exercises

Visualizing

Sit quietly, close your eyes, and relax your body. Think of the truths you would like to tell your partner, ones you now hold back. Imagine what it would be like to tell these truths. Do you think your partner has the strength to listen to the truth, or will he or she run away? Do you have the strength to listen to your partner's truth without taking it personally or running away? If you can speak and hear the truth, then you are ready to do the work that a relationship requires.

Journal Writing

Write about the truths you long to tell your mate. List them in your journal. If you are having trouble thinking of any, consider these typical areas of conflict:

1. Finances
2. Sex life
3. Your parents
4. Your partner's parents
5. Your children
6. Your job

Talking with Yourself

Find two characters within yourself, and engage in a dialogue about truth-telling. These are some questions you may ask:

1. Am I ready to speak the truth to my partner?
2. What is the most important truth that I wish to communicate to my mate?
3. Can I remain calm and get rid of my own defenses so that I become able to listen to my partner speak his or her truth?

Talking with Your Partner

Before you speak the truth to your partner, *read* and *reread* the following section on empathy. Telling the truth is danger- ous if partners do not commit to learning how to listen with empathy. Then sit together and use the Rules of Empathetic Listening on page 24 as you speak to each other. Be pre- pared for the unexpected. The unexpected may be a power- ful sense of relief that you are beginning to discard your masks; it may be the emergence of some frightening informa- tion that you or your partner have repressed; it may be a welcome intensification of the loving bond between you and your partner.

Empathy

♦ Roger and Ellen

I showed Roger and Ellen into my office. Roger was a rotund, balding forty-two-year-old of medium height. He wore a blue T-shirt, jeans, and wire-rimmed glasses. Ellen was the same age as her husband but looked younger. Tall and wearing her hair pulled back in a long braid, she wore flat shoes and a sensible skirt and blouse.

Several years before, Roger and Ellen had asked me to help them resolve issues of destructive jealousy in their marriage, and they had successfully worked to mend their marital wound. I was frankly surprised to see them again. They climbed the stairs to my office slowly and dutifully, like soldiers reporting for assignment.

"Who called this meeting?" I began.

"I did," Ellen said. "It's about his mother. She's coming to see us next week, and I don't want the same thing to happen that has always happened when she comes to visit."

"This is no big deal," Roger said. "Why do we have to pay Dr. McMillan's astronomical hourly fee to talk about this?"

"Because, Roger, I tried to talk to you last Friday when we were having dinner after the movie. I told you that I didn't want to get stuck with your mother when she came to visit. Then you started lecturing me, and thirty minutes later I could see that nothing I could say would make any difference. This time would be the same as last time, and I would be miserable. I can't talk to you."

"You don't listen to me," Roger said. "I explained that I have to work while she's here, and there's nothing I can do about it."

"Yes, you explained, and I listened," Ellen said. "That's how it always is, and frankly, Roger, relating to you has gotten me demoralized. I think I'm getting depressed. You talk, I listen. I feel bad."

"Well, I feel bad, too," Roger said.

"I don't understand, Ellen," I interjected. "Would you mind telling me what the problem is when Roger's mother comes to visit?"

"Roger's mother is an alcoholic who has been married six times. She smokes. She is not interested in our children, except maybe to give them money to buy a pushup bra or to tell them how she seduced her fourth husband. She is interested in my father, who has been widowed for five years. Like Roger, she likes to talk, talk, talk, and she badgers me to invite my father over for dinner or to take her to see him. And my father hates her, but he won't tell her so. Roger hates being with her, but he just stays away from home, leaving me with her to watch her smoke all day, take her first drink at 1 P.M., and drink till she collapses in bed at midnight."

"Well, what do you want me to do about it?" Roger almost shouted.

"I want you to tell her that she can't smoke in our house. I want you to tell her that we don't drink and that we don't allow alcohol in our house. I want you to take responsibility for her visit. I want you to take time from work, at least come home early and not go to meetings after 5 P.M. I want you to tell her to stop talking and to listen to her grandchildren. She's just like you. She talks and never listens."

"I can't change who my mother is," Roger said. "You're blaming me for my mother being who she is. There's nothing I can do about that. She is not my fault."

"Both of you are talking, and neither is listening," I said. "How about this? Let me see if I can listen to you both, so that each of you knows that someone has heard you, and then perhaps you can soften your positions a little. None of us can ever listen until we first feel that someone else has heard what we said, understood it, and acknowledged it. Now, Ellen, let me know if I have this right: the prospect of Roger's mother's visit frightens you, doesn't it?"

"Yes, it surely does," Ellen said, and instantly her tight face relaxed.

"It sounds as if Roger's mother exhausts you and destroys the social climate you are trying to create for yourself and your children."

"She sure does," Ellen said. She was looking at me now with interest instead of glaring at Roger. Her arms unfolded. Her fists became open hands, and she leaned back.

"Someone needs to set limits on Roger's mother while she is visiting your home. You believe that since she is Roger's mother, Roger should set the limits. You want Roger to tell her to not bring alcohol into your home, not smoke there, use appropriate conversation around the children, and show interest in them."

"That's right." Ellen was encouraged by my listening, and she enthusiastically continued with her requests of Roger. "And I want him to make plans to entertain her, and I want him to be there with her as much as possible."

"Yes," I said. "I hadn't gotten to that. You want Roger to take time from work while his mother is here and plan activities that will entertain her."

"Yes," Ellen said. "I don't want to aggravate my father by taking her to see him or by forcing him to be part of entertaining her."

"You want Roger to help you protect your father."

"Yes," Ellen said.

"Have I understood what you want?" I asked.

"Yes," Ellen replied.

"Roger." I turned to Roger and he looked back at me, eager for his turn to be understood. "You are feeling blamed for your mother being who she is."

"Yes," Roger said.

"And I would bet that those barbs about your being like her feel like insults."

"Well, they do," Roger said.

"Roger, you can't help the fact that this woman is your mother. I'm sure that you feel some pain from her behavior as well."

"Yes, that's true." Roger now leaned back and unfolded his arms.

"Nor is it your fault that you work and must leave home to earn a living."

"That's right. That's how Ellen wanted it. She says she is glad that she is able to be home with the children."

"So you are not leaving her at home alone with your mother on purpose."

"Well . . . Ellen is right, I do try to avoid being with my mother. It is so hard for me to be with her. Around her I feel ashamed, hurt, and angry all at the same time. So I do avoid her. She doesn't get to Ellen the way she does to me."

"How would you know?" Ellen interjected.

"Ellen, let me and Roger talk for just one moment, please." Ellen leaned back again. "So your mother is particularly difficult for you to be around."

"Yes, but she is my mother, and these are her grandchildren. I want my children to have a grandmother, and she is their only shot at that."

"So you feel it is your duty as her son to invite her to your home, and it's your duty as your children's father to give them a chance to know their grandmother."

"That's right."

"Have I understood how you feel?"

"Yes, thank you."

"Now, after hearing you both, since you both trust me, I could tell you what I think about all this, and probably we would reach a temporary solution. But if I did that, you would not know how to solve your own problems. Here is what I want you to do. I want you to do for each other what I just did for you both. Ellen, how did you feel when I listened to you?"

"I felt understood. I felt calm. I'm not so angry now. After you listened and understood me, I even understood some of what Roger was saying about his duty to his mother."

"So you were more open to Roger's point of view after you were listened to?" I asked.

"Yes, I was."

"And Roger, how did you feel after I listened to you?"

"I didn't feel much different toward Ellen, but I felt good about you. I felt you understood. While I was talking to you, I relaxed . . . but if I had to face Ellen's attacks again, I would be right back where I was."

"That makes sense," I said, "because Ellen hasn't listened to you. I have. So you feel safe with me but not with Ellen."

"What do you mean I don't listen to him?" Ellen retorted. "All I do is listen to him. I heard him, and I understand what he said. I'm not stupid."

"I'm not sure you have understood him," I said.

"Me either," Roger said.

"And that is the point. Roger isn't sure. He isn't sure because he hasn't heard his words and feelings reflected back to him out of your mouth. But he heard me repeat with compassion his point of view."

"Well, I don't have any compassion for his point of view—no more than he has any compassion for how I feel."

"Well, let's see about that," I said. "Roger, can you repeat to Ellen what she said were her problems with your mother's visit?"

"Well, she wants me to take off from work, and I can't do that."

"Roger, that's defending, not understanding," I said. "Place yourself in her shoes first. Imagine how you would feel if you were her, and talk about that to Ellen, not to me."

"Well, I'll try." He paused and looked at Ellen. "I know how hard Mother is to be with. I'm sure she wears you out. She does me, too. If you think it's hard on you, you should try being her son."

"Roger," I interrupted. "We are not trying to understand how you feel. We are trying to understand how Ellen feels."

"OK. Being with Mother is hard. She doesn't talk about the right stuff around the children. You are right. She doesn't know how to pay attention to them. She is mighty interested in your father. I'm sure that irritates him and you, and I don't blame you. Is that it?"

"No," I said, "but that was a very good start. Tell him what he left out, Ellen."

"Well, you conveniently forgot about her smoking and drinking."

"Ellen, it's hard for him to listen to you and not be defensive if you are going to attack him. Try that again."

"Oh, I see. I could leave out the 'conveniently forgot' part."

"Yes."

"You didn't mention her smoking and drinking," Ellen told Roger.

"No," said Roger, "but I am sure that bothers you. It would bother me, too, if I were cooped up with her all day."

"Yes, thank you," Ellen said.

"Good," Roger said.

"Good what?" I asked.

"Good, I'm finished."

"To know if you are finished, you have to ask Ellen."

"OK. Ellen, am I finished?"

"You left out the most important part—and that is, what are you going to do about it?"

"Nothing!" Roger blurted out angrily.

"See there," Ellen said, looking exasperated.

"Roger, listening and understanding do not necessarily mean doing," I said. "Our job now is simply to understand what Ellen feels and what she wants."

"She wants my mother to die. That's what she wants."

"That's not what she said," I said. "What did she say?"

"I don't remember anything except she wanted me to quit work for a week."

"That's not what I said either."

"Tell him what you did say, Ellen."

"I told you I want you to be the primary one responsible for entertaining your mother. She doesn't get up until 10 A.M., and she's not really out of her room until noon. I want you to be here as much as you can. I want you to plan things to do with her. She likes art galleries and craft shows. She likes theater and movies. Please plan things for her to do. And tell her she can't drink or smoke in our home. Tell her she shouldn't talk about sex and seduction with the children present, and please tell her to show interest in our children. That's all."

"That's a lot," Roger said.

"You don't have to do all those things," I reminded him. "You just have to repeat them to Ellen to show her you understand."

"OK. Since she is my mother, you think I should be the primary one responsible for her while she's here."

"Yes," Ellen said. "Thank you."

"And I think you have a point there, though I hate to admit it."

"Thank you again."

"What else?" I prompted Roger.

"She wants me to—"

"No, talk to Ellen," I said. Roger looked away from me and at Ellen.

"Ellen, you want me to tell Mother she can't smoke and drink in the house. And I can do that."

"Don't talk yet about what you can and can't do," I said. "The task now is to understand and be sure Ellen knows you understand."

"OK. Let's see, you want me to come home from work early and to take off a day or so. And you want me to tell her not to talk about sex and so forth around the children and to tell her to listen to them and to show interest in them. Did I get it this time?"

"Yes, you understood me. Thank you. That felt good."

"Now, Ellen, it's your turn to show Roger that you understand him."

"OK. You feel a duty to your mother to stay connected to her and to invite her to visit so I can take care of her."

"Ellen, is that what Roger would say?" I asked.

"I guess not the part about my taking care of her, but that's what happens."

"The task is not to tell what you think happens, but to understand Roger."

"OK. You have this damned duty to your mother. And I guess I understand that. I feel a duty to my father, too."

I glanced toward Ellen disapprovingly. She caught it.

"All right. I'm not here to understand my tale of woe with my father. My focus is on Roger. Roger does have a great burden with his mother. I know that. She is very difficult for him to be with. I can feel Roger tensing up a month before she comes. I know she terrifies him. And it makes me sad for him when I see her ignore Roger, too. He has accomplished a great deal. She has a fine son in whom she can take pride. Roger gets none of a mother's pride from her. And her drinking and smoking embarrass and irritate Roger, while they just irritate me. Is that right?"

"Yes," Roger said, "but that's not all."

"What did I forget?"

"You forgot about asking me to take off work."

"Oh, yes, the 'poor Roger has to work while I get to stay home with the children' song."

"Ellen, is that what Roger would say?"

"No."

"Well, say it as if you were Roger."

"OK, I'll try. We did agree that my work would be at home with our children and Roger's would be earning money. And I am grateful for our good fortune that we are able to give our children a stay-at-home mom. Roger is right. This is what I want."

I looked at Ellen and pointed to Roger. "Talk to him, not to me."

"Oh, all right. Roger, you are right. This is what I want."

"Thank you," Roger said.

"I know you must work, and I know you can't just leave work any time you want, but —"

"Would Roger say 'but'?" I asked.

"No. I know you can't leave work any time you want. You can't. Have I understood you?"

"I . . . guess so."

"You don't seem sure. What did she leave out?" I asked.

"I feel as if she blames me for —"

"Oh, yes, I know," Ellen said. "I blame you for your mother being who she is, and that's not right. Maybe I should blame her own parents, or the war for killing her father. You are right. Who your mother is is not your fault. I'm sorry that I implied it was. I never meant to."

"That was more than I bargained for," said Roger. "Yes, you have understood me."

"How do you feel, Roger?" I asked.

"I feel good. I really appreciate Ellen's listening to me, and while I was listening to her say those things, I began to change my mind. There are things that I can do."

"Good, because that's what's next," I said. "You have listened, both of you. And listening and acknowledging really does open you up to changing your minds. Now is the time to offer things you can do. You have heard each other, really listened and understood, and you have felt what the other feels. Those feelings matter enough to you that you are now willing to offer something that you weren't willing to offer before. But remember, it's important at this point not to give away the store. Give only what you can afford to give."

"I'll go first," Roger said. "I can't take off a week, but since she stays in bed till noon, I can go to work early and try to get home by lunch some days, and on others, by two or three. I don't have to go to any five o'clock meetings that week. I will gladly tell her not to bring alcohol and not to smoke in the house. She might not come, but that will be her choice. I don't know if I can talk to her by myself about the sex talk and the children, and I will not speak for your father in telling her he doesn't like her. And I don't think I'd be very good at planning activities for the week for Mother ... but I will work with you to make a plan."

Ellen looked at him. "I'm overwhelmed," she said. "That's more than I could have ever expected. OK. It's my turn." She paused to gather her thoughts and then began. "I know my tongue is sharp sometimes. I'm sorry I compared you to your mother. You are nothing like her ... except you have her eyes. I know you can't be at home all the time. I wouldn't mind if you even played golf on Wednesday, just so I would have some time to get away from her, too, and could leave her with you. We can plan your mother's activities together ... and I will be glad to talk with your mother with you about the children. I think she would like to relate to our children better. We can help her. It's my job to talk to her about how my father feels. That's right."

Roger and Ellen had not been able to talk with each other about important issues because they did not feel emotionally safe with each other. I provided them each with a safe person to talk to. Then they became able to provide emotional safety for each other. They did this by being empathetic—by listening, reflecting without defending, understanding with compassion, and acknowledging what was said and what was heard. Listening effectively can be hard work, and it may seem a tedious process at first. When done well, it is also highly rewarding work, as you can see by Roger and Ellen's resolution.

Being listened to changes a person. Notice how this opened up Roger and Ellen. As they felt they were being understood, their bodies changed. Each became more receptive to what the other one was saying.

Empathy changes the listener as well. Listening, reflecting, and acknowledging allow one to see things differently from when one uses the ears only to hear, and the brain only to invent a reply, and the mouth only to utter the next response.

The emotional safety established through empathetic listening and acknowledging is essential for truth-telling to occur. It is easily lost. But it can be reestablished with work and careful attention.

▼

▼ How to Use the Rules of Empathetic Listening

The following Rules of Empathetic Listening should be read and referred to many times. You will know that it is time to review these rules when you and your partner have become stuck in a fight or a power struggle, when neither of you feels understood, or when your frustrated feelings have become so powerful that you have no idea what to do next.

1. Listen when your partner tells how he or she feels. Do not defend yourself, and do not interrupt your partner with your point of view.

2. Never blame. Statements that begin with "you" usually lead to trouble. Avoid the word as much as possible. The exception is when you are wondering out loud how the other person feels. Then you might ask, "Do you feel like _____?"

3. Be quiet and listen, but only as long as you can remember what your partner is saying. When you begin to lose track of what your partner is saying, interrupt and say, "Before you go any further I want to be sure I understand. Are you saying that _____?" Use this interruption only to say what you have understood your partner to be saying thus far. Once you've finished and your partner agrees you have understood thus far, ask your partner to continue. Listen as long as you understand what is being said. Interrupt again if you need to.

4. The person who is speaking should stop after making one point so as not to overwhelm the listener. "Overtalking" is a serious danger. One can get drunk on being listened to and understood. When that happens, the speaker continues to speak without giving the listener his or her turn to be listened to.

5. When you find yourself engaged in a power struggle in which nobody is being understood and nobody is empowered, that is the time to have an empathetic talk. Listening with empathy is a skill that should be practiced until it becomes a natural part of you. It will become easier and more rewarding every time you do it.

_____ ▲

• Exercices

Visualizing

Find a quiet place, close your eyes, and relax. Think about what it would be like to be listened to. Have you ever felt that someone was really listening to you? How did that feel? Would you like your partner to be able to listen to you? Do you think you have the courage to listen to your partner? Do you think that learning how to listen with empathy would help your relationship?

Journal Writing

What are you afraid will happen if you really listen and understand? For most of us, our fear is that we may lose our sense of what is right for us, that we will give our partner his or her way and forget our own interests. Before you listen to your partner, record what it is that you don't want to lose or forget. After you have listened to your partner, it is time for you to speak. You may wish to come back to your journal list and ask your partner to listen to what is important to you.

Talking with Yourself

Before you try this empathetic listening exercise with your partner, engage in a dialogue with yourself. Ask yourself these questions:

1. Am I prepared to let go of my defenses when I listen to my partner?
2. Am I prepared to allow the unpredictable to happen as we communicate in this way?
3. Can I be patient with myself and my partner as we both learn the skill of empathetic listening?

Talking with Your Partner

Now it is time to talk. Find a time and place where you will not be interrupted and can give your complete attention to each other.

1. Sit across from each other.

2. Look each other in the eye as you ask questions of each other.

3. Listen while your partner talks, then "reflect" his or her truths back until he or she says you have it right. Do not let your partner talk beyond your capacity to remember. When you feel your memory is full, stop. Repeat what it is that you understand. When your partner acknowledges that you do understand so far, ask your partner to continue.

4. Being listened to can be liberating to the speaker. Listen for ten minutes, then stop. Get some closure on what has been said, then take your turn at talking while your partner listens.

5. Speak to your partner, then allow him or her to reflect your truths back to you, and say that he or she has it right.

Boundaries

♦ Steve and Amanda

In 1974 during my clinical internship at the Palo Alto V.A. Hospital, I worked with a couple close to my own age, in their late twenties, who had a hyperactive child. Our sessions were conducted in front of a one-way mirror so my supervisor and interested others could observe. My supervisor was Beth Richards, a brilliant psychiatrist beloved by all the trainees and staff in the Family Study Unit.

The couple and their child came regularly on Fridays at 2 P.M. Beth sat behind the mirror to observe me and take notes for a critique of my work.

I had seen the couple with their child for three sessions. As Beth observed these sessions, it had become obvious to her that there was considerable tension between the parents. The child's distractibility seemed to be at least partially related to this tension. She suggested that I ask the couple to come to see me together without their child, and she asked me to try to get to the bottom of the husband-wife tension. The parents, Steve and Amanda, arrived punctually.

As they took their places on the couch, Steve began to talk. "I'm glad we're seeing a young therapist like you, David. I believe you will have some understanding of what we're about. I know you think our son's problems are related to our marriage. If we're going to talk about marriage, I want to be sure we have a therapist who shares our belief in open marriage. Am I right about you?"

I was stunned and felt every small-town instinct in me rising to the surface. As a child, I had gone to the Presbyterian Church in Arkadelphia, Arkansas, twice every Sunday, and to the Baptist Church every Wednesday with my grandfather. Open marriage was not a subject I'd had much occasion to discuss. I struggled to find words. "What I think shouldn't matter," I said. "I'm not here to judge you. I'm here to support you, to understand your personal values and dreams, not to impose mine on you." As I spoke I twisted in my seat, crossing and recrossing my legs.

Knock . . . knock . . . knock . . . came a sound from the one-way mirror. Those in the therapy room generally ignored the mirror, but now it took on an inescapable presence for Steve, Amanda, and me. The knock signaled me to leave the room to counsel with Beth behind the mirror.

"Excuse me," I said to Amanda and Steve. "They want to talk with me for a moment." I left, appalled that I was doing so badly that I required rescue, yet at the same time I was relieved to have an excuse to take a break.

At the door was Beth's concerned face. Beth motioned me toward an empty seat beside her, and I sat down.

"David," Beth said, "what do you think about open marriage?"

"I don't know," I replied.

"Well, you'd better figure it out," she said. "Nobody in the world is without values. You can't hide behind the therapist role when a patient asks you a direct question about your own values."

"Well, I don't know what I think about it," I said. "I come from a repressed Southern town, and I suppose I'm intrigued with the idea of open marriage, but I don't see how it could work. I don't think I would be strong enough for that kind of relationship. What do you think, Beth?"

"I think a husband and wife sleeping with whomever strikes their fancy is utter foolishness, but they aren't the only couple in this crazy time to be caught up in the idea."

"Well, what do I do?" I asked.

"Go back in there and tell them the truth, just as you told me. Psychotherapy calls for creating a safe atmosphere in which people can speak the truth. Amanda and Steve don't feel safe enough with each other to tell each other the truth. If you risk telling the truth to them, they might trust you enough to tell the truth to each other in front of you. Go in there and tell them where you are with this. Remember: Never lie to your patients."

When I sat down across from Amanda and Steve, I was more shaken than I had been when I had left them. Amanda asked, "What happened behind the mirror?"

I remembered Beth's words: "Tell the truth." So I found my courage and said, "Well, they asked me what I really thought about open marriage."

"What did you say?" Steve asked.

"I said the idea of open marriage is intriguing to me, but that I don't think I would be strong enough to be in an open-marriage relationship."

"Strength," Steve responded. "It takes strength. I'm a mystical artist. I'm against ownership, private property, and possessiveness in relationships. This is what I believe, and this is the heart of my life's work."

"What did the others think?" Amanda asked.

"My supervisor, Dr. Richards, was the only one to express an opinion," I answered.

"What did she say?"

I was slow to respond, but I remembered what Beth had said: *Tell the truth.*

"She said she thought it was utter foolishness," I said.

"I'll bet she's over thirty," Steve offered.

"She is."

"Well, I'm glad we're seeing you rather than her," Steve said.

Well, I'm not, I thought to myself.

"I think she may have a point, Steve," Amanda said.

"What do you mean?" Steve glared at his wife as though warning her not to betray him.

"I haven't dared to talk to you about this, Steve," Amanda said, "but I've got to try...Maybe David can help us. We're both unhappy. We haven't had sex—with each other—in eight months. I feel as if you're constantly mad at me. You're always either working on your art or walking the dogs. You leave with the dogs and stay away for two hours at a time. I wondered what you were doing, being gone so long, so one day I followed you. I saw you rolling in the grass in the park, wrestling with the dogs. You were hugging them, pulling them down to you, letting them lick your face, and laughing. Oh, how I wanted to be one of those dogs! You don't have anything to do with me or with Jess anymore. Your son needs you . . . I need you."

"I don't see why," Steve said sullenly. "You have Fred."

"I know I have Fred, but I don't have my husband. Fred can love me without risking anything. He can leave any time he wants. Fred and I don't have a child together. I have no hold on him, nor does he have any on me."

"Well, that's how it should be," Steve said. "That's the way it was for me and Marilyn. It was great. The best sex I ever had. But then you had to go crazy. Your psychiatrist told me that my relationship with Marilyn was the reason. He said you couldn't handle it. Something about Marilyn. So I broke it off, thinking I would find a woman who was less threatening to you. I let go of Marilyn while you still had Jim. Then you dumped Jim for Fred. And I still don't have anyone."

"You have me," Amanda said quietly.

"I don't want you. I want us to be free."

"I was perfectly willing to stop it all at any time," Amanda began.

"I don't want you to stop," Steve interrupted. "I know it's hard to live out our values, but we've got to try."

"I have tried," Amanda said, "just as you wanted me to. But I can't share you. I'm not strong enough."

"Yes you are!" Steve shouted. His face was red and his teeth were clenched. "I'm not a piece of property, and neither are you. Monogamy is a social convention. Open marriage is fair. Women are not mistreated in open marriage, and men can be free. It's *fair.* If you love me, you'll make it work."

"I'm trying," Amanda said, "but it's obviously not working. I wish it *would* work. It sounds so perfect. But I can't help how I feel. It makes me sick when I think of you with another woman, especially with Marilyn."

"I told you it's fine with me if *you* pick the woman."

"But it's not just Marilyn, Steve. It's *any* woman. Maybe I'm a Neanderthal, but I get scared when I think you may find someone who touches you more deeply than I can. I know there's more to you than I've ever been able to reach. I'm afraid you'll discover a part of yourself with someone else and that you'll leave me and Jess for her. I've tried not to think about it, but I can't help myself. It makes me crazy."

"It's how you were socialized. You can rise above what your mother taught you."

"Steve, I know you're furious with me. You're mad that I have Fred and that you don't have Marilyn or some other woman. But you know I'm willing to let Fred go. I don't want him. The sex is not that important to me. I don't know what to do," she said helplessly. "If I stop seeing Fred, you'll be furious with me because you'll think I'm not trying to live our values. If I keep seeing him, you'll be furious with me because you'll think our relationship isn't fair and equal. I can't win!"

"Yes you can."

"Not really, Steve. You know, I can always find a man to have sex with me, but there aren't as many women who want to get involved with a married man. A smart woman knows it would be pointless, that it wouldn't go anywhere. She knows she has no future with you. Women see sex as being tied with their futures, Steve. In an open marriage, I'll always have the advantage over you because I'll always be able to find another man. I don't want that advantage, Steve. You hate me for it."

Steve's angry face softened. His eyes filled. He sat in silence for a while, looking at Amanda, then out the window, then back at Amanda again. Each time he looked at Amanda, his eyes filled. Finally he looked at me and said, "I don't know what I'm going to do." With these words, he put his head in his hands. "I don't want to give up . . . I don't want to give up . . ."

Amanda rose, knelt in front of Steve, and hugged him. After a few moments she said, "Steve, we came here for Jess. Our problems are sure to be affecting him. Let's take a break from open marriage for a while and concentrate on each other. Maybe that will help Jess."

"I know Jess needs me," Steve said. "I've been so hurt and angry that I couldn't make our open marriage work. I guess I've taken it out on you and Jess. OK," he said with resignation, "we'll try the 'picket-fence nuclear-family routine' for a while. I hate giving up, but maybe it will help Jess."

The story of Steve and Amanda is a complex one that speaks to issues of therapist/patient relationships, therapist training, and authenticity in the therapy room—but these issues distract us from the point that I want to stress. This point is that open marriage does not work. Boundaries are essential in a marriage for emotional safety to exist.[5]

If a couple doesn't observe a contract created to secure boundaries, competition from outsiders will eventually erode their trust in each other. The emotional safety necessary for truth-telling will disappear.[6]

An intimate relationship is difficult to sustain. Truth-telling is hard, and it is nearly impossible for a couple to feel safe if the threat of a third party lingers over the couple. Humans cannot avoid this fear. Amanda expressed the fear in this way: "I get scared when I think you may find someone who touches you more deeply than I can . . . I'm afraid you'll discover a part of yourself with someone else and that you'll leave me and Jess for her." She told the truth about her fear. And her fear was based on the realization that in an open marriage the partners have not drawn boundaries to set themselves apart as special to each other. As a result they cannot sustain trust in the idea that they are in fact special to each other. They cannot sustain belief that there is a sacred secret that only they can share. Without a clear boundary, the spirit that unites them becomes harder for each to feel and to rely on.

▼ How to Draw Boundaries around Your Relationship

The best way to avoid problems with boundaries in a relationship is to talk about them.

1. A couple must find regular time together that is private. This should include time to be physically intimate and time to share in joint adventures. The couple should establish boundaries to protect this time and keep everyone else away.

2. It is important that the couple set generational boundaries. The partners should establish places where neither children nor parents are allowed.

3. Partners may find they disagree about the need for boundaries in a particular area. If possible, each should support the other's need to have a boundary in the disputed area. If you offer this support, your partner may show the same respect for your own fear and insecurity. Yes, relationships involve bonds, and bonds bind partners to agreements. The individual not ready to be bound by mutual agreements may not be ready to work on a relationship. If this is the case, a couple may need the help of a therapist.

• Exercises

Visualizing

Sit in a quiet place, close your eyes, take a deep breath, and relax. Think about the boundaries in your relationship. Are they defined well enough so you feel safe in the relationship? Do you sometimes find the boundaries to be too restrictive?

Journal Writing

Write about the boundaries you perceive in your relationship. Think about these questions as you write:

1. How do I feel about the boundaries in my relationship?
2. What boundaries are especially important to me?
3. Is there anything I would like to change about my relationship boundaries?

Talking with Yourself

Before you talk about this subject with your partner, ask yourself these questions:

1. Am I afraid that my partner's ideas about boundaries may differ from mine?
2. Am I ready to listen to my partner's ideas about boundaries?

Talking with Your Partner

Sit together, and talk about things you think should be private, for your eyes, ears, and touch only. Consider all areas of your life together where you need boundaries, not only those of space and time but also conversational subject matter, friendships, financial resources, and limits on other resources, especially energy. Talk about how misunderstandings may have arisen if you have always avoided talking about boundaries. Be sure to use your empathy skills when having this discussion.

A Sense of Belonging

♦ Ruth and Bo

Steve was violently opposed to using the word *belong* when speaking of his relationship with Amanda, but belonging supports the spirit of love. The knowledge that one belongs is a magical thing. The more our partner or a group accepts us, the more we feel that we belong and are welcome. This feeling gives us strength and the freedom to act and to be ourselves.

The couple whose story follows faced the deterioration of a relationship in which partners do not share a sense of belonging. Ruth and Bo were both in their twenties, both teachers, and had been married a short while when they first came to see me.

Ruth sat on the couch, and Bo sat on a chair that was the farthest distance possible from Ruth. Ruth's hair was pulled back. She wore pearls and a white blouse, a blue skirt, and flats. Bo was dressed in slacks, a tie, and a sweater. I could see through the window behind Ruth that the sky was clouding up, and I sensed the same kind of storm brewing in my office. Ruth was the first to speak.

"OK, Bo, what is it? I've felt your anger since we got up this morning, before I even said a word to you. For the life of me, I don't know how it happens. But you can get angry in a vacuum—or that's how it seems to me. How come you're so unreasonable?"

Bo didn't answer. He stared out the window toward West End Avenue. I waited. Ruth waited. When I felt the silence had become counterproductive, I asked Bo, "Do you want to comment on what she said?"

"I'm not talking to her."

"Well, I do see that before you've even said a word, she's already declared you unreasonable," I said. That seemed to relax him.

"Yes, but she's also right. I *am* furious. I'm so mad, I'm afraid of what I'll do if I try to talk to her. I can't even look at her in the eye."

"Can you talk to me about it?" I asked.

"I don't know where to start," he said.

"Start at the beginning."

"OK," he said. He took a deep breath, looked around, and began. "I met Ruth two years ago at the National Education Association convention. That's when we began a long-distance courtship. It was clear she wasn't going to move to Kansas City to be with me, so I moved here to be with her. I got a job teaching with Metro Schools. We moved in together three months ago, and we married the next month. Then *boom*, it hit. 'Oh, by the way,' she said, 'my house is so small, there's no room for your furniture. Even if we had a bigger house, I don't like that furniture. I guess you'll have to leave it in storage. Can you sell it?' Then she said, 'Bo, I hope you'll understand, but I have to keep the second bedroom for myself.' I didn't know what that meant until one night she said, 'I'm going to sleep in my room tonight. I just need some space.' This happens about every third night now. Then last night we went to a large party at the house of one of her colleagues. As soon as we walked in the door, she bolted. I spent the evening looking for her or following her around, standing on the outside of all her conversations. Did she bother to introduce me or include me in the talk? No."

Ruth interjected, "But you knew these people. They came to our wedding."

"I met them one time. I didn't remember any of their names."

"I behaved just as I always do at parties," Ruth defended herself.

"That's right," Bo agreed, "you did. But you have me in your life now and that should change how you act. It was especially galling to stand behind you and watch you flirt with that art teacher. Boy, did you give him a good look down the front of your dress!"

This therapy session did not lead to any improvement in Ruth and Bo's marriage. Ruth did not know how to make a place in her life for Bo, or she wasn't ready to welcome him. They soon divorced, and Bo returned to Kansas City.

It's clear that Ruth did not understand or could not accept that living in a relationship is different from living by oneself. Each partner in a relationship must make room for the other. But welcoming your partner is not just a matter of moving over, the way you might make room on a bench for a stranger. Partners in a living relationship are not just sitting beside each other. This sitting together and making room for the other should lead to a feeling of belonging together. In this situation, making Bo feel welcome was Ruth's responsibility, as she was the person who was already established in the place where their married life began.

Bo was a stranger here. It was up to Ruth to make the gestures that would help Bo feel welcome and confident that he belonged. These gestures can be simple things: a smile or a wave and a "Hey, come over here" or "Here, let me move this, and you can sit by me." Ruth's failure to introduce Bo to her colleagues was especially painful to him and fed his feeling of being on the outside of her life. She perhaps should also have made room for his furniture, even if she didn't like it, as a gesture of acceptance: *The furniture (and you) belong here.*

There are things Ruth clearly should not have done if Bo was to develop a sense of belonging. She shouldn't have insisted on sleeping in the other room. She shouldn't have flirted with her colleague and given Bo the impression she was willing to share with another man what he thought was reserved for him.

For a love relationship to grow and endure, each partner must work to include the other and to make the other feel welcome. Each must find ways to communicate to the other: *There is a place for you in my life.* If the partners do not share that sense of belonging, their love will die.[7]

▼ How to Build a Sense of Belonging

There are concrete steps you can take to develop a sense of belonging in your relationship.

1. If you get home first, when your partner arrives be sure to greet him or her with a kiss and words that express "I'm glad you are home."

2. If you are together in public, be aware of where your partner is. If your partner moves toward you, create a space for him or her. If you are in conversation with someone else and your partner joins you, say something that invites your partner into the conversation: "Hello, _____, we were just talking about _____. What do you think about _____?" If your partner doesn't know the individual with whom you're speaking, introduce them to one another.

3. When you speak to your partner, look into his or her eyes. Making eye contact states that you are open, interested, and available.

4. There may be times when you don't want to include your partner. For example, when your best friend wants to talk to you alone, your partner will not be welcome. Explain the situation to your partner to eliminate confusion so that your partner will not intrude and risk being rejected.

• Exercises

Visualizing

Sit quietly, close your eyes, and relax. Think about how you and your partner fit together. Do you believe in the relationship? Do you believe that you and your partner belong together? You cannot have a relationship unless there is hope that the relationship is going to work. Do you fear sometimes that you do not belong together? Do you wish to work on strengthening the sense of belonging in your relationship?

Journal Writing

Write answers to these questions:

1. What about our relationship makes me feel my partner and I belong together?
2. Are there things about our relationship that make me sometimes think I do not belong in it?
3. What things could my partner do to make me feel more welcome in our relationship?
4. What things could I do to make my partner feel more welcome?

Talking with Yourself

Engage in an internal dialogue with yourself:

1. Is there truly a place for my partner in my life? Does there seem to be a place for me in his or her life?
2. Can I communicate my feelings about these issues to my partner?

Talking with Your Partner

Bringing all your empathy skills to bear, communicate your feelings to each other about whether or not you feel you belong together. If one of you does not feel welcome at times, explore ways that the other can help correct the situation. You may think of little things such as small gestures of welcome, or important rules such as consulting with each other when it is time to make a major decision.

An Expectation of Belonging

♦ Jan and Phil

Making someone welcome is a catalyst for love. Even the *expectation* that a person we approach will care about us and make room for us can give us a feeling of confidence and relaxed strength. We see this phenomenon at work in this story of a successful blind date.

Jan and Phil sat across from me on the couch. They were tense, having fought for weeks before making this appointment to see me. "How can I help you?" I began.

This set off a tirade from Phil about Jan's hypersensitivity, followed by accusations from Jan about the constant rage Phil had displayed since he lost his job. Angry silence followed as each folded arms and turned his or her back on the other.

I sat quietly for a while. As silence began to test my tolerance, I remembered the "How did you meet?" question, something I often ask couples. Relieved to think of it, I asked, "How did the two of you meet?"

Jan and Phil continued to sit with their backs toward each other, arms folded. Phil glanced at me, then at Jan, and then looked away again — but he seemed to want to say something. Jan appeared to slowly let her rigidity go, unfolding her right arm and putting her hand in her lap, then allowing her left hand to join her right. She looked down at her hands, then up at me.

"We met on a blind date," she said. "An old boyfriend of mine, Jack, fixed us up. I liked Jack a lot in high school, but I broke off with him to go to college. When I moved to Nashville, I called Jack and his wife. They were kind enough to include me in their circle of friends. Then I learned that Jack's best friend and college roommate, Phil, was going to move to Nashville." Jan's body relaxed into the couch. Phil's did as well.

"Jack began telling me about Phil, and every time he told me something, he also told me something he had told Phil about me. He said he had told Phil about the time he threw me into the pool with my prom dress on to see how I would look with my hair flat and my dress all wet. And how proud he was that I was such a good sport and that I punished him only by pulling him into the pool with me in his tuxedo! He told Phil how I liked to drive fast on curvy roads in my sports car and how much fun I was to tease. Phil liked to drive fast, too.

"He told Phil about the time I was homecoming queen and Jack escorted me in his football gear and I walked barefoot between two rows of football players, holding daisies instead of roses in one hand and giving the peace sign with the other. He told me that he thought Phil had developed an imaginary relationship with me. He said that I had become Phil's ideal woman and that Phil couldn't wait to meet me.

"So when Phil came to the door to pick me up on our blind date, I greeted him barefoot at the door, holding daisies and giving him the peace sign. He laughed, and I loved him. I have ever since." She looked at Phil, who was almost smiling now. "I just wish he would stop being so mad," Jan said. "He'll get another job."

Phil did get another job, and he and Jan resumed their zany loving relationship.

Before the couple even set eyes on each other, Jack prepared Jan and Phil to like each other. Phil was encouraged to believe Jan would like him simply because their mutual friend, Jack, had spoken fondly of him to Jan. And because Jan expected to be liked by Phil, to be welcomed by him, she had the courage to dress up as Phil's ideal woman, to greet him holding a bouquet of daisies and flashing the peace sign. It was an act of faith, faith in the idea that he already accepted her.

Jan and Phil believed they belonged together, and this expectation of belonging created a set of beliefs based on nothing other than imagination and hope. When you believe someone will like and accept you, you often let down your normal defenses and are able to open up and connect with another, as Jan and Phil did. Love flows more easily when you believe you will be accepted and when you share faith with your partner that you belong together.[8]

▼ How to Build Expectations of Belonging Together

Suggestions for building expectations that two people belong together may be more relevant for a matchmaker than for the couple themselves.

Here is my advice for a matchmaker: Creating an expectation of belonging is a myth-building project. Be careful when creating expectations. Myths that turn out to be accurate and to give meaning to what were once unrelated facts are helpful, while expectations that are far from reality will hurt relationships.

• Exercises

Talking with Your Partner

Expectations are the building blocks of hope and faith, and hope is essential to love. It is useful for everyone, including the partners in a relationship, to understand that expectations have power. We create reality, sometimes, with what we believe. When in the early stages of a relationship, you can help build positive expectations for the relationship.

1. Tell your partner what you believe you have in common.
2. Tell your partner what it is about him or her that you admire.

3. Tell your partner directly how and why you feel the two of you belong together.

Knowing the One You Love

♦ Claire

Her name was Claire. She was eighteen years old, tall, and pretty with auburn hair. I had first seen her when she was fifteen and experimenting with drugs and sex, and her concerned family had sent her to me for counseling. I had helped her then. Sometimes she came back to see me when she needed to talk. Often I was impressed with her maturity.

"I really liked him," she said. "When I first got to school, as a freshman, I thought he was the cutest boy. He was handsome and smart. All the girls liked him. But now I think there might be something wrong with me. He's the one I wanted, but I don't want him anymore. He makes me sick."

"Why?" I asked.

"He loves me. That's why. Or he says he does."

"Well, I'm sure he means what he says," I said.

"How could he?" she asked. "He tells me that he adores me, cherishes me. He told me this in a letter, that he worships me. That every move I make is exquisite. That every word I say is fascinating. That he can't keep his eyes off me. He says I am the object of his affections, his dreams, his hopes. He knows that I'm the woman for him, that we will have children together! He said all this in a letter.

"We've only talked a few times. I don't like this. I want to be loved, but I want somebody to *know* me and love me. He doesn't even know me, and suddenly I am his Helen of Troy. This feels like an insult, that he can come and look at me and grab me and put me inside his mind and make me into whatever he wants me to be. I am a person. I'm not a projection. I exist. This is not who I am—I am not confined to his imagination.

"But it's funny—he seemed at first to be the one I have longed for. I wanted his attention more than anybody's. And now that I've got it, I can't stand him. He is saying words I dreamed that he would say to me. Yet I hate hearing them or reading them! I just keep coming back to 'He doesn't know me. He doesn't even know me.'"

The young man's adoration of Claire was insulting to her because he was in love with love, not with Claire, a real person. Had he been willing to first learn who she really was, his adoration of her might have resulted in Claire's developing an authentic sense of belonging. She might have come to believe that she belonged in a relationship with someone who loved her for who she really was.

The greatest gift we can give our mates is to know and love them—not just to love them. This kind of acceptance cements a couple's sense of belonging.

▼

▼ How to Know and Love Your Mate—and Ask to Be Known and Loved

The most important thing about a sense of belonging in a relationship is that you be willing to really know your partner as well as be known by your partner. The goal is to have a relationship with a real person, not with a projection of your imagination. It is not a compliment if you profess to love someone you do not really know.

1. To accept your partner, you must know who your partner is. You must know your mate is not perfect. You must recognize your partner's character flaws. Your mate needs to know that you know and recognize the worst as well as the best.

2. You must be able to see that your partner's strength and your partner's weakness is often the

same thing. If you don't like one part of your partner's personality, you will probably discover that the part you don't like accompanies the part you do like. For example, if you are sometimes irritated when your mate looks at attractive people of the opposite sex, you might be able to come to accept this as being part and parcel of your mate's sex drive, a quality you truly enjoy.

3. Be aware how difficult a task it is for your mate to accept *you*. When you become aware that you are less than perfect—that you are not always a great prize—it is easier to be accepting of your mate and his or her imperfections.

▲

• Exercises

Visualizing

Sit still, close your eyes, and relax your body. Think about your relationship. Do you feel known—really known—by your partner? What would it feel like to be really known for who you are? How would it feel to understand who your partner is and to accept him or her without reservation?

Journal Writing

1. What are some things about me that I would be afraid for my partner to know?

2. What are some things about me that I would love for my partner to know?

3. What are some things about my partner that I have had trouble accepting?

Talking with Yourself

Begin your internal dialogue with questions such as these:

1. Am I willing to take a risk and let my partner know who I really am?
2. Do I think my partner is kind and strong enough to accept me for who I really am?
3. Am I ready to accept my partner for who he or she really is?

Talking with Your Partner

Sit down with your partner and ask these questions:

1. Do you feel that I really know you?
2. Are there things that I believe about you that are just not true?
3. Do you sometimes feel that I wish you were someone else?
4. In order to please me, do you sometimes act around me as if you were someone else?

The answers to these questions should be candid, and you should listen to the answers with empathy. When your partner is finished, give him or her your answers to the questions as well.

Summary

The Elements of Spirit

What is love's spirit? Where does it begin? We can't always say what produces the first spark of attraction between two people. A feeling of mystery and magic about the initial connection exists that is enjoyable and frightening all at the same time. We know that *truth-telling* fans the spark into a flame. The *sacred secrets* partners exchange are exciting but can be dangerous. Truth-telling requires the courage to do or say something whose outcome is unknown.

If the secrets are heard with empathy, truth-telling is safer. Abe and Sarah exchanged truths that she was pregnant and that he was surprised but loved her enough to face the challenge with her. They were able to do this in a place made safer by their compassion for each other and their mutual recognition of what the truth cost the other. Ernest had to speak the real truth hidden below his bitterness against Cynthia—that he was afraid of aging and losing power—before the spirit of love between them could be restored. That truth was finally spoken in a place made safer by the therapist's empathy.

Empathy, the skill of listening, understanding, reflecting, and acknowledging without blame, softens the impact of truth-telling and diminishes dangerous defensive power struggles between partners. Once the therapist showed Roger and Ellen ways in which they could listen with empathy to each other, they could begin to tell the truth to each other and recover the desire to help each other.

Before they can safely share truths, partners in a love relationship require boundaries. *Boundaries* establish lines that protect the couple. They limit who can intrude on the couple's private time and space together and exclude others from the sacred secrets they share. Steve and Amanda recognized that their open marriage had made them both feel unsafe to tell the truth. They learned that boundaries lead to safety and the ability to share sacred secrets.

The feeling that emerges for partners able to tell the truth to each other with empathy and within the safety of their boundaries is *a sense of belonging*. Part of the sense of belonging is the feeling that a place exists for you in your partner's life—a feeling that Bo never felt with Ruth—and an expectation of welcome, as felt by Jan and Phil. When partners share this sense of belonging, they more easily find the courage to share their truths and create their sacred secrets. As Claire discovered, a feeling of belonging and acceptance is not authentic unless the person welcoming you has some idea of who you really are.

Truth-telling, empathy, boundaries, and *a sense of belonging* all help to shape and nurture the original spark of attraction between two people. Carefully tended, it grows into something that we are not certain we fully understand, something that we are part of but which is greater than both of us: the spirit of love.

The Paradoxes of Spirit

1. Sharing true feelings, even negative ones, can bring passion and tenderness to a couple.

2. Remaining still as you listen to your partner can bring you closer to your partner.

3. When you "talk mean" about or to your partner, you are in reality saying something mean or negative about yourself.

4. The boundaries you set up in your relationship actually lead to more freedom, as they provide the safety to be your true self.

5. The same is true of belonging. Though some may object to the idea of belonging because it limits freedom, in reality a sense of belonging can provide the emotional safety that allows true self-expression.

6. Residing in the safety of a loving relationship does not mean you can go to sleep. You must remain awake to your feelings, to your lover's feelings, and to ways you can speak to, listen to, welcome, and accept your lover.

CHAPTER II

Trust

The Theory

A Relationship's Power

To develop a relationship, partners must decide who gets
what they want and when and how. It may be true that
partners have passion for each other. They can learn to tell
their truths and understand each other. But if they can't
decide what they are going to do together and when they
are going to do it, if they can't decide who is to lead and
who is to follow, they will become frustrated and bored
with each other and give up on the relationship. If they
don't know how to share and manage power, the relationship will collapse on itself.

Trust is a product of power and how power is used in
a relationship. Trust develops—or is destroyed—when
each partner observes how the other makes use of his or
her power.

Accepting this concept may be difficult. Some people
believe that the normal conflicts they have come to expect in
most parts of life, the conflicts that arise because we are all
human beings and we all want power and things, should not
be an issue in a love relationship. Two people in love may
assume that they just naturally fit together without having
to negotiate any issues. But this is the trance stage of a relationship; when the infatuation wears off, they will have to
negotiate all power needs. They cannot avoid this struggle,
no matter how much they love each other. The reality is
that successful loving means becoming conscious of the
power contract.

Partners must resolve a number of issues when establishing a mutually acceptable power structure in their relationship. In the following discussion we will look at (1) the
value of "paying dues" to the relationship, (2) the need for
an authority structure that can use information to make

decisions, and (3) the importance of established norms in building a stable relationship.

Paying Dues: Making Your Relationship Valuable

The first issue raised when a new relationship comes into existence is *Does the relationship matter to both partners?* Are both partners willing to sacrifice, to provide the resources that will allow the relationship to grow and thrive? I call this kind of loving sacrifice *paying dues*.

Paying dues in a relationship has several positive consequences. The first is that it becomes possible for the relationship to gain the resources it needs to grow.

One resource a relationship requires is time. A relationship suffers if partners are too busy to pay attention to each other. Child care, work, sports, hobbies, church, and other well-intended efforts can absorb so much time that partners have no time for each other. But if both partners agree to give the relationship the time it requires, their relationship gains the room it needs to grow.

Similarly, both partners must commit energy to their relationship. Each must be willing to go the extra mile for the other, to do what it takes to make their life together as pleasurable as possible. Providing energy to a relationship ranges from making small gestures of enthusiasm to shouldering the larger sacrifices partners are sometimes called upon to make for each other. It might mean agreeing to entertain friends for dinner. It might mean agreeing to take in a sick father-in-law until he recovers. In such cases partners are committing energy to the relationship.

Although sometimes considered unromantic, partners must pay dues in the form of money. Partners must be willing to do what is necessary to provide the money the relationship needs. This might require a second job or a tighter budget.

By committing time, energy, and money, partners will enjoy a more stable and satisfying relationship.

The second consequence of paying dues is that the person paying the dues acquires special feelings and attitudes about the relationship. Paying dues gives a person the sense that he or she has earned the right to be a partner. He or she feels entitled to a place in the relationship, a chance to make it work and to exert influence. A partner who has not paid dues might feel he or she has nothing of value to give or nothing the partner wants. The partner who *has* paid dues feels on an equal footing in the relationship, ready to express opinions about how certain issues—for example, about money, children, or friends—should reach resolution.

A person who commits time and energy and money to a relationship feels invested in it. This individual cares about the stability of the relationship and is motivated to solve problems threatening it. He or she is less likely to ignore signs that a relationship is in trouble because of not wanting to lose the relationship benefits. The person who pays dues to a relationship values the relationship, feels positive about being a part of it, and gains satisfaction in having a say in it.

The third consequence of paying dues to a relationship is the growth of positive feeling in the person to whom the dues are paid. When one partner receives dues paid by the other, the receiver feels valued and cared for. A partner who receives dues of time, hard work, and money feels confident that he or she is loved and valued. This confidence leads the receiver of the dues to make willing reciprocal sacrifices and offer reciprocal dues to the initial payer. In this way, paying dues in a relationship begins a cycle of give and take, pay and receive.

If we are not willing to give up something we value, to invest our time, energy, affection, and money, then it is unlikely our relationships will survive. But if both partners are willing to pay dues to a relationship, each will feel valued by the other. Both will feel pride in the relationship, and they will have laid the foundation for trust.[1]

Nothing good comes of a relationship in which one partner pays his or her dues, makes sacrifices, and gives away power if the other partner does not reciprocate. Trust is developed in a relationship only when power given away returns in power gained.[2] If one partner, for example, creates time in his or her schedule to see the other partner regularly, but the other partner frequently calls at the last minute to cancel the date or often forgets to mark the time on his or her calendar, the hope of trust between the two quickly begins to evaporate. The partner who has committed the time and energy to the relationship, perhaps by sacrificing time at the office or perhaps by spending money on flowers or housecleaning, receives nothing in return for these sacrifices and gains no power or influence in the relationship. Relationships of this kind can grow dangerous in the extreme if one partner is abused or if one partner begins to hoard power in a way that prevents him or her from being influenced by the other.

Partners often find themselves struggling for dominance in a relationship instead of struggling as equals to make clear to each other what they want, expect, or need. This happens because they have lost mutual goodwill or because one partner is not strong enough to let himself or herself be influenced by the other. Exhaustion sets in when one partner must give away power constantly while getting little power back in return. With exhaustion comes a refusal to give away power, and then the partners find themselves in a continual power struggle.[3]

When a relationship becomes a power struggle, the only way out is for each partner to find more power. This can be accomplished if each partner is willing to find ways to give power away and ways that he or she can be influenced by the other. As each partner gains more power, each finds the strength to disengage from struggle, to compromise, and to build a new consensus without loss of face. Only when partners begin anew in this way to pay their dues to each other will the power struggle be replaced by a growing trust in each other.

Making Your Relationship Powerful: Who's the Boss?

It is clear that a relationship has power over us. For its sake we pay our dues and give away power in the belief that power will be returned to us. But how do we come to have power over the relationship? This is a question about authority. And how do we establish the authority? This is a political question. You find politics in a marriage just as you do in the government of a country.

Authority in a relationship is similar to the government of a country. Decisions must be made, and actions must be authorized. The authority structure provides ways to receive information, evaluate it, make comparisons, and transform the information into decisions and plans of action. When the authority structure is clear, partners in a relationship know what to do and how to use their energy effectively.

Governments of countries vary in the degree to which the people of the country participate in decision making and in how they are allowed to exercise their influence. At one end of the spectrum is a totalitarian régime, in which the ruler or party or military body currently in power makes all the decisions and the ruler may change laws at his or her discretion or on a whim. At the other end is a democracy, in which people possess certain rights that cannot be violated by anyone, including the government, without punishment and the people possess the means to control and direct the government. Somewhere between these extremes is a government that has a king or ruler but has laws that even the ruler must follow.

In a democratic relationship, partners work together on authority issues to create a structure in which each has power or influence that feels equal to the other's. Most of us probably desire this type of relationship. Some relationships work well, however, with a kind of "boss" authority structure, as long as the boss does not make decisions that are capricious or cruel. But whether a relationship is democratic, vests authority in one person, or is some combination of the two, a way for decisions to be made must exist in all cases.[4]

Nothing can destroy a relationship faster than the inability to make a decision. All of us have experienced a version of the following:

> She: Where do you want to go to eat?
>
> He: It doesn't matter. Wherever you want to go is fine with me.
>
> She: I want to go where you want to go.
>
> He: Well, I don't know. Can't you think of somewhere?
>
> She: Anywhere you want.
>
> He: No, I want the choice to please you.

A little more of this indecision and you may conclude that it is easier to eat peanut butter sandwiches for dinner — alone. While relationships may occasionally experience small bouts of indecision, extended periods of it will soon undermine trust between partners. Neither will feel confident that the other can be relied on to get something done, and neither will be certain who should make the decision or take the required action.

We might want to insist that a democratic authority structure is the only kind in which partners may have a relationship built on mutual trust. But while a balance of power between partners may be desirable in most relationships, we must recognize that a balance is not always necessary for there to be trust between partners. Indeed, a democratic balance of power may not always work best in some relationships.

In a relationship in which one partner is considerably more mature than the other, for example, a democratic relationship may not be possible to achieve for some length of time. Think, for example, of an older man, a widower, who marries a woman his children's age and begins to raise a second family. His second wife may reasonably defer to his authority on the question of how to raise children. She may quickly come to rely on his experience in child-rearing. It may comfort her to know that her partner has "seen it all before" and that she can trust him to be right when he is alarmed about the children or when he is not.

Or think of a young woman who has successfully supported herself for many years. She marries a young man dependent on his parents for support until the time he marries. He would be correct to defer to her experience in setting budget goals.

In both these marriages, one partner is more mature in a significant way than the other. In some cases the other partner may be expected to "catch up" with time and experience, but until that time a less democratic authority structure will work best for both partners.

Some undemocratic relationships are indeed happy ones. But most of us long for a relationship that obviously empowers both parties. This might mean that all decisions are reached by a negotiated, well-talked-through consensus. Or authority may be delegated and balanced. One may handle investments, for instance, and the other determine budget allocations. The partners' trust in the idea that the authority structure of their relationship is a democratic one requires that they feel their specialties are equally important. One partner trusts the other to defer in the area of the specialty. In successful arrangements of this kind the partners enjoy each other's dominance in their specialty: "Susan manages all our investments. She's a genius at it." "John picks out all our furniture. Isn't his taste wonderful!"

Democratic relationships, just like democratic governments, are complex. They require that both partners are interested in sustaining a viable authority structure. They require that partners make compromises and engage in the transfers of power necessary for creating a balance of power. Citizens of a democracy, however urgent their concerns, must choose legal means to influence governmental policy. They vote or write letters to their representatives or organize protests or contact the media to exert their influence on the authority structure. The same is true of democratic relationships. A partner in a democratic relationship will not plan a vacation or put a down payment on a house without consulting with the other partner. The partners must respect the authority structure and not threaten or subvert it in order to gain power.

This means the partners must be disciplined, flexible, and capable of making the compromises and engaging in the transfers of power that occur in democratic relations. Children and some adults do not have this kind of flexibility. They can only think in two categories: "I have power" or "I do not have power." Democratic relationships require mature partners who can relate to each other in a variety of ways to achieve the goal of shared power in the relationship's authority structure.

At some time in a relationship one or both partners will probably test the authority structure of the relationship. We may wonder if our relationship can process information so that a decision is made, but we may also wonder if we can tear down the authority structure in a test of wills. Can our relationship contain our lust for power, our desire to have our own way? Is the relationship strong enough to resist our worst self and protect us from becoming someone we hate? If the authority structure cannot contain our impulses, then our partner is not safe, and we are not safe from ourselves.

Using Relationship Norms: Another Road to Freedom

Whether the authority structure of a relationship is democratic is really not as important as whether it is *clear and predictable.* Partners can find security and competence in decision making only in a clear and predictable structure.

One of the functions of a healthy and stable authority structure in a relationship is the generation of *relationship norms*, rules that tell the partners what is expected.[5] Establishing and observing such rules results in security for both partners. This security allows partners to bring all their resources to the relationship.[6]

Relationship norms in countries and in marriages are created only when decisions are made consistently over time by a healthy authority structure. When partners have established relationship norms, they know what is allowed in the relationship, what is expected, and what the relationship will bear. They do not have to struggle with every small decision as it arises.

Relationship norms cover a large range of decisions. They govern who usually takes the car in for servicing, who usually plans the menu, who usually sees to it that the house gets painted or the lawn gets mowed. They govern whether in-laws are usually invited for the holidays and for how long. They govern whether risks are taken on investments and how much time is given to hobbies, sports, or friends outside of the relationship. They determine how much time a partner can give to a profession before the relationship suffers. They say whether flirtations are permissible. They govern (but do not control, of course) whether the relationship expands to include children, or more children. When partners have established relationship norms they know the small rules and large laws of the relationship; they know which can they can bend and which they cannot break.

The contracts we make around touching—when to touch, how to touch, whom to touch, and who touches—are essential to the survival of a relationship. Some people marry and say to their partner, *You will make the commitment to monogamy, but I don't expect to be required to meet your sexual needs.* Unless the partners have a healthy and effective agreement around the sexual norms for the relationship, there won't be enough trust so that both feel they are making the appropriate sacrifices to be together. This can even mean that sometimes a person has sex just because that is what the partner wants.

A relationship that has and knows its norms is like a group of jazz musicians who know each other and have an understanding of the beat and the melody of their music. Together these musicians can be as creative as their artistry and talent allow. A relationship with well-defined norms may also be compared to a team of basketball players who know what to expect from their teammates. On a fast break, a no-look pass will find a teammate above the basket ready to slam the ball through the hoop.

For a couple, norms give the partners the ability to dance the dance of intimacy. They know when and what to say, where to stop and where not to, what to touch and how to touch. This knowledge comes from practicing and learning what to expect. This knowledge becomes the relationship's normative structure and allows trust to develop.

The stories that follow illustrate how the three issues of paying dues, establishing an authority structure, and producing relationship norms are interrelated when creating a foundation for trust in a relationship. All these stories remind us that it is necessary for trust to develop and grow stronger for love to endure in a relationship.

Stories

How Paying Dues Opens Doors, Entitles, and Creates Pride

♦ Meg and Peter

A therapist, of course, does not learn everything about relationships from conversations behind the office door. One of the best stories I can offer to illustrate the consequences of paying dues to a relationship was told to me at a dinner party by friends who were describing their courtship. They both related their versions of how their relationship developed. First, here is Meg's story.

"I was not particularly attracted to Peter," Meg began. "There was no great chemistry in the beginning for me. We met in the parking lot at college behind the dorm. I had a flat rear tire, and I was staring at it when Peter walked up. 'Can I help?' he asked very politely. 'I guess,' I said. I wanted the help, but I didn't want to admit that I couldn't do it myself. His strength did come in handy, but I screwed the lug nuts off and on myself.

"The next week he sat down beside me in psychology class. We were teamed up in a class project. Then I got mono, and Peter had to do most of the work on the project. The school doctor told me to stay in my room, so Peter got special permission from the dorm mother to come to my room for the project. He would always bring me a pizza and a strawberry milkshake. (The doctor said I needed to eat all I could.) I could smell the pizza coming before I heard the dorm mother yelling, 'Man in the hall!' as she escorted Peter, the milkshake, and the pizza to my room. After that we started to date. He took me out to some great places, and he was a great kisser.

"My father died six months after we started dating, and Peter came to the funeral. He was so kind and understanding. I don't know how I would have gotten through everything without having his arm around me. The rest seemed to follow naturally."

The more Peter did for Meg, the more valued she felt. He changed her tire, catered to her when she was sick, took her to some "great places," and was there for her when her father died. His interest and sacrifice boosted her self-esteem at a critical time. This feeling of being valuable to Peter opened her heart. She felt safe and comfortable with him. She trusted him, and the love began to flow.

Peter responded with his version of their courtship:

"I had seen Meg around campus. I had been attracted to her for months, but I was too afraid to approach her. Providence must have flattened that tire. If I had thought about it, I would have hammered a nail in it myself. After I helped change her tire, I was a little less afraid. When I first walked into psychology class and saw her next to that empty seat, I turned around and walked out the door. Then I remembered that I had changed her tire, and I got up my courage and walked back into the class. I sat down in the empty seat, and that ensured our destiny.

"I was sorry she got mono, but I was glad to have the chance to worm my way further into her heart. The more I did for her, the more I wanted her. Toward the end of the semester, I decided I didn't have too much to lose by asking her out.

"I took her to the best restaurant in town. The maitre d' brought me the wine list, but I didn't know Boone's Farm from Pouilly Fouissé. Luckily Boone's Farm wasn't on the wine list! I think I showed her a good time. When she came back in the fall, I got two tickets to see Peter, Paul, and Mary—it was a great concert! But even though I had two hits in my favor, it took a lot of courage to try to kiss her. When that seemed to work, I was beside myself.

"I was sorry to hear that her father had died, but I think her father's death gave me my real courage. She was so hurt and seemed so glad to see me when I arrived at the funeral in her hometown. That was the first time she had ever introduced me as her boyfriend. When I heard her call me her boyfriend, I said to myself, *That's right. I have been a good friend to her.*

"She was sad for a long time. We would go out, and she would cry, and I would hold her. One of those sad moments turned into a warm moment between us, and as Meg said, it was very natural from there."

The more Peter did for Meg, the more invested he became in the relationship. In his words, "The more I did for her, the more I wanted her."

When we make a sacrifice for a relationship, we feel we have a right to be in that relationship. We feel entitled. Peter's hard work gave him the title of boyfriend and all the privileges which go with that title.

♦ Howard

Another delightful outcome of sacrificing for a relationship, or paying dues, is the resulting feeling of pride in the relationship. This can happen in a couple's relationship or with a group, as illustrated by this story of Howard's experience with the National Guard.

"In 1969 I joined the National Guard as a way to appease my patriotic father as well as to avoid the draft. When I went through Fort Dix Reception Center, where I had my head shaved and immediately had to start picking up cigarette butts, I promised myself that I would do nothing to further the cause of the military. I was assigned to Basic Training Company A. We were drilled in marching until we could march together. Now, I saw no harm in marching. In fact, it seemed like a dance, and the sergeant sang lewd cadences while we marched.

"Company A became a team that moved as if it had one mind, like a choreographed ant farm. Every day, morning and evening, we did what they called P.T., physical training. This included calisthenics and a two-mile run. Twice a week we would force march to the 'weapons' range.

"In the army, you didn't use the words *rifle* or *gun*. The M-16 everyone was issued was called a weapon. Any time one of us was overheard using the word *gun*, we then heard, 'Drop and give me fifty!' That meant fifty pushups. The forced march was ten miles long. We did it in an hour and twenty minutes in the heat of August. We all hated our captain, and we hated our sergeant even more.

"The day before graduation from boot camp, we were taken to a football field surrounded by a track. In order to graduate we had to run a ten-minute mile, throw a mock hand grenade at least thirty feet, complete fourteen rungs on a monkey-bar set before dropping off, do twenty-five pushups in a row without stopping, and run through two rows of tires. If we did well in these exercises, our company would get an award that took the form of a ribbon pinned on our captain's chest. As we walked onto the field, I remembered my promise to myself. I decided I would do the absolute minimum: run a nine-minute, fifty-second mile, do fourteen monkey bars, throw the grenade thirty feet, and so on.

"I started with the mile run. I don't know what happened, but my legs really moved, and in the last 880 yards, I sprinted. My time was just over six minutes! Next came the monkey bars. I did fourteen, then held on until I'd done thirty-four. Pushups were next. I passed twenty-five, and then went on to fifty-five before I was exhausted. I threw my grenade seventy-five feet.

"Our captain won a ribbon. My performance confused me. I wasn't sure what had happened.

"But now I think I know. I had invested so much in my platoon group that I couldn't help but feel pride in it.

In spite of my best intentions, the more I invested in the platoon, the more I valued it."

So sacrifice creates pride in a relationship[7] — a point that generates discomfort in some people. Does this mean that love can be bought, that the spirit is for sale? Of course not. It simply means that *we value what we work for.*

▼

▼ How to Make Dues-Paying Work

If you are not willing to give up something to be in a relationship, the relationship's passion is not strong enough to inspire the kind of behavior that will make the relationship work.

1. A person who pays dues to another and to their relationship feels *a sense of entitlement.*

2. A person to whom dues are paid (or for whose benefit dues are paid) feels *valued.*

3. Partners who pay dues to each other and to their relationship acquire a feeling of *pride in something that is more than either one alone.*

4. You may pay dues to your partner and to your relationship in many ways. Food and flowers are obvious ways, but partners can offer each other alternatives such as resources of time, energy, and money to help their relationship grow.

5. Allow your partner to make sacrifices. Do not be the one to make all the compromises or to take most of the risks. If your partner makes sacrifices to be with you, he or she will value you and your relationship.

Be aware of how much you have given up for a relationship. But it is no less important to be aware of the rewards you have received from being in the relationship. Become aware of what you have received for the dues you have paid.

▲

• Exercises

Visualizing

Go off by yourself, sit down, and close your eyes. Be still and ask yourself: What did I give up to be in this relationship? What have I lost? What have I had to grieve and let go of in order to be here? Let these thoughts roll through you.

Journal Writing

Write about what your sacrifices meant to you and how it felt for you to make them.

Talking with Yourself

Ask yourself these questions:

1. Did giving up these things bring me closer to my partner?
2. Are there some things I should not have given up?
3. Have I been willing to let my partner sacrifice for the relationship?

Talking with Your Partner

Sit down with your partner and talk about the value of your relationship. What have you received for the sacrifices you made? What has your partner received for the sacrifices he or she made? Discuss your sacrifices so that you are both aware of how much you gave up to be together. Was it worth it? Do you value the sacrifices you have made? Are you giving enough resources to each other?

Discuss your rewards so that you become aware of how much you both value the relationship. Talk to your partner about how being in the relationship makes you feel. Tell your partner what you are proud of. Ask your partner to tell you his or her feelings about the relationship.

The Power Struggle

♦ Charles and Loraine

It was the Wednesday-night meeting of my Compose Group, a therapy group for violent families. Near the end of each session, participants talked about problems they had during the week with the hope that my consultation and the skills they were learning in our group could help them resolve their problems without violence.

Charles, a neatly dressed man with a shaved head, raised his hand. Beside him sat his wife, Loraine, a stylish woman whose hair was a flow of tight braids.

"OK, Charles," I said. "What you got?"

"Well, it's about church. I go to one church, and she goes to another. I don't want to go to hers, and she doesn't want to come to mine. Neither of us thinks it's a good idea to go to different churches. We both think it would be good for us and best for our children if we attended the same church. I suggested that we shop for a church we both like. I nominated a particular church, thinking she would like it. We went. But she didn't like it, she said. Then two weeks later one of her friends invited her back, and now she wants to join that church."

"Well, good, problem solved," I said.

"I guess, but it hurt my feelings. I think the only reason she didn't like that church at first was because it was my idea. When someone else thought of it, then suddenly it was a good idea."

"He's reading your mind, Loraine," I said. "He can't do that, but he can ask you if he is right about his speculation."

"Well, he's sort of right. He makes all the decisions for us. It has to be his way, his idea, his plan or nothing. I get tired of it. And I'm not going to let him tell me where I find God. When my friend suggested the church to me, it sounded better because she told me she was a member and that several of our mutual friends were members, too. I didn't know this until she told me. I liked the thought of having women friends where I go to church. Since I rejected that church the first time, choosing it again was not his idea. It was my idea this time. And now, because it's my idea, he won't go, just out of spite."

"Do you both agree that this is a power struggle? It's not about the church or what is best. It is about who has the power, right?" I asked.

"Yes," they both agreed.

"The way to get out of a power struggle is simple. The principle you must embrace to get out is that you get more power by giving power away. Loraine, what did Charles say that you do support?"

"I think he's right that we should go to the same church. It would be good for our relationship and our children, but—"

"No buts," I said, "just tell Charles the ways you support him."

"OK, Charles, you were right to pick that church. It was a good idea. I'm sorry I didn't see it at first."

"All right, Charles, it is your turn," I said.

"What do you mean, my turn? That sounded pretty good to me. She said I was right. We got a deal."

"Well, you do have a deal, perhaps," I said, "but how much of what she said do you support?"

"Well, she's right about this: I like things to be my idea. I'm sure that's hard on her sometimes. I'm glad she found out about having friends at the church. She didn't know that when we went the first time."

"Loraine, can you let go of the power struggle now?"

"Yes. I appreciate he recognized that I had a point, too. And I can see how I might have hurt his feelings."

"Charles, can you let go of the power struggle?"

"Yes. I am glad Loraine understood me."

"So you agree to attend this church for now anyway?"

"Yes," they both agreed.

Most of us recognize Charles and Loraine's power struggle as the kind of situation we have participated in all too often. But unlike Charles and Loraine, we may have had difficulty recognizing that a disagreement is a power struggle. And we have probably not been able to see our way out of the struggle.

Power struggles happen when we believe we don't have any influence on our relationship. If we can't have power, we decide, then no one will. When this happens, we cannot make decisions. The relationship exists, but it exists without direction or focus and without any way to find consensus.

To get out of a power struggle, power must be added to the relationship. Both parties need more power in order to have the strength to disengage and cooperate instead of compete. Loraine gave Charles more power when she allowed herself to be influenced by his words. She listened to Charles's words and told Charles that these words mattered to her. Charles then felt empowered. He almost made the mistake of taking his influence over Loraine and ignoring his responsibility to empower Loraine as well. If he had done that, Loraine probably would have locked them into a new power struggle later to stop Charles from exploiting her. Luckily, Charles reciprocated. He listened to Loraine's words and acknowledged that they mattered to him. With each of them giving power to the other where possible, there was enough power for no one to lose face and for both Charles and Loraine to compromise.

▼

▼ How to Avoid Power Struggles

Do not believe that love's spark can compensate for the fact that you have no power over your partner. It cannot.

1. A power struggle signals that one or both parties feels overpowered by the other.

2. When caught in a power struggle, recognize that your partner is, of course, often right. Listen to

your partner and tell him or her what you agree with and what he or she has said that has influenced you. This gives your partner the power and confidence to give power back to you.

3. Try giving this kind of power for some time, but do not do it forever if your partner cannot reciprocate. If your partner cannot also empower you, get out of the relationship.

4. Sometimes when a power struggle takes place in one aspect of a couple's relationship, the power struggle becomes endemic to the relationship. The couple can avoid this if the couple agrees to limit disagreement to this particular area so that they can cooperate in the rest of their relationship. Agreeing to disagree means that you both know you may be wrong, you respect your partner's position, and you want your partner to think independently and to be "true to self" even if you disagree. Recognize that on the subjects of politics, religion, and other philosophical issues, mates may need to agree to disagree.

• Exercises

Visualizing

Sit in a quiet place, close your eyes, and relax. Think about the balance of power in your relationship. Do you feel powerless at times? Are you willing to express your desire for more power? What would it feel like if both partners in your relationship had more power and influence?

Journal Writing

Write about an incident that occurred between you and your mate that you now recognize as a power struggle. What was said (or done) by each partner which showed that certain power needs were not being met? Who "won" the struggle?

Talking with Yourself

Ask yourself these questions:

1. Do I have influence over my mate?
2. Is my level of influence enough for me?
3. Am I willing to allow my mate more influence over me?

Talking with Your Partner

If you have determined from your individual exercises that you do not have enough power in your relationship, discuss this lack of power or influence with your mate. You may be surprised at your mate's response. Your mate may be more than willing to help you achieve more influence. If your mate feels a lack of power or influence, try to help him or her in the same way. Remember, if both of you have plenty of power, you won't need to have a power struggle.

An Authority Structure in Crisis

◆ George and Helen

I had worked with George and Helen several years before when they came to see me about their daughter who had an eating disorder. George had at that time been a bright, commanding attorney who wore blue power suits with red somewhere in his ties. He knew how the world worked and how to provide for and protect his family.

Then he had a stroke at age fifty-six. He had recovered a great deal, but the left side of his face remained collapsed with paralysis and his left hand often shook. Today he was dressed in a cardigan sweater, polo shirt, slacks, and loafers.

Helen was dressed just as she had been years before, in a flowing skirt and blouse with a sport coat. Helen began the session.

"I married George because I knew he would make all the important decisions. I didn't want all the pressure of making a living and deciding what to do, and George seemed to love being in charge. When we went somewhere, George drove. I liked that and George did, too. I was the passenger in our marriage as well. If there was a problem, I could relax, and George would handle it. His decisions always seemed right to me. I was very happy until George had his stroke. George changed. I hoped he would recover and take over again, but he didn't."

"George, how do you feel about the change in your marriage?" I asked.

George looked down. There was a long pause. He seemed to be piecing together a response. Finally he spoke, his words slowly coming forth. "Well, Doctor, I'm not the same man I was. I'm just not as strong physically or mentally as I was. I feel like I have lost my face. I can't go to court anymore. I used to know what to do. I don't now. I look to Helen for that."

"And how do you feel about this change?" I asked.

"Well, I know Helen is unhappy with me. I think we have enough money for her to leave me if she wants."

"He is talking about the disability insurance payments," said Helen. "George had a good disability policy. It pays twelve thousand dollars a month. That is plenty of money for both of us if we were to divorce."

"Is that what you are considering?" I wondered out loud.

"No," Helen said. "I married George for better or for worse. I don't like this turn of events, and George now is a different man from the George I married, but I still love him. We raised our children together. He is my husband. I view marriage as a commitment. I'm not afraid to sacrifice.

I knew life would be hard. It could just as easily be me with the stroke. He withstood all this pressure by himself for a long time. Now I have to do it. I'm just not prepared." Then she turned to George.

"George, I don't want to leave you. I just want to get used to my new role."

"George, how do you feel letting Helen make the decisions now?" I asked.

"OK," he responded quickly. "She does better than I can now. I'm sorry I can't do for her like I used to. I liked it then, but I can't. At first I was mad at myself for what I couldn't do. I couldn't talk. I couldn't stand up. I couldn't use my left hand. I am grateful for what I can do now. You don't know how blessed you are until you lose something and you think it will never return. When it comes back, even part of it, you are so happy. Helen is so good to me. I just wish I could be more helpful."

"It sounds as if you trust Helen," I said.

"I do," George responded.

"It seems to me that George is adjusting to being the passenger, but the difficulty is that Helen is having a hard time being the driver."

"That's right," Helen said. "My grandmother always said that you can't run away from what you are not. I have never had a talent for keeping track of what needs to be done from day to day: home repairs, paying bills, all the decisions big and small that come up every day. I could always do what needed to be done if I had guidance from someone else. But now I must become a good driver as well. God is giving me a challenge to become all that I am. I know I can drive, and now I must."

Democratic arrangements are not always the best for every relationship. Before the stroke, Helen was happy to have George in the role of "benign dictator." George, after his stroke, was happy to have Helen in this dominant role.

The most important attribute of power in a relationship is that it reside in some person or in a decision-making structure shared by both partners. Helen and George had always had a clear authority structure that worked because it served both their needs. They could make decisions. Ambiguity and chaos did not overwhelm them. The relationship had been good for Helen because, for whatever reasons, she was frightened of the responsibility that comes with power. George had been happy to be the benign dictator because he was frightened by anyone who would compete with him for power. But when George was unable to function in this role, the couple had to create a new authority structure so that they could continue to make decisions. They used me to help them make the transition into their new roles. With a little practice Helen found her stride, and I was out of a job.

▼

▼ How to Diagnose Your Relationship's Authority Structure

Consider your relationship's authority structure.

1. The important thing to remember is that decisions must be made, and your relationship must have a way to make them. Decide how authority is distributed in your relationship:
   (a) A boss
   (b) A boss who is ruled by law
   (c) A form of democracy

2. When diagnosing your relationship's authority structure, *look at how decisions are made.* Most relationships exhibit some combination of democracy and delegated authority. Sometimes one partner is in charge, sometimes the other. Identify the areas in which you share authority, the areas in which you both have agreed to defer to a principle of a higher authority, and the areas in which one partner makes the decisions.

3. The only one of the three major types of relation-ship authority structure that is probably unwork-able is the first one, in which the "boss" makes demands without any consistency. A relationship in which conditions change rapidly on the whim of the dominant person is a frightening one for the other person. It is impossible to feel secure or safe when one never knows what to expect.

4. Partners in a democratic relationship should rec-ognize that in some situations it is best for one partner to take the lead in making decisions (with the influence of the other), and other issues are best resolved by both partners having an equal say. For example, sex and child-rearing work best when both partners share equally in establishing the rules. But one partner may be better equipped temperamentally to cope with a health emergency. One partner may have more knowledge or experi-ence that will benefit the relationship in a financial emergency.

▲

• Exercises

Visualizing

Sit quietly, relax, and close your eyes. Think how you feel when you must make a decision. Are you sometimes fright-ened when you have to make a decision? Are you more frightened by allowing someone else the power to make a decision that affects you? Do you feel happiest when a deci-sion is made by consensus? Are you comfortable deferring to a "policy" or a "higher authority" when you must make a decision? Your personal feelings about making decisions will be a factor as you and your partner struggle to devise a rela-tionship authority structure that is acceptable to both.

Journal Writing

If you are having trouble diagnosing the authority structure of your relationship, write about how decisions are usually made in some of these areas:

1. How are budgeting and purchasing decisions made?
2. How are child-rearing decisions made?
3. How are recreation and vacation decisions made?
4. How are decisions about "who will do which chores" made?
5. How are housekeeping and home decoration decisions made?
6. How are vocational decisions made?

Talking with Yourself

Ask yourself if you like the authority structure of your relationship. If both you and your partner are happy with it, you don't have a problem. If one or both are unhappy with areas of your relationship's authority structure, you need to discuss and probably change your authority structure.

Talking with Your Partner

If either partner is dissatisfied with the authority structure, both should discuss how you might revise it and set goals to work toward creating a mutually satisfactory structure.

The Power of Relationship Norms

◆ David and Marietta

Therapists learn important lessons from patients behind the closed doors of their offices and from others outside their offices. They also learn from their own mistakes. I tell the following story from my marriage to relate an experience that taught me to respect the power of relationship norms.

I had just returned from a golf trip with some of my buddies. I walked in the house Sunday evening at about eight o'clock, having been away since Thursday evening. I saw that Marietta had finished eating dinner and was watching television. She seemed indifferent to my return.

"There's a TV dinner in the freezer," she said, without getting up from the couch.

I unwrapped the frozen dinner and put it in the microwave. I carried my bag upstairs and unpacked. When I went downstairs, the microwave was beeping, so I took out my dinner, got a plate and drink, and sat beside Marietta on the couch.

"What are you watching?" I asked.

"*Masterpiece Theater*," she said.

We both watched the television while I ate. Finally Marietta broke our silence.

"Can you tell I'm mad at you?" she asked.

"No," I answered. "Are you mad at me?"

"Yes." She kept her eyes on the television as she talked. "You come in the house. I don't say a word to you, and I don't get up, but you don't realize something is wrong. I guess that's because if I had come back from a trip, you would be glued to the TV set too, and you wouldn't say a damn thing to me except for a few grumbles."

"What are you talking about?"

She used the remote to switch off the television, and she turned to look at me.

"When I go on a trip, I call you every night," she said.

"That's true," I said. "You wake me up at midnight when you get back from some party or something."

"See, you don't care."

"I don't care about what?"

"You don't care whether I call you or not."

"No, I just don't care for the phone calls that wake me up in the middle of the night."

"When we do talk, you act as if you don't care about me. You never have much to say."

"I wonder why," I mused.

"Well, I'm just treating you the way I would like you to treat me. When you go on a trip, I would like you to call me. It would make me feel better to know you're thinking about me. And"—she gave me a hard stare—"I asked you specifically to call me when you got to your hotel Thursday night."

"I got to the hotel at 11:30. I didn't get to my room until after twelve. I didn't call you because I was treating you the way *I* would like to be treated."

"David, I worried about you all night. Believe me, you wouldn't have awakened me. I was awake, reading, waiting for you to call, until three o'clock in the morning."

"How was I supposed to know that?"

"You were supposed to call the way you said you would. I've been worried about you all weekend—less so as time went on, because I figured the highway patrol or a hospital would have called me if you had been hurt."

"Well, I wasn't hurt," I said, trying to look on the bright side.

"It would have been better if you were," she said darkly. "Then you would have had an excuse other than that I don't matter to you."

"You know you matter to me," I said.

"How am I supposed to know that? If you called me, it would help me know that you care."

"Look," I said, "you have one set of ideas about how the person who leaves should behave, and I have another. Neither of us is wrong."

"I'm sorry," she said, "but I think you are wrong. Sometimes I feel we're drifting away from each other. We need to pay attention to our relationship. I love you, and I love us, but we have to work to protect our connection.

We can't just take it for granted. When you're on a trip, you should call me no matter how late it is so that we have a chance to remind each other that we are loved and are important to someone. We need to put some rituals or something in place to help us. When I come back from a trip, you should get up off the couch, turn off the TV, and come kiss me and talk to me. We need a reentry ceremony to help us recognize that one of us has been gone and has now returned."

"Maybe we should kill the fatted calf," I said.

"You make me furious."

"I'm sorry, I'm sorry," I said hastily. "You're right. I'm getting your point. I'll call you when I go on a trip, no matter how late it is."

"And I'll always call you," said Marietta. "I don't always do it because I want to, though I do sometimes. I don't do it because you want me to, because you don't. You would rather be asleep. I do it because we need for me to. It's important for our relationship."

Marietta was trying to establish a relationship norm. She was insisting that our relationship be ruled by law, not by neglect or by personal judgment. Without a norm that we both agreed on—that I would call when I arrived at my destination—she had no way to know that I was safe. She was afraid. She pictured me falling asleep at the wheel and hitting a bridge abutment. She had to use her own strength to realize that if she hadn't heard from the state police, I must be safe. This realization gave rise to another problem: she began to wonder how much I really cared about her if I didn't care enough to call to let her know I was safe.

This anxiety could have been avoided if I had done what I had agreed to do by calling her. I had failed to respect what she wanted me to accept as a consensus norm. Her trust in our relationship was threatened by that failure.

Some may dismiss this incident as an illustration of the differences between the needs of men and women and take the lesson that in this case it was wise for the man to "humor" the woman's request. But this is too facile an interpretation. When partners agree to a relationship norm, they are tending to the well-being of something bigger than either of them: the authority of their relationship.

We humans choose to serve relationship norms for love as well as for our own selfish reasons. We enjoy being part of a social consensus, something that is greater than ourselves. Norms that transcend the personal reinforce the relationship and give us the satisfaction that we are part of something "bigger than us." The power of the relationship norm is in how it turns us toward the relationship as a higher authority and away from selfish or careless choices. Creating and honoring these norms are the ways in which we build the trust on which love relies.

▼

▼ How to Create Relationship Norms

We establish relationship norms in order to "make up the rules of the relationship."

1. Creating relationship norms is an ongoing process. Do not overwhelm your partner with a massive list of expectations that must be put into practice all at once. A relationship norm may arise naturally when one partner says, "I like it when we do _____. Let's do it every Friday." A relationship norm may be established when one partner feels neglected in some way and recognizes that establishing a loving ritual, such as a kiss when coming together at the end of the day, may take care of the problem. Partners can establish relationship norms when they recognize that chaos threatens their relationship; norms help them get their lives under control.

2. If you have a democratic relationship, norm-making always involves conflict and negotiation. Assert the rules you need to have in a relationship.

Allow your partner to assert rules that control you in reasonable ways. Once you both know what to expect of your relationship and of each other, you can dance harmoniously.

3. A set of norms that is right for one couple is not necessarily right for another. One couple may decide that turning off the television at dinnertime means that you care enough about each other to give each other your full attention at the dinner table and that this rule is never to be broken; another couple, just as caring, may decide that gathering around the television to eat dinner in front of a favorite weekly television show is a practice that both partners enjoy.

4. Keep your promises. You can't have shared norms if you don't do what you promise. Integrity is essential to an effective partnership. Being loved creates expectations. These expectations become binding.

▲

• Exercises

Visualizing

Close your eyes, take several deep breaths, and think about relationship norms. Can a little ritual or "usual way of doing things" be that important? Can you think of a norm in your own relationship that appears insignificant but actually symbolizes something about your relationship that is very important?

Journal Writing

All relationships have unspoken understandings and expectations. What are your understandings and expectations of your partner and of your relationship? Write down as many of these as you can.

Talking with Yourself

Think about the concept of the "relationship norm." Ask yourself these questions:

1. Am I convinced of the power of relationship norms? Am I willing to live by them for a time to see how they work?

2. Have I recognized the norms that already exist in my relationship?

Talking with Your Partner

Talk with your partner about your expectations of him or her and of the relationship. Articulate as many of these as you possibly can. Ask your partner to tell you his or her expectations of you. This will probably cause a disagreement. But working out your disagreements so that your norms become clear will strengthen your relationship. Talking about expectations is like a relationship tune-up and should occur from time to time. You might even want to write down the consensus you develop as partners.

Democracy as a Relationship Goal

♦ Nancy and Ty

A democratic relationship is one in which each partner respects the right of the other to share in decisions. What is sometimes more difficult to see is that a democratic relationship requires that each partner demand a share of power. Ty and Nancy were struggling with this issue when they consulted me.

> Nancy wore a long, flowing off-white dress. Ty wore blue jeans and a cotton button-down shirt. They had fallen in love five years earlier. When Ty first met Nancy, he smuggled marijuana and had several casual sexual partners. He credited Nancy with turning his life around and

giving him a moral and spiritual compass. Lately their relationship had been turning sour, and today things between them seemed particularly tense. Nancy appeared worried and Ty sad. They weren't sitting on the couch together as they usually did. Nancy was sitting in the large overstuffed blue velvet chair, looking at Ty, and Ty was sitting on the couch, his head in his hands.

"I don't want you to leave," Ty said. "And I don't want to leave you."

"I know," Nancy said, "but I must go."

"I don't understand," Ty said. "Is there really no one else?"

"No. I still love you."

"You love me, and I love you, and there's nobody else. I don't get it. I thought we were married."

"We are. Our marriage ceremony was beautiful, and we have the calligraphy of our vows on our bedroom wall, signed by all who attended."

"But marriage means being *together*. What have I done?" Ty asked. "What can I do to change your mind? Is the problem sex? Is it another man?"

"I don't think the problem has anything to do with you. It's not sex. It's not another man. You've done nothing, and there's nothing you *can* do. This doesn't mean — to me, anyway — that we're not still married. I'm still committed to you. I don't want anyone else. I just feel a need for some distance. For me, our relationship is not the same as it used to be. You've remained the same, I think. I'm the one who's changed. Everything you once did that I used to think was charming irritates me now. I just need to get away from people and be alone."

"Can't we find another solution?" Ty pleaded.

"I've been praying about this for months," Nancy said. "I've thrown the I Ching about it every day. You've seen some of the readings. You know what they say."

"How long is this for?" asked Ty.

"I don't know."

"Can we find a compromise?"

"We've been over and over this," Nancy said. "Love doesn't require compromise. If two people love each other, neither should have to change. I don't want to change you."

"No, you just want me to get the hell out of your life."

"I just want more distance, that's all," said Nancy. "I don't see why you don't get this. Love means that we're both free. Love means we should be able to fit together without having to compromise. Love is the oil that should take care of any friction. If you ask me to compromise, you want to *possess* me. That's not what love is about."

"So you see love as being like oil, Nancy," I observed. "I wonder if love might not really be more like glue?"

"No," said Ty. "Nancy has to be right. I've learned more about spiritual life from Nancy than from anyone else. Nancy spends an hour a day in prayer, consulting the I Ching, looking at our astrological charts. She spends another hour collecting her visions and recording her spiritual wisdom in her journal. Nancy is a prophetess. Before I met her, I thought I was a lost soul. My life was a failure. I was ashamed to be living until I met Nancy. Nancy is my link to God. It has meant more to me than I can say to be a part of her spiritual journey. I believe her spiritual path will someday be followed by millions of people."

"Aw, come on," Nancy said, "I don't care if people follow my teachings. But I do believe that it is God's will that I live alone now. I cannot compromise on this. Love never requires compromise."

"I would like to offer a dissenting opinion," I said reluctantly. "For a mutually loving relationship to work, both people need to have influence in the relationship — and that requires compromise. It sounds to me as if Nancy's God speaks for *both* of you. It's as if you have two bodies and one head. I wonder if Ty could have a vision of what the relationship could be. And if he could, how much influence would his vision have on you as a couple?"

I turned to Ty. "I think you should trust more in your own spiritual connection and not depend so much on Nancy for your answers."

"I tell him that all the time," said Nancy.

I took a deep breath. "If Ty did have his own connection to God, independent of you, Nancy, I think the two of you might disagree even more than you do now. How would you work out your disagreements without compromise?"

"Love," Nancy answered.

"I'll move out," Ty said. "I don't want you to have to leave your home, Nancy—your spiritual place. I know how important it is to your spirit."

The relationship between Nancy and Ty ended a short while after this meeting. It is possible to feel sympathy for Ty and impatience with Nancy, but that's probably not fair. Ty gave up all of his personal power in the relationship to Nancy, and Nancy took it, as most of us would. When Nancy got this power, she found herself burdened with the responsibility for Ty's life as well as for her own.

She was trapped because she bought into the idea that she was a prophetess. Ty helped trap her by contending that Nancy was a spiritual leader and his own "link to God." Nancy couldn't give up her power, and yet she was burdened by having all the power in the relationship. She couldn't get Ty to claim his own power, and she was weighted down by being required to know what was best for both of them all the time. Inside herself, though she was afraid to admit it, she didn't want to handle that responsibility. In this relationship, as in most relationships, placing all the decision-making authority in one person was too much for one to bear.

In Nancy and Ty's relationship, one person ruled. Ty wanted influence, at least when it came time to decide the fate of the relationship, but he refused to claim his power. He had not insisted that their relationship contract be based on democracy. Nancy wanted a democratic relationship, but she may not have had the strength to respect her mate and share power.

Nancy and Ty had no way to make decisions for their relationship when Nancy abdicated her role as ruler. Because there was no way to deal with the power vacuum left by Nancy's withdrawal, ambiguity enveloped the relationship, and no decisions except the decision to end the relationship could be made. Though there are exceptions, democratic relationships tend to work best to meet the needs of both parties. Democracy requires equality.[8] Achieving the goal of democracy in a relationship requires that both partners assert their right to influence the relationship and make their claim for a share of the power.

There is one caveat, however. After working seriously to establish a democratic balance of power in your relationship, you may be chagrined to suddenly discover yourself in an old-fashioned game of teasing your partner as you "run away," or perhaps you may find yourself "pretending to be the boss"—and enjoying it! What is the truth about your games of power?

People enjoy power games. We have been playing these games for thousands of years, and we will continue to play them. A power game in a relationship may be something like *hide-and-seek*, *predator-and-prey*, or *dominance-and-submission*. There is nothing wrong with these games as long as they don't diminish you in your own eyes or in your partner's eyes, or diminish your partner in his/her or your eyes. If a power game results in one person emerging as more valuable than the other, this will diminish the relationship, and that will harm both people. Another thing to be wary of is "getting stuck" in roles that you no longer enjoy. If this happens, it is time for discussion and change.

▼ How to Create a Democracy in Your Relationship

Clients often ask me, "How do I get my mate to let me have influence?" The answer is that you cannot. The spark described in Chapter 1 should inspire each partner to be willing to let the other partner have influence. "I love you" should mean "I love you enough to let your feelings matter to me, even to control my behavior to some degree." Even in a relationship in which most of the decision-making power resides in one person, the loving "dictator" will take into account the expressed feelings and desires and needs of the other partner. If the love you receive from your partner does not give you some influence in your relationship, then something is wrong.

1. In a democracy both parties have equal value. One is not more precious than the other. Be sure you believe what Aunt Nellie says in the musical *Oklahoma*: "I ain't no better than nobody, but nobody's better than me."

2. Relationship contracts get defined in the beginning. It is possible to change a contract once it is established, but it is easier to start off right than to change in the middle. Insist from the beginning that you have a say in relationship decisions. Be sure to voice disagreements you have with your partner about sex, money, friends, and family.

• Exercises

Visualizing

Sit in a quiet place, close your eyes, and relax your body. Think about what a democratic relationship would mean to you. Do you have such a relationship? Are there areas that you wish were more democratic?

Journal Writing

Write about a time when a decision was made in your relationship and it felt as if one person was dictating to the other. Did something about it feel "wrong" to you? This may be a sign that you would like to work on making your relationship more democratic.

Talking with Yourself

Have a dialogue with yourself:

1. How important is it to me to have a democratic relationship?

2. Can I stand the conflict that might result when my partner and I work to make our relationship more democratic?

Talking with Your Partner

Building a democracy means you will have many conversations. When you talk about relationship issues, advocate for what you believe is right. This often means conflict. Conflict is a given in a democratic union. Declare what you want, and together search for a win/win solution.

Justice and Authority

♦ The Holland Family

I was seeing the Holland family: mother Lillian, father Jim, and adolescent son Jimmy—who was heavily involved in taking drugs, although his parents didn't know it. This boy was smart, and not just "work hard–straight A" smart— he was one-in-a-million smart. And he knew it, too, but he thought he was a little smarter and more special than he was. He thought he was an avatar, the next Jesus Christ. He thought he could become your personal savior.

His parents had sent him to me because they were concerned about a sudden change in his personal habits—the way he dressed, hair length, and frequency of baths—and a complete disregard for schoolwork. They said they were unable to "get through to him" anymore. When he first came to see me, he made it clear that his plan was to take me on and convert me, making me his first disciple by convincing me that the path to spiritual enlightenment began with marijuana and proceeded to acid. He looked the part—torn baggy jeans, T-shirt with pocket, shoulder-length hair, and sparse mustache and beard. He explained that marijuana and hallucinogens were God's drugs, and alcohol and cocaine were the devil's. He said he had a mission to convert others to this belief. He wanted my help in getting his parents to recognize his special mission on earth and, incidentally, to get them off his back.

We met with his parents the next week. His father, Jim, a college professor, was a tall man wearing a tweed jacket and wire-rimmed glasses. His mother, Lillian, wore similar glasses and a cable-stitched white sweater and skirt.

Jimmy chose the armed swivel desk chair—the power chair—for his seat. Lillian sat near Jimmy, on the end of the couch. Jim looked around the room. It was clear he didn't like the choices that remained to him: the blue velvet chair was too far away from his wife, but the couch would put him in a position lower than his son's. At last he chose to sit on the couch next to his wife, though he shot her an irritated glance before he took his seat.

I opened the session.

"Jimmy has told me some interesting ideas, and now he wants you to hear them. I'm sure you will be interested in them as well. My only request is that you wait until Jimmy is finished speaking before you comment."

Jimmy seemed pleased to have the protection of this rule. He explained his ideas about his own importance in the cosmos and his discovery that the use of drugs—the right ones, of course—provided the path to spiritual enlightenment.

Jim, trying to sit quietly on the couch, could barely contain himself. He listened to Jimmy for a bit, got up, changed his position, and cast his eyes at the ceiling, at which point Lillian, keeping her eyes on her son, patted Jim's leg as if to settle him down. Occasionally she cast a sour glance at her husband's disapproving body language as if to make him behave himself. Jimmy finished by saying, "To show you what I'm talking about, I would like to invite you to drop acid with me tonight. If that's too much for you, then Kathy and I will turn you guys onto marijuana. Dr. McMillan, you're welcome to join us. Well, that's it. What do you think?"

Jim looked straight at me. "Is it the drugs, or is he psychotic?"

"He's not psychotic," I said.

"How could you even think that about our son?" Lillian asked her husband. "That's Jimmy's problem. You don't try to understand him. Jim, if these drugs are so important to him, why don't we try them with him? He needs our support."

"Look, Dr. McMillan," Jim said, "do you see what I'm up against trying to raise this boy? She always protects him when what he needs is a kick in the pants. And now it's come to this. She wants us to seriously consider taking LSD with our son." His voice was dripping with contempt. "If I were not living this, I wouldn't believe it. God help us."

This family was stating the Oedipal triangle once again, but I was impressed. I had never seen a version quite like this one.

I started with the mother, because I thought she was the key to solving the problem and also had the most to gain from a change in the situation. "Lillian, have you always been caught in the middle like this? I'll bet you feel pulled apart as you try to love both of them."

"I do," she agreed. "It's horrible. Sometimes Jim gets so mad that I think he might try to kill Jimmy—or that he might die from a stroke. I know things aren't right with our son, but I just can't leave him to his father. I think his father hates him. I can't trust Jim. I know from personal experience that his anger is very scary. But I can't trust Jimmy, either; he does everything he can to provoke his father."

"Do you think he could have presented his father with a scenario more likely to send him through the roof?" I asked.

"No, but Jimmy is just a child. Frankly, I expect more from his father, but sometimes Jim acts as much a child as Jimmy does."

"I'll bet you feel sometimes as if you have two children," I suggested.

"I do," she agreed. "I really do. I'm so glad you understand that."

"I'm more worried about you, Lillian, than I am about them," I said. "All fathers and sons have contests, some meaner and more bitter than others. Somehow fathers and sons come to terms with each other—or they don't. There's not much you can do about it except get chewed up if you try to get between them."

"I feel as if that happens to me," she said, "as if they're both eating me alive. Sometimes I wish one of them would die. It wouldn't matter which one."

Jim was shocked. "What! That is awful. Lillian, I had no idea!"

"You should have had an idea. I've been pleading with you for years to be kind to Jimmy, as a father who loved him would. I don't care how you treat me; I can take it. But Jimmy—"

"To me it's seemed as if you always took his side against me—that you loved him, but you didn't love me,"

Jim asserted. "When I felt Jimmy needed someone to jerk him up short, you were there for him—never for me. You think I like wearing the black hat? I don't. But someone has to stand up to the boy, or he'll continue to be lost. Look at him. He thinks he's Jesus Christ."

Lillian turned to me. "What have we done?" she asked.

Things weren't going at all as Jimmy had hoped. His mother's defense had turned into betrayal. It was becoming clear to him that she had never really believed in him, she had just been coddling him. He sat stunned, mute, watching his parents' passion and shame for him emerge from their conversation.

I tried to answer Lillian's question. "You haven't done anything that millions of families before you haven't done. But Lillian, I think you are the key to helping this family change. To begin, it's obvious that you don't trust your son *or* your husband."

"I don't," she said. "I can't trust Jim to control his anger, and I can't trust Jimmy to keep from provoking his father. They can't do it on their own, so I try to control both of them—but I'm not doing a good job of it."

"I wonder if you could give up trying to control them," I suggested.

"I'm afraid to," she said.

"I think you're their prize, Lillian."

"What do you mean?"

"I think Jimmy, like any child, is trying to keep his mother for himself. He has learned that he can actually succeed at this by reducing his father to a fool. When Jim loses his composure and becomes a fool, you psychologically divorce him and join your son in order to protect him from his foolish, angry father. Thus Jimmy wins the prize. The prize is your love and allegiance."

Lillian's voice was small. "So you're saying I'm the problem?"

"Partly," I said. "I'll bet they get along better when you're gone for a few days. And I'll bet they even know how to talk civilly if you're not in the house."

"That's right!" Jim said. "When Lillian's not around, we do get along better. When Jimmy was younger, he and I used to go camping. While Lillian was around watching us load the car, we would fight, but when we got in the car and drove off, things got better between us." He looked at his son. "We always had a good time."

Lillian's eyes were full of tears. Her constant smile was beginning to fail. "So they're better off without me?"

"No, no, no," I said. "I'm only suggesting they're better off when they don't have you as the prize."

"What should I do?" asked Lillian.

"Have they ever hit each other?"

"No," she said.

"Then you need to join your husband, Lillian. Marry him, not your son. Make it clear to your son that you are, first of all, your husband's ally."

"But I'm afraid for Jimmy."

"I wonder if you're not really afraid for yourself," I said gently, "because Jim is so angry at you."

"He's always been angry," she agreed. "I've never been able to please him."

"So you use your son to prosecute your case against your husband."

"I never thought of it that way," she said.

"You have tried to ignore Jim's anger toward you," I said. "But your own anger at his unreasonable behavior hasn't really gone away. It's just pushed you into becoming the protector of a son who doesn't need your protection. What he needs are the challenges that his father can give him. I wish you could let go of your son, and you, yourself, protect yourself from Jim. Hold *Jim* accountable for how he treats you, not Jimmy."

"I've always tried to help them get along," she said. "I talk to Jimmy in the morning when I fix his breakfast.

I ask him to consider doing one thing that day that would please his father, to cut his hair, take a bath, clean his room, maybe mow the lawn. Sometimes he does one of them. Jim never notices, unless it's the yard, and then he just notices to criticize."

"When he mows the yard, it looks as if it was mowed by a drunk," said Jim roughly.

Jimmy spoke for the first time in a long time. "I'm mowing it by the clouds, following the lines I see in the clouds. The yard is a painting of the spirit."

Jim spoke to me. "I'm beginning to see what you're saying, Dr. McMillan. He does these things because they're guaranteed to get to me. And then I go off and that pushes his mother away from me as she runs to protect him. I have been a fool."

"Yes," I said. "But Lillian, you said you try to control both of them. What do you do to control Jim?"

"Every night before we go to bed, I ask Jim if he can find something good to say about Jimmy and tell him about it. Then I pray out loud for them to get along."

"Boy, that really puts me in the mood," Jim interjected.

"Maybe that's the point," I said directly to Jim. "I'm not sure that making love to a constantly angry man is very appealing." I needed to get Lillian's attention to help her finally see her predicament clearly. "Lillian, you're like a traffic cop in Jim and Jimmy's relationship. First you direct Jimmy to be good, then you direct Jim to notice it. But relationships are like two people dancing together, with both of them moving all the time. Directing them one at a time will only confuse them. In a dance class, a good dance teacher stands outside the couple, not between them. They will never learn to dance with you in the middle. Love between two people means that each person gets to influence the other and the relationship all at once. It's like dancing to good dance music."

"But they can't dance, and the music they make will be an earthquake," said Lillian.

"How can they learn another way?" I asked her.

She said quietly, "It's obvious things are not working now. Maybe I could try what you're suggesting, to get out of the middle and support Jim and stop protecting Jimmy."

I said, "Jimmy is obviously a brilliant fighter. He's been winning the fights with his father. One day Jimmy will be stronger and know more about how the world works than does his dad, but that's years away yet. He needs his dad."

"He may already be physically as strong as I am," Jim said.

"I have another suggestion to make to you, Lillian," I said. "Fight your husband about how he treats you. His anger toward you seems unnecessary.

"Now, Jim," I said, turning to Jim.

"Believe me, I get it," Jim said. "I have been a fool. You're right. I'm not going to let that little asshole beat me again."

"Jim, you're still a fool," I said.

Jim looked startled. I wish I could have thought of another way to talk to him, but at that moment it was the best I could do.

"And you will remain a fool until you can stop calling your son an asshole. Jimmy needs an effective father, not a rival sibling. You behave like a child when you call him an asshole. Your son is a child. Every time you join him in child territory, he'll defeat you, because that's his territory. Your job is to act like an adult, which you do not do. Your anger is poisoning your relationship with your son, and that's bad. But your son will survive. The most important thing you can learn from all this is that your anger is poisoning your relationship with your wife.

"Your son wants you to notice him," I continued. "He will get your attention. He's good at that. If you like, you can notice him for something positive. What can he teach you? We all know he's got a lot he can learn from you, but he wants to have something special to teach you as well. He can either teach you about drugs or about something you would like to know. Does he have anything to teach you that might interest you?" As I said this and looked at Jimmy, I wondered if I had not asked too much of Jim, but he responded immediately.

"Computers," said Jim. "Jimmy's a whiz with them. He's learned computer language and has made his own computer programs. I wish Jimmy would teach me how to work with computers."

"Will you do that, Jimmy?" I asked.

"Sure," he said.

The Holland family's story says much about the importance of establishing relationship norms. They are necessary not only for preserving trust between the partners but also for establishing clearly to all members of the family what the authority structure will allow. In this case the partners had not made clear rules about how Jim was to respect Lillian. She felt that Jim was always angry at her, that she never pleased him. Lillian feared challenging Jim with limits on his behavior toward her. Instead she tried to establish norms for Jim's relationship with his son.

But Jim felt Lillian disrespected him when she interfered in this way. Jim automatically resisted Lillian's attempts to control his treatment of their son, and consequently no one served as an adequate authority for their son. Jim and Lillian had no co-parenting norms. Neither respected the parenting style of the other. The only person who attempted to create and obey norms for how to treat the others was Lillian, and no one cared about how Lillian wanted to be treated. She could tolerate this disrespect from her son, but she was deeply hurt by the way her husband treated her.

Lillian would not get the respect she wanted from her husband until she demanded it. When she did insist on receiving this respect from Jim, they would have to struggle to develop norms for how she was to be respected. And when

Lillian no longer attempted to make rules for Jim's relationship with his son, the two of them, left to their own devices, would develop norms for their father-son relationship.

In the Holland relationship, influence became blocked. No one in the family allowed himself or herself to be influenced by the others, except for Lillian, and she did not have any real influence over her husband and son. When influence became unblocked—through decisions made by each family member to change behavior—it flowed in all directions at the same time. Jim and Jimmy allowed themselves to be influenced by each other, and Lillian discovered that she had real influence over both of them once she gave up her fruitless attempts to control them.

The Holland family's story makes it clear that justice, or an environment in which everyone receives his dues, is achieved only when each member demands respect and can accept the discipline of self-control and respect for every other member. Jim had to learn to control his anger and childish temper in order to meet Lillian's demand for respect; Lillian needed to side with her husband or stay clear of his disagreements with his son to meet Jim's demand that she respect his need to establish his own relationship and authority with his son. When both met these norms, they could support an authority structure that could withstand their son's manipulations, and he would benefit from having a secure authority structure in place. He would learn to trust its stability and trust his parents' love for him.

The Miracle of Trust

I knew from following the local news that the Hollands had started a family business that was now worth millions. Jim had observed that mail-order companies and companies that did lots of business by phone needed special computer software. Jimmy had developed his father's idea into high-quality software packages. Jim, a business-school professor, had applied marketing theory in selling these software packages to businesses. Whiz-bang—a family success story.

In working with the Holland family, I met only with Jim and Jimmy and with Jim and Lillian. I never worked with the three of them together again after the session related in the preceding story.

Some years later I got a letter from Lillian. I rarely receive letters from patients telling me how well they are doing and thanking me. In part it's because it's my job to become invisible after I'm finished and for people to go on with their lives as if I weren't there. This made Lillian's letter special to me.

Dear Dr. McMillan,

I am writing to thank you for what you did for my family.

I have continued to learn since we stopped seeing you. I had to fight. I couldn't just be sweet. I wonder sometimes if being sweet is a woman's disease while being mad is a man's. I don't know. Anyway, Jim changed. I didn't believe it was possible, but he did. I guess I did, too. Once I wasn't afraid of Jim anymore, and once I let go of controlling my husband's relationship with our son, I saw something wonderful—Jim and Jimmy began to get along. They trusted each other, and I began to trust both of them.

You were right. Jimmy was a good fighter. And he has plenty of other strengths I hadn't recognized. He and his father fought just as they always had at first, but in the middle something would happen. They would bring the fight to me to choose between them. I chose Jim. He started acting more respectful of Jimmy, and they would work things out. The problems between them became fewer and fewer.

Jim had, of course, been right to insist that Jimmy stop drugs and that we give him random drug screens. Jimmy agreed to the tests, but he later told us that he could have gotten around them with some health-food-store vitamins that fool the drug screen. But he didn't try that because he wanted to see if he and his father could get along. It is a credit to both of them — Jimmy began to grow up.

Jimmy taught Jim a lot about the computer. With each lesson, Jimmy's self-esteem began to rise. He was so proud that he had something to teach his father. Jimmy's hair is still long, but he doesn't wear it like Jesus anymore. He pulls it back into a ponytail. I'm afraid he has my father's genes, and in a few years there won't be enough hair to make a ponytail.

It is a pleasure to watch my two Jims now, but the greatest pleasure is that Jim and I now have a warm, loving relationship for the first time since before Jimmy was born. Before I had no influence in our family. Now they both listen to me and care about what I say. I find the more I let go of trying to control them, the more control I have. Trust creates trust. Faith creates faith. I no longer have to always be on my guard around Jim. I used to live in fear all the time, and now I don't.

Lillian's letter described what partners in a strong, mature, and viable love relationship often experience as the miracle of trust: it empowers those who give power away. When partners establish order through relationship norms that support a mutually acceptable authority, one based on principles of fairness and justice, they can trust that the sacrifices they make of their own power and control for the sake of the relationship's authority will return to them in power gained.

▼ ────────────

▼ How to Avoid Problems with Power and Build Trust

Negotiate a good relationship contract right from the start. Be aware that early in the relationship, when both partners are enchanted with each other, their eagerness to please will often lead them to avoid asserting themselves. As a couple emerges from this first stage, partners begin to deal with issues of power. As soon as you have agreed to be a couple, start defining what you want and what you are willing to give.

1. Observe the movement of power and influence in your relationship. Find where influence is blocked. Do one or both of you feel you have little power or influence? Do one or both of you refuse to allow yourself to be influenced? Do what you can to unblock the situation. This might begin with empathetic listening. If you need help, consult a therapist.

2. Are you in a relationship with an immature partner who insists on being the boss? If you are, do you want to remain in that relationship? If you do wish to stay, and yet you want the authority structure to change, you must demand respect and be willing to fight, not physically but by demanding that things change and that you receive equal respect. If this doesn't happen, you must be willing to leave. If your partner loves you and is not addicted to power, he or she will work with you to find a solution that works for both of you. Remember, there are a million options. There is no one right way.

3. If your partner won't participate in decision making, your partner has set you up in the oppressor role and has chosen the passive victim role. If you don't like your role, be patient. Refuse to make a decision until and unless your partner states a preference. If and when your partner does state a preference, include your partner's interests in your negotiated decision. In this way you can begin to achieve a more democratic partnership.

▲

• Exercises

Visualizing

Sit quietly, relax, and close your eyes. Think about the level of trust in your relationship. Can you see the connection between the level of trust and how power is used in the relationship?

Journal Writing

Write about a time when someone in your relationship was not treated with respect, or when things were "just not fair." Is such a situation symptomatic of your relationship?

Talking with Yourself

Before talking with your partner, ask yourself these questions:

1. What do I want in this relationship that I am not getting?
2. Am I willing to fight for it?
3. Am I willing to listen to what my partner wants?

Talking with Your Partner

If you have little power or influence in your relationship, you will need many conversations as you fight to get what you want. If there are others in your family, don't express your frustration by fighting someone else's fight. That will never work. Be direct. Fight your own fight when you speak to your partner. Doing so will give the outcome value for you.

Summary

The Elements of Trust

When trust exists in a relationship, it may seem miraculous and beyond explanation. More often than not it represents the hard work of both partners. It represents their mutual self-discipline and respect for each other and their desire to preserve and improve and enjoy their relationship.

Meg discovered early in her relationship with Peter that he was capable of making sacrifices in a way that led her to develop trust in him and in the relationship. Howard was amazed to discover the loyalty and pride that emerged within him as he made sacrifices for Company A, a group he had at first regarded with distaste.

Trust does not develop when one person tries to hold onto power. Charles and Loraine were able to reach consensus over which church they would attend only after they were helped to resolve their conflict by each allowing the other influence or power. George and Helen were faced with the challenge of changing their authority structure to cope with the new life circumstances created by George's early stroke. Helen had to learn how to assume more authority, and George had to learn how to let go of authority for their relationship to adapt to the sudden life change. Only then could they trust their relationship to provide the security they needed.

The story I have shared from my own marriage illustrates how democracy in a relationship is not static but challenges partners to face up to conflict, examine their expectations, and understand the rules on which their trust is built. Without this kind of energy from partners, even the most democratic of relationships will suffer lapses in which partners feel their trust in each other is betrayed.

Like George and Helen, Nancy and Ty were challenged to create a new authority structure, one that altered the balance of power between the two of them. They were unable to meet this challenge. Ty could not step forward to stand on an equal footing with Nancy, who was demanding a more democratic relationship. The question of whether Nancy could have made the compromises required by this more democratic relationship was never tested because the relationship ended.

The Holland family, Lillian especially, did challenge themselves to reform their authority structure, and from their efforts flowed new relationship norms that allowed each member more influence. They built a new foundation for trust.

It is important to remember that *there is no one right authority structure.* George and Helen had enjoyed a secure relationship for many years that satisfied both of their expectations before their trouble began. In their relationship, George was the dominant member. In the new structure they worked to create, Helen accepted greater authority than George. Trust was achieved in both arrangements. Other people in these stories—Charles and Loraine, Nancy and Ty, the Holland family—were all struggling to develop *democratic relationships.* Democratic relationships are most often likely to meet the needs of both partners because in them each partner is allowed power to influence the relationship, and most people want power.

What sacrifices did you make for your relationship? Do you have influence over your partner? Does your partner have influence over you? Do you do things not just for your partner but for the relationship? Is the authority structure satisfactory to both partners?

It is a worthwhile challenge to both partners in a relationship to resolve these questions so that trust may develop. Strengthening trust will ensure that the spirit of love has a secure foundation on which to thrive and grow and meet the surprises fate may have in store.

The Paradoxes of Trust

1. You get more power by giving power away.

2. When you allow your partner to influence you, you acquire more influence over your partner.

3. You have more control over your own life and over your relationship when there is an authority that controls both partners.

4. Having an authority structure to make decisions gives us more freedom than it takes away. Obeying that authority protects us from indecision, ambiguity, and chaos.

5. Contrary to the "happily-ever-after" myth, true love will blossom only with a fairly detailed definition of power and how it is to be used in a relationship.

6. Relationship norms are the basic rules we use to become creative lovers. With no rules at all, and never knowing what to expect, partners cannot become a creative team.

CHAPTER III

Trade

The Theory

A Relationship's Value

With truth told and safety for intimacy assured, with expectations clarified and order in place, and with trust established as the basis of power, two people are ready to sit at love's table. But if love is a feast where people satisfy their human desires, how can they learn to eat the right amount and not eat too quickly or too much? How can they make sure both people bring enough to the table and receive fair shares? The answer is the third principle in the McMillan Relationship Theory: Trade.

Our romantic spirit balks at the notion that love requires trade. We may wish to believe that love's passion and spirit are enough to sustain a relationship. It seems cynical and perhaps even "dirty" to consider love in the context of trade. But though love involves spirit, it also involves basic human appetites and desires—and these are satisfied through trading.

Psychology has devoted considerable time to complex experiments proving what most of us would accept without experimental proof: that people have wants and will persist in satisfying those wants. It is helpful to think of *what people want from love* in terms of three kinds of resources.

The first kind of resources people seek in love are those they use to keep them safe from physical harm. Love relationships can help people find food, shelter, clothing, and other materials they can use to protect their physical selves from pain and discomfort.

The second kind of resources a relationship can provide are those used for protection from emotional pain. The greatest enemy of the soul is shame. A love partner can offer protection from the great narcissistic wounds that come from shame and loss. Most social psychological research on the topic of emotional trading has been aimed at rewards that can be used to inoculate people from shame.[1] Status is one such reward. We often trade for social position as we attempt to find a social niche where we believe shame can't reach us.[2] Social psychological research has also focused on the ways that people trade for competence.[3] The competence of a partner can help us get pleasure as well as protect us from shame. Status and competence are just two emotional goods that people trade for. (I believe that social psychology has barely scratched the surface in its investigation of this topic.[4] There are probably as many kinds of social trades as there are people.)

The third kind of resources people seek in a love relationship are those they can use to serve their creativity. Almost all people want to express themselves and contribute their unique gifts to the earth and the human community. The impulse to seek joy in the risks involved in creating is as basic as the drive to seek protection. Love relationships offer a playing field for creativity and support people in being and expressing their unique selves. This kind of trading is most rewarding to people as they mature and grow spiritually.

Social-Emotional Trading

In a love relationship material benefits may be exchanged for emotional benefits (for example, one may trade financial resources for emotional support or for enhanced social status), but the most powerful medium of exchange is *emotional sharing*. Though trading for protection, material goods, status, and competence is essential, it is social-emotional trading that can help a relationship grow strong and endure happily.

In emotional trading, one partner offers his or her true feelings in exchange for knowing the other partner's true feelings. Social scientists call this *self-disclosure*.

Not all such trades are of equal value. The value of an emotional exchange depends on the level of risk entailed in the self-disclosure. To compare self-disclosure or truth-telling (as defined in Chapter I) with money as a medium of exchange, consider the value of your partner telling you what he or she thought about last year's weather in December. This would be of only slight interest to you, worth, say, one dollar. Then imagine your partner telling you how he or she felt when last December's snows prevented a holiday visit with relatives. A self-disclosure that includes a feeling about other people is of more interest and value than a simple thought about weather—worth, say, five dollars.

Now consider that your partner tells you how he or she felt about not being able to be with you because of December snows. The value of this self-disclosure increases because your partner is telling how he or she felt about you. Let's make that worth twenty-five dollars. Finally, suppose it's December right now, and your partner says to you that he or she wants to stay with you right now, snuggling in front of the fire, and never wants the snows to come between you again. Now your partner is taking a serious risk of rejection, exposing feelings about you in the "here and now" moment. This disclosure might be worth a hundred dollars in our comparative medium of exchange.

Feelings expressed about what it feels like to be with each other in the present moment are the most valuable currency in a relationship trade. But a relationship must mature to a place where these most valuable trades can be safely exchanged. Sometimes one partner wants to hasten development of intimacy by declaring his or her love for the other early in the relationship. This can be a form of emotional blackmail. If a person pushes a relationship into premature declarations of love, that person is often running away from the important awkward, frightening negotiation of a relationship. He or she is probably trying to push the relationship past the risky trading stage where there is always potential for rejection.

In most successful long-term serious relationships, emotional trading builds slowly. One partner declares an interest in spending time with the other. The other accepts. They have a date. One partner tells the other that he or she enjoyed the time. The other concurs. They date until one of them has the courage to risk a kiss. The other shares the passion in the kiss. The relationship proceeds at this incremental pace. Some relationships that explode into intimacy do survive, but more often distrust develops because partners have not learned enough about each other to feel safe. Because their trades have not developed slowly and carefully, they are not certain of their value to each other.

Three basic phases occur in the social-emotional trading of a relationship: (1) trading to confirm similarities, (2) trading to exploit differences, and (3) transforming trades.

Trading to Confirm Similarities

In immature or early relationships, people often trade to confirm what is similar between them. This is because acknowledging what they have in common helps protect them from fears of being unworthy or even shamefully deviant. When two people discover similarities between themselves, they feel more confident that they will be accepted because they are alike. It is a great relief to discover that a new person you are attracted to also loves to bowl when the last person you asked to go bowling laughed in your face! More significant similarities, for instance, in religion or race or social class, can increase people's confidence that they will be acceptable to each other. As partners trade information about their similarities, they confirm their identities, validate each partner's right to be, and protect themselves from rejection and emotional pain.[5]

In spite of these advantages, such trading does not create a real exchange because both parties already have what is traded. Differences between partners create the possibility that one has something the other needs.

Trading to Exploit Differences

In this second trading stage, relationships shift their search from looking for similarities to recognizing differences.

When a relationship can survive the threat raised by differences between partners, a search for differences becomes the process that makes real trade possible.

During this phase partners seek to inventory the differences each brings to the relationship. She, for example, may be more daring and experimental and will encourage him to buy the sports car he's always wanted and can afford. He, on the other hand, may have a better sense of humor and will help her learn to laugh more at life. Discovering and accepting these differences helps build what I call *complementarity* in the relationship. Rather than fearing their differences, partners will come to rely on them to varying degrees. The partners learn that they can segment and delegate relationship tasks to the partner who has the resources and skills to cope with a particular challenge. Each partner feels that someone stands beside him or her, someone who can see what she can't see or cope with what he can't face.

Couples with children frequently must turn to each other for the particular strength or skill or just plain staying power when one partner runs out of energy for a time. The focus of this second phase is on delegating and coping, though the couple who is trading for differences will find many opportunities for giving and receiving pleasure and the joy of creative self-expression. To be interested in self-expansion and personal growth, one must be interested and open to differences.

It is important, especially in the initial phases of a relationship, that the trades between partners be fair trades. People need to feel that they get back equal measure for what they give. If in a trade one party gets the best of the other, trust is destroyed. People in an intimate relationship expect to enjoy a long-term mutually rewarding relationship. How many of us would return to buy a car from a dealer whom we felt outtraded us? Intimacy without equitable value will be no more rewarding than a bad bargaining session on the car lot. For a relationship to last, trades must be win/win trades. Both parties should feel equally rewarded.

Sometimes a complementary trade is fair, and sometimes it is not. It's important that it be fair.

Partners seeking to explore differences will often discover their differences are complementary, and they can gain strength from this complementarity.[6] People who discover in someone else what they feel is the other half of themselves feel excited and attracted by this discovery. They often use the term "my better half" to describe their mate. It is as if they have found something in the other that fills out the part of themselves they felt was missing. Now they feel whole.

But what happens when the differences between partners repel them? Think of Professor Henry Higgins's question about Eliza Doolittle in *My Fair Lady*: "Why can't a woman be more like a man?" Sometimes people are attracted by their differences and repelled at the same time. In order to fit together they must first discover some significant way in which they are similar.

Finding this similarity will create safety and goodwill and the faith that the two partners are on the same team. The important similarity for a couple may be that they grew up in the same part of the country, or perhaps that they both place a high value on thrift and honesty, or perhaps that they have a religious tradition in common. With their similarity established, the two will feel safer to explore their differences.

Sometimes partners cannot find out where they fit together, and their differences continue to be a source of confusion, repulsion, and pain. In such a case, the help of a therapist may be needed. Both partners must trust the therapist, and if the therapist can use this trust to create an atmosphere of goodwill, then the two partners may be able to find creative ways to work together.

Transforming Trades

In the third phase, trades become transforming trades that teach and help each partner grow. Often in marriages this third phase comes after the crisis management of childcare is waning. Partners in this third phase know what they can and cannot do. They are chafing to grow beyond who they are. They want to learn to do what they couldn't do while they were complementarily engaged in crisis management. Instead of segmenting tasks as they did during the complementary phase, they want to do the things they once didn't have time to learn. Those who have been restricted to childcare may want to pursue a career. Those who have been exhausted by their careers may become more interested in nurturing friendships and relationships with children.

If a relationship doesn't explode from the natural impulse of the partners to free themselves of their limiting interdependence, each person can learn something from the other. Trade in this third phase is a matter of each partner teaching and learning from the other partner. The barter is no longer "I will do this if you will do that" but "Look, I can also do this, and I believe you can also do that." To work together in this third phase, a couple must achieve a consensus that they are mostly safe, and they must agree to teach and learn, each one to and from the other. With these agreements in place, a couple can begin the halting crossing-over into sharing new beginnings and collaboration in helping each other become whole persons.

Acquiring Grace

At first in a relationship, partners keep score to be sure they're not being cheated. At a later stage, scorekeeping becomes a way of being sure we bear our part of the burden because that is what we want to be sure to do. At this stage partners begin to give for the sake of giving—not for getting.

There are many examples in relationships where exchanges between partners have nothing to do with getting a good trade.[7] We often see this kind of giving for its own sake when a person cares for his or her mate at the end of life. Mature relationships can grow more spiritual and less interpersonally demanding as their love becomes well defined. Partners may begin to give to each other for the pure pleasure of giving to someone they love. Compassion and love for another is a gift to the self. Loving relationships that don't ever become strong enough to allow partners to quit keeping score eventually become empty and shallow because the partners never experience this joy of giving for its own sake.

In the religious world this giving for its own sake is called *grace*. In a love relationship grace is the unexpected, unpredictable culmination of telling the truth, trusting, and a history of mutually rewarding trades.

Grace is a gift. It is not something we can demand or expect from each other. It may seem strange, but we actually enjoy life more fully when selfish goals become less important. Life is lifted out of the ordinary when we lose ourselves in a transcendent purpose such as loving another.

The significant role that trade plays between partners in love relationships is evident in the stories that follow. In these stories people struggle to avoid bad trades and learn to identify fair trades. Their conversations shed light on questions about trading for competence, for status, for sex, for protection, and on the conditions under which giving purely for giving's sake can occur. Their partnerships testify to the risks and advantages inherent in the differences any two people bring to a love relationship. They make clear that the spirit of love and the bond of trust between partners are not above bartering but in fact are nourished by partners who welcome the work of learning how to trade fairly.

Stories

Similarity as the Basis for Trade

♦ City Boys and Country Boys

When I was in the fifth grade my mother sent me to
Mississippi to visit her sister—my aunt Jane—and Aunt
Jane's husband, my uncle Wilbur. I went under protest, not
wanting to give up a moment of my summer at home.
Mother drove me to El Dorado, Arkansas, bought me a bus
ticket, kissed me, loaded my bag on the bus, and watched me
ride away, my hands pressed against the bus window glass
and my eyes clutching at my last vision of her for the next
two weeks. I rode alone to Greenwood, Mississippi, where
Aunt Jane met me. On the drive to her home she told me
about a neighbor boy across the street. His name was Jack
Rhea Tannehill. "Jack Rhea is a year older than you," she
said. "I know you will like each other."

I didn't answer, but I was thinking that grownups often
made the same mistake. Just because they liked someone's
parents, they were sure the kids would get along. My father
had once taken me to Little Rock on a business trip. He was
good friends with a Little Rock lawyer, and the lawyer had
a son my age. He dumped me at the lawyer's estate in the
middle of the city. The son had a go-cart dirt racetrack in
his backyard, and when I arrived he was driving go-carts
with a friend. There were only two go-carts. I was the hick
kid from Arkadelphia. They were the urban kids who knew
about engines and were the proud owners of Champion
spark plugs. After I watched them race a few races, they got
out of their go-carts, and the lawyer's son's friend asked,
"How can we get rid of this hillbilly?" The lawyer's son
answered, "We can't. My daddy's making me play with him."

I was remembering that day in Little Rock when Aunt Jane mentioned Jack Rhea to me.

When we got to Aunt Jane's house I had supper with her, Uncle Wilbur, and my girl cousins Elisa, Carol, and Susan. Uncle Wilbur mumbled a three-second blessing, and as soon as he finished, my cousins were talking about Jack Rhea. I gathered that he was coming over the next day for breakfast.

After supper I went to my room and went straight to bed. I had been riding the bus for eight hours. I missed my mother and I dreaded meeting Jack Rhea in the morning. I quickly escaped my sadness and fear by descending into a deep sleep.

The next morning Aunt Jane's voice awakened me: "David, it's time to get up." I slowly rolled out of bed, dressed, and shuffled down the hall to breakfast. Sleep had almost helped me forget about the coming ordeal of meeting Jack Rhea. "David, you help Carol set the table," Aunt Jane ordered. I was caught up in that task when the doorbell rang. "That must be Jack Rhea. David, go answer the door," my aunt commanded.

I was slow to respond.

The doorbell rang again. "David, go on," she said.

I did. I opened the heavy front door to see a mess of a boy chewing bubble gum and holding a baseball glove just like mine. The first words out of my mouth were, "You have a baseball glove like mine, a Pee Wee Reese auto-graph Wilson."

"I like it," Jack Rhea said. And he walked into the house as if he belonged there.

Aunt Jane peered around the corner. "Jack Rhea, spit that gum out, go wash your face and hands, and tuck your shirt in before you come into my kitchen."

Jack Rhea laid his glove down on a chair in the foyer and strolled down the hall to the bathroom. He tried to open the door. It was locked. Susie yelled, "I'm in here,

Jack Rhea. *Just wait a minute!*" She came out carrying her brush and comb, glaring at him as she left the bathroom.

Jack Rhea came back without gum, hands and face washed, and shirt more or less tucked in.

Once Uncle Wilbur finished his three-second mumbled blessing, Jack Rhea and I began our inquiry. "Do you have baseball trading cards?" "Yes." "Do you have Mickey Mantle?" "No." "Do you play marbles?" "Yes. Do you have any steelies?" "Only a small one. I don't have a big one yet." "Do you like the Beach Boys?" "Yes. Do you like Elvis?" "Yes. Did you see the movie he was in?" "Yes."

We talked like this for half the morning before we went downstairs and played Ping-Pong. During that two weeks we became best friends. We went everywhere together, to the Neshoba County Fair, to the swimming pool, to my first boy/girl dance. We liked the same girl and we fought over her. But even when we had differences, we always were able to retreat to the comfort and support of the things we had in common. I will never forget Jack Rhea and my summer visits to Mississippi.

Differences threaten immature people; they can be used as weapons to hurt, shame, and draw boundaries that exclude. When we observe six- and seven-year-old boys and girls at play, we often hear, "Oh, she can't play. She's a girl," or, "I don't want to play with him. He's a boy." Children use similarities to bond and differences to reject. The two boys who excluded me in Little Rock were only doing what most of us have done and frequently still do when we meet a new person. The Little Rock city boys were searching for ways to reject the country boy—ways I was different that would prove they were better. Shame became their goal in a better-than, less-than hierarchical game. They used my differences to bond more closely at the expense of the country boy. That experience filled this Arkadelphia boy with fear and suspicion. I felt enormous relief when I sensed Jack Rhea was looking with me for ways we were similar.

When Aunt Jane ordered Jack Rhea to wash his hands and Susan got mad at him for intruding on her space, I knew I had discovered a kindred soul, one subject to the same adult and female forces as myself. Jack Rhea and I quickly discovered we shared many interests, and these similarities became the foundation of our friendship. We came from similar backgrounds and knew each other's etiquette. This gave us confidence that we knew how to behave in each other's world. We were comfortable together. Over the three summers I visited Aunt Jane we discovered differences, some of which became resources to trade and some of which created problems for us. Always, our similarities gave us the faith we needed to overcome our differences.

▼

▼ How to Use Similarities in a Relationship

When people consider the possibility of a friendship, they first search for similarities. The trade they are making can be expressed as "I will validate your likes and dislikes if you will validate mine." In beginning relationships, and in relationships between immature people, similarities are the most powerful bonding forces.

1. Don't begin a relationship by talking about how different you are. Begin by comforting yourselves with discoveries of how you are alike, the things you have in common, the interests you share. When beginning a relationship, look for shared challenges and shared opponents.

2. If you discover differences at this stage, do not use them as a source of shame. Be careful not to embarrass your potential partner with ways that you are not alike.

3. In opposite-sex relationships, differences are a given, and men and women may not develop inter-

ests that overlap. It is a delight, however, to discover shared interests and activities. After the relationship's initial stages, a man and woman may
forget the interests they once shared. Don't forget
these interests. Cultivate them together.

• Exercises

Visualizing

Close your eyes and relax, taking several deep breaths.
Think about the ways in which you and your partner are
alike. If your relationship is new, you will probably perceive
more similarities than you will if you are in a long-standing
relationship.

Journal Writing

Continue to think about how you and your partner are similar. Where do your similarities lie? In shared history, in
similar upbringing, in similar beliefs, in similar goals? Write
about the ways in which you and your partner are alike.
Remember, partners who are "too much" alike may have
little of value to trade. But it is necessary to discover at
least one important similarity in order to create a safe place
in which real trading can begin.

Talking with Yourself

Ask some questions about your partner and yourself:

1. Do our similarities afford a strong foundation for
    the relationship, or are we so similar that boredom
    may sometimes be an issue?
2. Am I willing to discuss this topic with my partner
    so I can learn how he or she feels about it?

Talking with Your Partner

Talk with your partner about the ways in which you are similar. Be sure that both of you listen with empathy, for your ideas on this subject may be different from your partner's. Discuss the meaning of the similarities in your relationship. Are you so similar that your relationship might be enhanced by a search for and acknowledgment of differences? Or perhaps you feel you are so different from each other that you need to find an important similarity which will increase goodwill and faith in your relationship. Some couples may begin a search for an important similarity by agreeing to see a trusted therapist.

Setting the Speed of Relationship Trades

♦ April and Carl

I have mentioned that in love relationships the most important medium of exchange between partners is emotional sharing. The value of an emotional exchange depends on how much a person risks in terms of self-disclosure. Sometimes partners have difficulty setting the pace of these emotional exchanges and their ability to make fair trades is impaired. April and Carl were facing a crisis of this kind when they came to see me.

They had been dating for four months. Both were in their thirties. I had helped April through her recent divorce. She had been sexually abused as a child and physically and emotionally abused in her previous marriage. She was amazed and delighted by Carl's kindness and his interest in her. But she was afraid to enter another relationship, and she didn't trust herself to decide about this one with Carl. She wanted me to meet Carl so I could advise her on what to do. I agreed to meet with her and Carl to help them sort out their relationship.

They came to see me on a hot, humid August day. Carl wore slacks and a golf shirt. April was in her usual neatly pressed slacks, blouse, and sandals. Once they were seated April began.

"It is all going so fast. Carl took me to look at rings last night. When I tried one on I panicked, took it off, and ran outside for air."

"Is it going too fast for you, Carl?" I wondered.

"Not fast enough, Doc. I love this woman. I want to marry her and take care of her the rest of her life."

"But Carl, I've been divorced only six months."

"When did you feel, April, that you began to go too fast?"

"On the first date. Carl told me all about his first marriage, why he had no children, about his alcoholic mother and his first sexual experience—all that first night."

"How did you feel about that?" I asked.

"Guilty. I felt that he had exposed himself and I was supposed to reciprocate, and I couldn't. I wouldn't. It was just too much. It's all too much for me. He gives so much. I've never met anyone so generous. I feel as if I don't have anything to give back."

"Well, you do, honey," Carl said.

"Carl's talking about sex, Dr. McMillan. Do you see my predicament?"

"Not right now," Carl interrupted. "I know, darling. But after we're married, in time you will get comfortable with me. All women, if you love them right, like sex. And I'm going to dedicate my life to loving you right."

"Carl," I asked, "do you think all women like sex if they are approached right?"

"Of course. Don't you, Doc?"

"I don't. Women have different levels of sexual interests for a number of reasons. One reason might be because of wounds they have experienced to their feminine sexuality."

"Wounds to feminine sexuality? What does that mean, Doc?"

"Have you told Carl your sexual history, April?"

"No, but I wish you would."

"I won't, but I think you should sometime if you want to pursue this relationship."

"OK, all right, I will," April spouted angrily. "Carl, I was sexually abused when I was twelve—by my eighteen-year-old stepbrother. This went on for a year. He told me he would kill our little sister if I told. He eventually went to college and left me alone. My marriage failed in part because I could never share myself with my husband fully. He responded by being a brute! I was always frightened. I don't know if I will ever enjoy sex."

"I don't believe that. Do you, Doc?"

"What don't you believe?"

"That she will never enjoy sex. What an awful thing to say. I'm sure if I'm patient and tender she will."

"Well, Carl, I'm not sure she will. I hope she can recover from this sexual wound, but some people never get over something like that."

"Well, I don't care," Carl said. "I'm in this now. I've given myself to her. I'm in deep."

"Well, I'm not in that deep," April said. "And I do care. I don't know if I can live under your constant warm gaze hoping that any minute I will become some sort of wild woman for you. It's going so fast. I feel that it's all out of balance. What do you think, Dr. McMillan?"

I hesitated to answer. But I didn't see how I could not. "It is not a bad thing for serious relationships to take time," I said. "Sometimes a big risk of self-disclosure such as Carl took on the first date can be a desperate attempt to pull the other person deeply into the relationship."

"Well, I do need her," Carl said. "I'm ready to love now. I want to get married."

"But Carl, April says she's not ready for a relationship to develop. And she says your readiness scares her. Usually when a relationship begins, each person takes a small risk and exposes something about herself or himself.

They gradually share more, deepening their relationship together slowly. April can't give as much as you can give, Carl, partly because April takes relationships seriously and wants to approach with caution, and partly because April is wounded and doesn't have it to give right now. She doesn't know if she ever will."

"And Carl," April said, "you want to give me a big flashy diamond and a mink coat. I don't want a big diamond. I'm afraid it will attract a robber. And Carl, I don't believe in wearing animal skins."

"That's silly, April. You wear leather shoes and leather belts."

"Yes, I do, but I don't like that I do. I certainly don't want a mink coat. And Carl, I love the symphony. I gave you a CD of Debussy's music with my favorite piece, 'Clair de Lune.' That piece means so much to me. And Carl, you haven't even played it, have you?"

"Well, not yet."

"Carl, what you have to give I don't value, and what I have to give you don't value. I'm always delighted by your attention and interest. You are the most generous and kind man I've ever met. But Carl, I'm not ready for you. You deserve someone who can appreciate all you have to give."

The session ended. Carl left devastated, and April left righteously validated. She came to see me the next week.

"Well, I don't think my relationship with Carl is going to last much longer. You helped me see how bad he is for me."

"Did I do that?"

"Yes."

"Why do you think Carl is so bad for you?"

"Because we are so different. We are not a good fit."

"I'm not sure being similar is all that great. It might make things easier, but it might not provide the challenge and excitement that being different offers. In fact, it is the difference between men and women that attracts them to each other."

"But the difference between us was just too much. He doesn't even like Debussy, and he expects me to wear animal skins and a huge diamond that will attract muggers."

"One of the differences between the two of you is that you live in constant fear and Carl doesn't. He has the courage to face daily life, to express himself and attract attention, a courage you need. You are afraid to leave your house sometimes."

"That's true, but he doesn't even like music."

"You don't really know that yet. He pushes too hard. He needs so much to be involved, just as you need to keep your distance and move closer slowly. He needs a partner with taste, poise, and grace, things he doesn't have. No wonder he is attracted to you."

"He does need some softening. I have some things he doesn't. And he . . . is so sweet to me. How do you overcome differences like ours?"

"It takes hard work. The first thing you must be willing to do is recognize that you have weaknesses and decide whether you need his strength. Then differences can become advantages, something you can trade. But Carl must also be willing to admit he has weaknesses that your strength compensates for. If he insists that he is perfect the way he is and that your need to go slowly and your present inability to enjoy sex make you a lesser person than he is, then you should end the relationship."

"This seems so hard. I'm afraid to be alone, and I'm afraid to be with anyone. Carl is rough around the edges maybe, but he has a good heart, works hard, and is kind. I trust him more than I have any other man."

"It is hard work. You may not be up to it. Carl may not, either. You don't have to do this. You may want to wait until you have gotten over your divorce before you take on another relationship."

"I'm afraid that if I wait until I'm over all my fears, I will be dead. I want to try. I want to ask Carl to try with me. He was kind enough to come with me here once. Will you help us if I can get him to come again?"

"Sure, I will be glad to pitch in with the two of you."

The currency of exchange between April and Carl was self-disclosure, but their levels of risk were out of balance. Carl was a bit foolhardy in his emotional risks, and April may have been overly cautious. Their pace of self-disclosure was not in sync. This frightened April and frustrated Carl. April was too locked up in her fear to expand her risks toward Carl. In working with me later, Carl was able to move with smaller steps. When April saw Carl working to rein himself in, she opened up and took more risks.

The McMillan Relationship Theory recognizes that people bring to a relationship different wounds, strengths, and skills. Not all women are alike. Not all men are alike. To love someone means that first you know who they are, their character flaws and their emotional strengths, information that should be divulged at a pace that feels comfortable to both. Certainly relationships challenge us to grow as April and Carl's relationship did, but people must be willing to accept their partner as they are, not as they want them to be and/or believe they will become. No amount of investment or trading will make your partner into something he or she is not.

This story presents an issue often found in relationship conflict. It is the issue of fit. April said to Carl, "What you have to give I don't value, and what I have to give you don't value." Couples in troubled relationships often feel this way. What it often indicates is each partner's inability to admit his or her own flaws. When both parties believe they are perfect as they are, they fail to see value in what the other has to offer. In a righteous position few people can find a comfortable fit with another.

If you are a conflict avoider, you should consider whether it will help you to choose a partner who is also a conflict avoider. Are you certain that avoiding conflict is always best? If you feel righteous about your way as being the best way, you narrow your trading options. You reject the positive value sometimes associated with people who are unafraid to face conflict. When April was able to admit that she faced a negative side in her fear and caution, then she could value differences and stop demanding that Carl be like her. When Carl was able to admit that he might not always be completely right on what a woman needs, then real trading between them could begin.

When a couple finds that their differences make them incompatible, they must seek help or disintegrate. April and Carl had enough going for them so that they only needed an "honest broker" third party, someone they could both trust, to help them recognize and value their differences.

▼

▼ How to Pace Relationship Trades

1. Tell the truth. But be sure your partner is interested in hearing your intimate secrets before you tell them. Your partner may not be ready for that level of sharing and may not be able to reciprocate. This may create pressure and guilt you don't wish to create. It may develop into roles in which you are the active self-discloser and your partner is the passive (bored) listener.

2. Raise the risk of your trades slowly. Don't meet your partner's risk level unless you are comfortable. You have a right to your defenses and to let your defenses down at your own pace.

3. If your partner begins to use guilt to coerce you to give something you are not ready to give, stop. Your partner may be using guilt to gain sex, a commitment to marry, a decision about having children, an approval of an expenditure, a decision about friendships. If you feel your partner makes excessive gifts or inappropriate confessions in order to gain your affection, explain that you cannot be bribed to feel

love. Tell him or her that guilt won't force you to give what you do not want to give.

4. There is no such thing as a perfect fit between partners. Creating a fit requires work and the recognition that differences between the partners are opportunities for each to grow. Differences enlarge both partners, and we should celebrate them.

▲

Recognizing a Fair Trade

♦ Maria

Maria had first come to see me for help when she was going through a divorce. Now thirty years old, she was trying to adjust to single life. She worked as a manufacturer's representative for women's sportswear. She had been a gymnast and now was dedicated to running and working out. She arrived at 8 A.M. on a Friday morning in her jogging suit. After we got settled Maria began to tell me what was on her mind that day.

"I really enjoy running with Karen. She's fifty and she's kept her figure and her health. I admire her. She has been through a divorce. She was single for eight years, and now she's happily married. I consider her my mentor in some ways.

"I was telling her about my relationship with Hank. He is really interested in sex, but I'm not sure this interest has much to do with me. Hank wants us to have sex. I didn't tell him this, but I really am not sure that I trust him. I did tell him that we don't love each other. He said love has nothing to do with it. He says it's just about our giving pleasure to each other.

"I confess I'm very attracted to him, and we've talked about taking precautions, so I feel safe. I haven't had sex in over a year, and I would like to again, but this doesn't feel right to me. When Karen and I were running last Saturday, I told her about how I felt and asked her what she thought. What she said made a lot of sense to me."

"What did she say?" I asked.

"'You probably won't get pregnant,' Karen said, 'but to have sex with Hank you'll probably take the pill. Does Hank have to take the pill? Will Hank's body swell with water retention? Does he risk high blood pressure and the possibility of cancer? And aren't we more vulnerable to sexually transmitted diseases? And how many times do prophylactics break? He is not risking pregnancy. You are. What if you do get pregnant? People do, even on the pill. You are the one who will have to carry the baby for nine months and go through the pain of childbirth. You are the one who will have to nurse it and take care of it after it's born. Or you will have to go through the physical pain and emotional scarring of an abortion. If something happens, Hank can just walk away. Don't let him convince you that it is the same simple deal for you as it is for him.'

"I told her, 'I have a friend who doesn't have a boyfriend right now, but she has a sexual "arrangement" with an old boyfriend of hers. She doesn't expect to have a baby with him, and she doesn't expect him to marry her.'

"'That is her choice,' Karen told me. 'Apparently she is either not aware of the hazards of such a deal, or she has made a decision that the risks are worth taking to get what she wants. But didn't you tell me once that when you get into a sexual relationship, you always become emotionally involved? To be fair to yourself, I would think you would want to be sure you trust the person you get involved with.' She reminded me that I am the one who would suffer the consequences, that it is my responsibility to be sure that the time is right, that the relationship is strong enough for me to feel good about taking this step.

"I think women have an instinct for when things are right for sex and when they are not. Men don't have that instinct. They depend on women to set the sexual pace."

"There's a feminist faction that would criticize such a statement," I said, smiling, "but you may be onto something there."

"Karen and I talked about what happens to a sixteen-year-old girl when she has sex with a boy on the first date," she went on. "The girl likes the boy. That's what he says he wants. She gives it to him. Why doesn't he come back? Why does he run away? The answer is simple, Karen said. The powerful event of sex was too much too soon. The boy knew something was wrong. He just didn't know what. He felt ashamed. But what was really happening was that he was afraid. There was too much danger. His female partner was not in charge of being sure that this was the right time and place. This meant no one was in charge. That is why he runs away.

"I remember the first time I had sex. It may not have been the perfect time and place, but I thought it was good enough. I misjudged my boyfriend. He didn't understand what had just happened to me. I went back to my sorority house afterwards confused, excited, glad to get that test behind me, afraid I might be pregnant, ashamed of what my parents might think of me now. I'm sure he went back to his dormitory excited and proud.

"The next day I went to class with the fear of what I had done getting stronger. I didn't see him. He didn't call. Days passed with not a word from him. When I finally ran into him three days later in the student center getting mail, I told him we had to talk. I asked him why he didn't call the next day. He said it never occurred to him. He had no idea what I had been going through. Men just don't get it. He'd gotten pleasure and so had I, but mine vanished in my sense of what was at risk.

"Sex for sex is usually not a good trade for a woman. Especially for a young girl, the trade is usually her risk, fear, and exposure for his pleasure. And for me . . . I guess it would be stupid to do something that I am not sure is good for me just because another person has presented it as a good, fair deal. I think I need to be the judge of what is a good deal for me!"

Often partners think they have something of value to trade in return for something they want only to find out that their partner doesn't value what they are offering. Partners who want to make a fair trade must understand value from each other's point of view. If Maria had agreed to the sex-for-sex trade Hank proposed, she would have gone against her own instincts and good sense. She would have betrayed her own sense of timing and would have put herself at risk. Hank, if he cared about Maria, would have been distressed to learn that he was giving something he thought was valuable but which actually caused Maria a great deal of anxiety.

Sex can be fairly traded. A fair sex trade might occur when a woman agrees to share herself sexually with a man she loves if he agrees to be committed to her and whatever comes from their union. If sex is treated as a sacred trust between them, it can become a wonderful trading resource for a couple. Others may not require as deep a level of commitment, but it is always important to be aware of your own expectations and needs when contemplating any trade.

If a sexual relationship is treated casually and the implications are not understood by both partners, it can become a source of great hurt and emotional pain. Each person should be aware of what is really being traded—especially the person who is the most at risk.

▼

▼ How to Make a Fair Trade

1. Consider how much of a risk you are taking in a trade with your partner. If you don't feel the risk is balanced by giving, don't make the trade. Wait

until you understand what you feel is unfair about the trade, then explain your feelings to your mate.

2. If a trade seemed fair at the time it was made but later doesn't, you can't change what has happened. You can change what you both agree will happen next. Don't make that same trade again.

3. Listen to your partner. You may not have seen what he or she feels. When you do see the risk from his or her point of view, the trade may seem more fair to you.

4. Remember, a trade always involves risk. The risk results in part from your reliance on your partner to honor his or her part of the bargain. The risk also results from the unpredictability of life. If you trade a share of stock and the whole market falls, it is not any one person's fault. Don't blame your partner for something he or she could not control.

5. Don't trade impulsively. Trades can have serious consequences. Be sure that your partnership can weather the consequences. Ask for but do not rely exclusively on the advice of others. Be cautious and use good sense.

▲

Trading to Become a Team

♦ Tina and Townsend

Tina was a dancer, now more than fifty, but still a dancer. She was the artistic director of a well-established dance company. Her husband, Townsend, had died the previous year. He had been her dance partner and co-founder of the company as well as her husband and the father of their two now-grown daughters. Tina was still small and lithe and had a face filled with character. She was dressed in sweats when she came to see me during a break in her rehearsal schedule.

"I need your help," she began. "I think one of my dancers is bulimic, and I don't know what to do. I think she began to purge when Townsend died. Without him I come across too hard, I think."

"I'm sure you miss him in more ways than this."

"I do miss him, so much sometimes I just don't want to go on."

"What do you miss about him?" I asked.

"I miss how I felt when I was with him. We were such a team. I knew him inside out, and he knew me the same way. When I was too hard on the dancers, he knew how to smooth their feathers. When we danced, he could throw me into the sky, and I was so tiny that I made him seem like Hercules."

Tina paused for a moment. She glanced out of the window and continued looking as she spoke. "It was like that for us always," she said. "I was thinking about the time we first crewed on a sailboat. We didn't know what to do, but we knew each other. We anticipated each other's moves. When I zigged, he zagged. We were so good together. Townsend had things I didn't, and I had things he didn't. He wanted the grace of a tiny woman. I was that for him. Sometimes I longed to be a strong man, and he was that for me. I was tough. He was tender. Together we were one. I never felt any greater joy than dancing with him. Everything we did together was like a dance. I feel as if when Townsend died he took my last dance with him."

Tina turned a firm gaze on me again. "But that's not what I came here to talk about. What should I do to help my bulimic dancer?"

Tina and Townsend had something wonderful together, a sense of fitting together and gaining power from their partnership that many would envy. There is a great reward to couples when their complementary power as a team transcends what they can accomplish and enjoy on their own. In these relationships each person brings to the partnership resources that the other values and that produce real rewards for both partners.

The rewards Tina and Townsend found in their partnership extended far beyond the limits of a comfortable style. Together they felt whole, empowered to act, and joyful. When Tina consulted me about how to help her dancer, she was grieving for this lost sense of wholeness and joy.

The risk to the kind of complementarity or mutual interdependence that Tina and Townsend shared is that these trades work and feel best only in the face of a challenge that the partners can overcome together. Tina spoke to me about crewing a sailboat with Townsend, running a successful business with Townsend, dancing with Townsend. Without him she no longer felt capable. She believed her dancer's problem was related to her own hardness, a quality Townsend would have balanced with tenderness. With Townsend, Tina felt she could have met the crisis. Without him, her dancer was sick, and she needed my help to find a remedy.

Tina lost her partner, but sometimes partners who enjoy the same kind of mutual interdependence lose their challenges instead. A couple who have based their relationship on their dependence on each other to raise their children well, or people who have enjoyed the challenge of struggling to build a business or improve a community, may find their enjoyment of each other reduced when the crisis they were so good at managing is over. There is no longer a need for the teamwork at which they excelled. They may resign themselves to a feeling of loss, but they will always want more. It is the fortunate couple who can move on to the next trading stage in a relationship, the stage of transforming trades.

▼ How to Make a Good Team

1. Know your strengths and weaknesses. Look around, experiment, find out what works best for you in a partner.

2. Practice. In order to know what you and your partner will do under pressure, you must rehearse. Don't back away from disagreement or threats from outside the partnership, but regard them as learning experiences.

3. In Chapter II we talked about authority battles, conflicts to see who will take charge of a partnership. Learn your patterns when these conflicts appear. See your respective characteristic roles in the drama. Understand that such conflicts are natural in any relationship and any system. Working through authority conflicts is simply working through systems problems; such conflicts do not have to threaten the existence of the relationship.

4. Never envy or punish your partner for the resources that you depend on him or her to supply.

5. Take care that the resources you seek in a partner will enable you to make real and not merely cosmetic improvements in your feelings of self-worth. In other words, make sure that you value the resources you acquire with your partner, that their value does not lie only in how they appear to others.

6. Enjoy your teamwork as you meet your challenges, but cultivate interests that allow each partner fulfillment outside the partnership as well. And cultivate interests that will allow you to enjoy each other when a crisis is over.

7. Both partners bring to a relationship their own *mishegosh* (Yiddish for "craziness"). Each partner carries around certain baggage. In a good team, partners learn how to watch each other struggle with their baggage. One partner's struggle with authority or struggle with self-control need not threaten the other partner. The partner does not get angry at the other for this personal struggle, nor does the partner try to fix it or solve it for the other. What a partner *can* do is give encouragement to the other until the other becomes more effective at coping with his or her personal struggle.

▼ How to Get What You Value from Your Relationship

Wanting is essential to passion in a relationship and should not be denied. Usually when a partner's desire for some quality of the relationship is extinguished, the relationship itself fizzles. Wanting something your partner can give flatters you both. It affirms your partner's quality as valuable and, in turn, sanctions your desire for that quality.

Here is the right way to trade for differences:

1. First, know what you want from the relationship. It is sometimes helpful to make a list of what you want.

2. Recognize that a relationship should give the partners status and enhance their competence. Think how unsatisfactory a relationship that did not do this would feel. Partners in a strong relationship are proud of their association and conscious of the benefits each gains from the other.

3. Accept that differences are an advantage to a relationship. They enable people to make complementary trades. Do not ignore, minimize, or be afraid of differences. Think instead of how these differences can be made to benefit the relationship.

▲

• Exercises

Visualizing

Sit down in a quiet place and close your eyes. Breathe quietly for a few moments and allow your body to relax. Think of ways that you are proud to be with your mate. Think of a strength your mate brings to you.

Journal Writing

Write about the things that you receive from your partner. Write about the things that you want from your partner.

Talking with Yourself

Ask yourself these questions:

1. What do I have to offer to my partner in our trading partnership?
2. Am I satisfied with the trades that are made in our relationship?

Talking with Your Partner

Ask your mate if he or she is satisfied with the trades that are made in your relationship. Tell your mate about the things that he or she brings to you that you value. Talk about the differences between you. Be sure you both recognize that differences bring excitement and value to a relationship. Think about how you can make your differences into trading assets. If you are having trouble doing this, consider consulting a therapist for help.

▼ Trading for Competence and Status

As mentioned, most social psychological research on emotional trading has focused on rewards, such as status and competence, that can be used to inoculate people from shame. With a nod to the prevalence of social psychological research—as well as acknowledging that trading for status and competence is part of the trade in any relationship—I offer the following simple rules for making successful trades. If you scorn individuals who measure status by invitations to "high-society" balls or by a partner's good looks, perhaps you will find a soul mate who believes with you that these things are shallow and that enhanced social position should be based on qualities such as intelligence, ability, or reputation for doing good works.

Our creativity comes into play when we decide for ourselves the kind of status that is important to us, and our maturity may be seen when we honestly look at what status really is. Perhaps we are wise at those moments when we realize the emptiness of status and, indeed, of many of the things we trade for. We are also wise when we don't punish ourselves for participating in the universal human search for status. It is as much a part of the life force as is any desire, and it can be used in positive or negative ways. Mature people have learned to view this drive (and other human traits) with a sense of humor.

Remember, there are many things besides status and competence to trade for. In the best relationships, people are able and willing to provide for each other a wealth of things that each desires. As you return to your journal from time to time and engage in discussions with your partner, bring into awareness the things of value that each of you provides for the other.

▼ How to Trade for Competence

Usually a trade for competence is an attempt to cover a base you don't feel you can cover yourself.

1. If you find yourself attracted to someone who can meet people well and you hope they will somehow compensate for your shyness, then you are trading

for their competence. The trick is to know yourself. Celebrate your partner's strength and be careful not to later punish your partner for the very thing that attracted you in the first place.

2. Often a trade for competence is a search for a match. You can dance alone as creatively as your talent will allow. But if you choose to dance with a partner, your partner's skill will affect how well you can dance together. Frequently, when dancing or playing a sport, people don't enjoy having a much weaker partner. They want partners whose competence matches their own. Be sure you know whether your partner has the strength you are looking for.

▼ How to Trade for Status

Whether we admit it or not, we are all status-seekers.

1. Know clearly what in your partner makes you proud of your relationship and conscious of an increased feeling of status. Is it her brains, his good looks, her good reputation, his social ease? Do not mislead yourself or a potential partner by failing to understand the kind of person you want to be associated with.

2. Don't deny the significance of status in choosing a partner. Consider whether you would be comfortable bringing home as a potential mate someone who spoke crudely, had terrible table manners, and didn't enjoy reading and music, or someone who made a large show of his or her wealth and was condescending to waiters, store clerks, and secretaries. If you find yourself bringing someone like this home, be honest with yourself about your motivations. Do you truly know and care for the wonderful person beneath an exterior of which

others may disapprove? Or are you showing rebellion or trying to get revenge on someone with your choice? When you choose a mate, you are making a statement. Be sure your choice corroborates your statement about yourself.

3. Often relationships end when one of the parties feels shamed by the association with the other. Sometimes this is because they come from two different worlds. One of the parties may not be able to negotiate the difference as being merely descriptive and begins to think in "better than/less than" terms. This often happens after infatuation ends. It can begin, for example, in a fight over whether to buy carpet now on credit or wait until you have saved enough to pay for it completely. If one partner feels shamed by the other for this disagreement, that partner may strike out in anger. It is important for both partners to know their own and their partner's values before they create a binding relationship.

▲

Transforming Trades

◆ Sylvia and Dan

I was surprised to see Sylvia and Dan's names on my appointment schedule. They had come to see me several years ago when they were having problems with their eldest child, a fourteen-year-old girl who had begun sneaking out of the house at night to be with boys and do drugs. That had been a serious challenge for their marriage, but Sylvia and Dan hadn't blamed each other for the trouble and had successfully worked together to help their daughter. I had counseled them briefly when they faced problems with their four younger children and remained impressed with how well they worked together as a team. Now that their children were launched from their home, I was curious about what possible problem they might be facing together.

Sylvia led the way into my office. A short, spunky woman with blonde, curly hair, she was an energetic fifty-five. Her husband, Dan, a good half-foot or more taller, quietly followed her. Dan still worked full time as an orthopedic surgeon at a large private hospital. Sylvia spoke first.

"I'm so bored, I don't know what to do. I can't believe that I'm a stereotypical empty-nester, but my life was so incredibly full raising our children that now it seems terribly empty. My children always had something to tell me. I know it was wrong, but I got involved vicariously in their dramas. You may remember you had to help me detach a little from our daughters. But I so enjoyed their struggles and adventures. Dan never talks to me. He just reads medical journals every night and worries silently about managed care and hospital committee work."

"How do you know what's on his mind if he doesn't talk to you?" I wondered.

"I don't," Sylvia said, glancing at Dan for the first time. "I'm just guessing. That's what I would be worrying about if I were him. He won't talk to me about his work, so I just have to imagine what his struggles must be."

"Is she right, Dan, about what she imagines?" I asked him.

"Not exactly," Dan offered after a few moments of silence. "I used to worry about the hospital committees and managed care, but the truth is, I'm not interested in that so much anymore." He paused. "I'm tired of work. I have to work, and I guess I still want to, but it doesn't occupy me the way it used to."

"Well, if it's not work, what *do* you think about?" Sylvia asked him.

"I think a lot about the children. I don't know them the way you do. They don't come to talk to me the way they come to you," he said, looking at his wife. He looked back at me again. "Sometimes I think about how I could become good friends with the men in my Catholic Craisio group, too. Sylvia has friends, lots of friends. She knows how to be a good friend. She's right that I don't talk enough. I don't know what to say to connect to people the way she does. I've always depended on her to make our friends. But lately I've been thinking that I want to make friends of my own. I don't want to depend on her. In fact I get angry at her sometimes when the children come to visit. I feel as if she's in the way."

"Well," Sylvia said, her voice surprised and a bit hurt, "I didn't know you felt that way. Why didn't you say something? I wouldn't mind giving you more time with the children. I'd welcome it, really. I love being their mother, but that's not *all* I think about. I'd like to do something else with my life, but I just don't know what."

"Well, I wish you would," Dan said, squirming a bit in his chair. "I feel as if you never ask me about anything except the hospital. I don't want to talk about work. It already gets too much of my attention. I think it would help if you'd find your own career."

Sylvia was quiet a few moments. She looked at her husband and then smiled. "Well, we agree about that, but I still don't know what to do. I've been reluctant to do anything because I thought you would resist any radical changes. You like dinner to be ready when you get home. You like me to travel with you when you go to conferences. You like me to organize the entertaining we do." Sylvia glanced back at me again. "And now that we have a grandchild on the way, I've been thinking I should be available to help my daughter as much as she needs me. I thought everyone would say that I was too old to go back to work and that they needed me to stay the same."

Sylvia and Dan both sat quietly for a short while. Dan broke the silence.

"You were an OB nurse," he said. "You could take refresher courses and do that again. I could help you find a job."

Sylvia colored a little. "Actually," she said, "I've been thinking about how I could combine law and medicine. I never enjoyed hands-on nursing that much, but the ethical questions involved in medicine really interest me."

Dan considered Sylvia carefully. "Ted Fredrickson, the malpractice defense attorney at the hospital, always works with a nurse assistant when he develops his defense. Is that the kind of thing you mean?"

"I'm not sure what kind of work I mean," Sylvia ventured. "I've followed in the papers the debates over reproductive technologies. People have so many more choices today, and sometimes I wish I could participate more helpfully in that debate. Maybe as a counselor for the young women who face these choices. I don't know for sure. How do you suppose you get the training to do that kind of work?"

"I don't know," Dan said, "but I'll ask. Maybe someone on the nursing staff could give us some leads. Maybe if we look at the nursing curriculum we'll find answers. I'd like to help."

Dan and Sylvia both fell silent. Sylvia still seemed a bit embarrassed by her admission, but they both looked excited and pleased with their discussion.

"Well, Sylvia," I said, "Dan has given you some good ideas, but I wonder if you could help him with his problem."

"Which problem?" she asked.

"He wants to get closer to your children and to find out how to make friends more easily. Can you help him?"

"Oh, that's easy," Sylvia said. "Everybody likes Dan. He's a good person. He's just reserved, so people are reserved with him. He needs to be more outgoing." Sylvia smiled eagerly at her husband, but Dan didn't seem to share her enthusiasm. He smiled briefly and then squirmed in his chair again.

"How would you suggest that he become more outgoing?" I asked Sylvia.

Sylvia paused a moment. "Well, the easiest way to get to know people better is to invite them for dinner. Maybe instead of me being in charge of the dinner, Dan should do it. I would help, of course, but he could decide on the guests, he could plan the dinner, he could cook it, and he could get all the credit for throwing a great dinner party. Maybe if his friends saw the party was all his idea, they'd see how much he enjoys their company, and they'd all warm up more." She looked at Dan. "We could try it anyway, Dan."

"OK," he said, smiling more openly now. "I'll give it a try."

"You don't have to do that much to get closer to your kids, Dan. They're crazy about you. Just make an effort to spend more time with them. Samantha walks in Percy Warner Park every morning at six. You could walk with her now and then. She'd love it if you called and asked to join her. You could do it on Saturday, when you don't have to operate. And you could go to New Orleans by yourself to visit Ben. We've always gone together, but I wouldn't be hurt if you said you wanted to go alone, and I know Ben would get a kick out of spending time alone with you there. He's found a place out in the bayou where you can fish and get a bowl of jambalaya that he was raving about the last time I talked to him.

"And when Julia comes home next month, you two should go out alone together one night, see a movie or have dinner. She'd love it. I know she would. Dating is practically impossible with her work schedule, and she worries about it. You could treat her to a night out and tell her to stop worrying. She's only twenty-five, for heaven's sake."

Sylvia's enthusiasm was contagious. By the time they left my office, Dan had been filled in on the current details of his five children's lives and supplied with many practical suggestions on how to forge closer ties with each of them.

Helping Sylvia and Dan was easy. They had a long history of making good trades and being an excellent complementary team. They had a basic trust in each other that allowed them to move beyond that complementary phase of their relationship into a new phase that matched their newly awakening desires to be more than part of a team.

What they discovered was that there was more to learn about each other. Sylvia had ambitions beyond mothering. Dan longed for more intimate ties to his children and friends. They had performed their complementary functions so successfully for so many years that they had grown to depend on each other in a way that prevented each from becoming a more integrated whole self.

Because Dan depended on Sylvia to nurture the children and make friends for them as a couple, he had not developed his own ability to grow in that direction. Sylvia, on the other hand, had depended on Dan to provide financially for the family and supply a link to an important professional world outside the family. Once her children were raised, she longed to participate in that other world, but she imagined that she couldn't play any role other than the one that had complemented her husband's in raising their children.

They discovered that if they were to move beyond being each other's complement to a place where each became a whole integrated self, they would have to make the kinds of transforming trades that encouraged each to move toward wholeness. They needed my help to facilitate their movement in this direction, but they had such a good history of telling the truth to each other, making fair trades, and building trust that they needed only a nudge from a therapist to help them move forward.

▼ How to Change from Complementary to Transforming Trades in Your Relationship

If you have enjoyed a long, rewarding relationship, the time may come when you and your partner want something more.

It is important to avoid becoming "the teacher." If you become the teacher, it is difficult not to be seen as trying to be "the boss." You can teach and consult without becoming your partner's instructor. Point your partner to the places where you learned.

This phase requires patience. If your partner is learning something that you do well, be careful not to gloat or stand on your mate's shoulders by telling how much better at that you are. Be aware of your own awkward learning as a beginner. This will help you avoid arrogance.

• Exercises

Visualizing

Go off by yourself, sit down, and close your eyes. Be still and ask yourself these questions: How does my relationship feel to me now? Is it helping me accomplish what I want to accomplish? Have my partner and I learned to work together as a team? If so, do I feel satisfied by our work together as a team? Is there something more that I would like to do or experience? Is the time right for exploring new possibilities?

Journal Writing

Think about some things you have always wanted to do but never have done. Perhaps you have only recently felt the desire to do or learn something new. Write about these unexpressed desires.

Talking with Yourself

Ask yourself these questions:

1. Does the time seem right to discuss new directions with my partner?
2. What kinds of things do I not know? What part of what I don't know do I want to know? Do I believe my partner can help me as I turn to new goals?
3. Am I willing to help my partner if he or she expresses new ambitions?

Talking with Your Partner

Ask your mate if he or she is willing to consider new directions in your relationship. Discuss whether the two of you think you can help each other with new goals. Be prepared to list skills your mate has that you don't have. Ask your mate to do the same, listing skills you have that he or she does not. Then ask each other what you each have to offer to help the other learn.

Replacing Justice with Compassion

♦ Marsha and John

Marsha and John consulted me regularly in their married life. They had come for twelve sessions of premarital counseling. They saw me a couple of times when Marsha was pregnant with their first child, Cory, and then again after Marsha delivered Jan, their second. I saw them as a family when Cory went through an adolescent period of anorexia. Marsha and John were both academic psychologists of some note. On a cold, wet November day, I nodded to them in the waiting room full of people, and they followed me upstairs without a word spoken. They found their place on the couch and sat down slowly and carefully. Marsha began.

"I went to the neurologist six months ago and received a diagnosis of multiple sclerosis. We're ready to talk about it now. We invited a group of colleagues to our house last night. They came as I knew they would, husbands and wives, all good friends.

"We separated. I met with the women, and John met with the men. I told the women that I was worried about John. The disease may someday make me an invalid. I may become a burden to John, and I don't want that. I asked them to help John and insist that John put me into a nursing home if the disease becomes advanced. I want them to help John make that decision. It will be difficult for him to make alone. I don't think he will do it.

"They promised me they would help, and they asked about how *I* was feeling. I told them I was not afraid of the disease so much. It comes out of remission and then goes back into remission. I might live a normal life. Some people do. I have so much I want to do. No, I'm not going to give up on life. I'm sure of that. I just don't want to drain the life out of John on my way out."

"That's my decision," John interrupted. "I don't see life being much fun without you. While Marsha was meeting with our women friends, I was meeting with the men. I told them about Marsha's diagnosis of MS, that it was like having a cruel intruder enter our home, a poisonous spider that we cannot find which will bite Marsha at unexpected times. Though I loathe this disease, I am grateful for it, too. It has made all my moments with Marsha precious.

"I told them about a ceremony we do once a week. Marsha takes an experimental drug that she must inject herself. A nurse came to teach her how to do it. After Marsha did it once, the nurse reinforced her with the comment, 'Good job.' Now every week while Marsha injects herself I sit beside her, and after she completes the chore I offer her a supportive comment like 'Well done,' or I give her an accolade like 'A woman with a big heart.' Every week I think of something different to say. Marsha seems to really appreciate this attention. I can't explain exactly what happens to us in this moment, but it is good. I look forward to it every week.

"Last night I told my friends that I needed their help. Marsha likes to be a player in whatever game is being played. She hates to be on the bench. She doesn't have to excel or win. Power is not her objective. Her goal is simply to participate and contribute. I'm afraid people will use this diagnosis to marginalize Marsha—to dismiss her as a lame duck, a retiring player. She would hate that. I asked my friends to be sure to include her in decisions in our church and at the university. Don't protect her by keeping her off important committees. Invite her to play. She will if she can, and the invitation will give her a chance. That is what I am most worried about. I want Marsha to live all the life she's got in her.

"They asked about me. How was I and all that. I told them that I was more awake than I had ever been in my life. Every moment seems so important to me. The moment I was telling them about Marsha seemed rich. This moment that we have with you, David, right now feels full and profound. I'm not worried about me. I am concerned for Marsha. If I can, I want to help her beat this thing."

Marsha and John's story is about grace. For a portion of their lives they were not concerned about fairness, justice, or value-for-value trades. The normal concern for justice had been replaced by mutual compassion. Life was transformed for both of them. They found reasons for their existence that they never knew before.

They did not remain in this state of grace. As they became used to the disease and learned to cope and live with it, their normal self-interest returned. One morning John went out to get the paper, half-conscious, and Marsha asked him what the temperature was outside. "How should I know?" John answered. "You were just outside, that's how," she replied. "Well, if you want to know what it feels like outside, go yourself." They told me about this morning fight proudly as an example that normal life had returned to them.

Marsha and John could not stay forever in a state of grace any more than anyone else can. Some relationships never have such an experience. But if we continue to make good trades that are mutually rewarding, it is more likely that grace will come to us.

For most human beings, our self-interest and sense of self will eventually return, along with a fear of merging, and we will again look for a victory or, at the very least, for justice and a fair trade.

▼

▼ How to Encourage a State of Grace in Your Relationship

1. Setting up conditions to encourage a state of grace in your relationship is a difficult task. In fact, it may be impossible. It is important not to be disappointed or angry if you and your partner cannot reach this state of mutual compassion.

2. For those who pray, you can use prayer to open your heart to feeling compassion for your mate. For those who don't, you can meditate on opening your heart and feeling for a moment your mate's pain in living.

3. You can have empathy or compassion without losing your own position. You can see how your partner feels and yet feel your own feelings too.

4. Remember, you can feel compassion for your mate, but you can't make your mate feel compassion for you, and you can't control the emotional climate in the relationship. Don't expect too much.

▼ How to Give without Keeping Score

1. We have seen that relationships most often progress through three phases: trading around similarities, trading to exploit differences, and transforming trades. This takes time and creates a history of fair trades that partners rely on to say what trades are necessary and beneficial in the relationship. Without confidence in a history of mutually rewarding trades, partners will feel anxiety when they risk giving for giving's sake and will very possibly disappoint each other.

2. Try giving without expecting anything in return. If it feels good to do this, ask yourself if such giving will anesthetize your partner to your needs. Will he or she stop considering what you need? If the answer is that your partner doesn't similarly enjoy such giving, your relationship may not be ready for this. And that needs to be OK with you.

3. If you stop keeping score in your trading, take stock after a period to be sure that fairness is still a part of your relationship.

4. Be careful not to indulge yourself in the hero role of giving, taking all of the strong giver's self-esteem for yourself and leaving only the weak taker role for your partner. Allow your partner to give to you.

▲

Summary

The Elements of Trade

The happiest relationship stories are those in which partners never completely lose their attraction to each other. Their respect for each other, enjoyment of each other, and pride in their relationship grow together steadily over the years as they share more and more challenges and rewards. The details of these stories always involve some degree of risk, uncertainty, painful truth-telling, admission of imperfection, compromise, and bargaining. And in these relationships, the partners have over the years learned how to trade fruitfully with each other.

People seek in relationships rewards that will protect them from pain and provide pleasure. Initially they seek similarities between themselves and others in order to feel safe and to protect themselves from shame. This trading for similarities is typical of relationships between children and immature adults, and it most often characterizes the first phase of relationships between mature adults. My youthful relationship with Jack Rhea was based on our enjoyment of our similarities, which made us both feel secure and provided us with activities and conversations to share.

This kind of liking for what is familiar in another person is the way that most people begin to gravitate toward each other. They exchange similar things: similar professional interests, similar tastes in art or music or a general appreciation for culture, similar enthusiasms for sports or politics, similar religious ideas, similar social assumptions, even similar degrees of physical beauty. The rewards they find in these similarities make them feel more confident of being accepted and valued.

Most adults, however, must learn to accept and enjoy differences in each other in order to sustain their relationships.

As the partners seek differences in each other that will strengthen their union, they can deepen their relationship. They welcome the way in which they complement each other and enjoy the power they gain as a team. April and Carl, Tina and Townsend, and Sylvia and Dan all had something to gain from what was different about their partners. They could trade qualities of equal value to each: April's refinement for Carl's courage, Tina's toughness for Townsend's tenderness, Sylvia's maternal competence for Dan's professional competence. Each couple could move to the second phase of trading that is based on trading differences to form a complementary relationship. Once partners begin to trade in this way, they gain more power from their partnership. Each partner supplies some quality that the other needs and values, and together they accomplish more.

Some partners wanting to establish complementary emotional trades experience difficulty in setting the pace of their self-disclosures. April and Carl clearly had problems of this nature. Carl was moving much too fast to respect April's sense of privacy, her fear of self-disclosure, and the wounds of her sexual abuse. Maria and Hank were also out of step, but Maria's insistence on honoring her own sense of timing prevented their relationship from running headlong into a sexual experience that she feared might create anxiety and pain for her.

In each of these relationships, the level of risk the partners suffered was out of balance because the partners either did not disclose their true feelings to each other or one partner raised the level of risk too quickly for the other. They did not properly value self-disclosure, the currency of relationship trades, or they used it inappropriately.

Complementary relationships may falter when the challenge or crisis the partners have successfully managed is over. Tina experienced not only the grief of losing someone she loved when Townsend died but also the emptiness of losing her other half. She had relied on Townsend in order to feel whole, and when he was gone, not only did she feel incapable of making good decisions, she felt only half-alive. Sylvia and Dan experienced a similar uncertainty about what they would accomplish on their own once the challenge of raising their children was over, but aging and the prospect of death did not cheat them of a chance to enter a new phase: a phase of transforming trades when each partner could become a more autonomous and wholly integrated self. Their aging challenged them to become all that they were before it was too late.

Sylvia and Dan shared a long history of fair and mutually rewarding trades that supported their trust in each other. They were secure enough, and what is also important, they had the freedom to encourage each other to explore further to see what each could accomplish. Sylvia agreed to exchange her parental competence and enthusiasm for Dan's professional competence and connections.

Marsha and John had also shared a history of fair and mutually rewarding trades that laid the foundation for a relationship of trust. They were able to experience from time to time a state of grace arising after the discovery of Marsha's serious illness. In this state, neither cared so much about receiving something from the other, but each felt and showed compassion for the other. You cannot plan or create this state.

It is a joy to lose one's self in something that transcends us. It is sad that grace often comes in the shadow of death, illness, or tragedy. Would that we could find it all the time and hold on to it forever.

The Paradoxes of Trade

1. Wanting and desiring something is more important than getting what we want. The human drive to want gives our lives a sense of direction and purpose. When we get what we want, we lose that direction.

2. When you trade to win, you lose. A good trading partnership is more valuable than getting the best of any one trade. If you get the best of your trading partner, your partner will stop trading with you, and you will lose a valuable trading resource.

3. Giving is just as satisfying as receiving.

4. When you receive graciously, you give self-esteem to the giver.

5. Carefully keeping score in a trading relationship creates an atmosphere in which the score will eventually matter less and less.

6. Trading solely for status and power can sometimes diminish our personal value.

7. A gift to someone not ready to receive it can become an insult and create an emotional wound.

8. Love will die if partners do not address concrete practical matters by exchanges of value for value. Romantic love is not enough.

9. Trading is risky: There are no guarantees that you will get what you want. But choosing to avoid the risks of trading does guarantee failure, isolation, and disappointment.

CHAPTER IV

Art

The Theory

A Relationship's Meaning

My mother and I were riding in the car together, returning from the doctor's office. We had just heard him speak words that meant death. "Mrs. McMillan, the tests are positive for pancreatic cancer." Mother seemed relieved. "I thought so. David, I'm tired. Take me home."

I was still in shock and felt numb as we began the drive home. I heard her saying to me, "Remember the time you fell out of the second-story window and landed headfirst in the flowerbox?...Remember how the team bus would wait outside your father's office while Toney ran in, stripped off his shirt to expose his hurt back, and lay down on your father's desk, and your father would tape him while he talked to his clients?...Remember how Aunt Margie used to go to her farm, pick lima beans and black-eyed peas, and shell them with me on the front porch while we looked after you children playing in the front yard?...Remember...?" All during that long drive home, she called up family memories, making sure they were spoken and not forgotten. Even in the lucid spaces between the comas that followed, she loved to remember—and I loved hearing her remember.

The power of parents to create art out of history for their children was wonderfully and painfully impressed on me during my mother's last illness. With each memory my mother was calling up the past, investing it with meaning, and passing it on as a gift to the people she loved. She was offering us the story of our lives together.

Partners give to each other in the same way when they share stories of their relationship. "Remember when...," they say to each other, and they tell stories that give their relationship meaning.

If truth-telling makes fire and trust provides a relationship infrastructure and trade creates a relationship's economy, then *art* provides a way for partners to take note of themselves and celebrate the good fortune of being together. The art of a relationship represents the transcendent values inherent in the relationship's bonds. The raw material of relationship art is a relationship's history.

Relationship art is created when a couple takes their shared history and truths and acknowledges them through stories, pictures, rituals, traditions, and symbols. Creating art together ennobles a relationship. It allows people to move above selfish smallness to transcendent things that are more important than either person. People need to remember and think about the wonderful assets of their relationships. They do this by creating relationship art.

Partners who make their history into art create for themselves and their relationship a sense of identity and clarity. They become certain of what they mean to each other, why they are together, and what they have learned together. Often couples who have not done this can learn how to acknowledge and symbolize their shared experience and thus celebrate each other and their union.

How to Make History by Spending Time Together

Without spending time together it is nearly impossible for a couple to build the shared history that is the raw material of relationship art.[1] It is difficult to develop a sense of history for those couples who have long-distance relationships and whose time together is severely infringed upon by their jobs, their children, their parents, illness, or other events that frequently separate them.

But a couple need not be present together in time and space in order to share an event. Partners who are divided by war can share the fear and the experience of longing for each other that war creates. Partners who sometimes must live apart can create a shared history through letters, regular telephone calls, and memorable rituals of reunion.

A couple can even create part of their history from events that precede their partnership. One couple I met through my practice bonded around the event of John Lennon's death. They were not partners at the time of his death, but both had been ardent Beatles fans, both watched the coverage of his death on television, and both were affected by his death in the same way. The event of his death became a part of their shared history.

What Makes an Event Memorable?

In order for a couple to remember an event as part of their "story," they must satisfy two conditions: The event must be shared, and the event must be dramatic.[2]

To experience an event as shared, both partners in the relationship must see themselves in the same boat sharing the same consequences of the event. When Jackie Joyner Kersee pulled out of the Olympic Heptathalon in 1996, she didn't pull out of that contest alone. When she withdrew, her husband and coach, Bobby Kersee, felt the same painful loss. Five days later, when Jackie returned to win a bronze medal in the long jump, she and her husband shared the triumph.

To be memorable, something about the shared event must turn on, arouse, excite, or energize both partners in some way. This quality may be danger, competition, seduction, conquest, or another dramatic quality. Almost always, the event is one that poses a challenge to the couple. In a previous version of the McMillan Relationship Theory I used the word *valent* to describe such an event. *Valent* in this case means "dramatic."

It is a strange part of the human genetic programming that when we are free of challenges which make demands upon us, our minds drift into depression and despair. When we achieve a goal and have nothing more to do, what do we do? We become dissatisfied, create another goal, and get back to work, unhappy that we haven't yet achieved our new goal. We are never long content with what we have achieved.

Sharing a challenge brings a new level of satisfaction and joy. There is a great feeling when a runner wins a race, but there is a different, stronger, longer-lasting feeling when a team wins together. When one person joins with another to face a shared challenge, each gains a feeling of joy that transcends the self. Athletes often say that a team victory means more to them than any personal achievement. Most people feel good when they believe they are part of a team or a group that is serving the common good.

When we lose ourselves in a transcendent purpose, when we don't have to defend ourselves against the rest of the universe alone, when we are joined, we know there is more to life than just pleasing the self. For partners in a relationship, these shared challenges can range from coping with a financial loss to weathering the death of a parent to overcoming the threat of infidelity. Possibly no greater shared challenge exists for partners in a relationship—no more meaningful dramatic history—than their story of the birth of a child.

What Makes an Event Worthy of Becoming Art?

Several aspects of a dramatic or valent event can distinguish it as being the raw material of art. The first aspect is *the amount of investment the partners have in the outcome of the event.*[3]

Some partners may not recall much about finding the first home they shared together. They may remember that it was smaller, cheaper, and less well-furnished than their current home. Other partners may remember the acquisition of their first home as the first challenge they met together. Perhaps they saved and scraped and bought a home they'd always dreamed of owning. They slowly restored it, one room at a time, and gradually they built together the home in which they live today. It stands as a symbol of their shared dedication. Finding this home was a dramatic event in their relationship, an event whose outcome they both deeply valued. They weave the story about their home into the myth they create about what two people sharing a dream can accomplish together.

A second aspect that determines whether an event becomes art is *the level of ambiguity associated with the event*.[4] The level of ambiguity should be low. Myths most often have clearly drawn archetypal characters who represent universals such as good, evil, temptation, the familiar, the unknown, the fallen, the resurrected. Chaos may be represented in a myth, but at the end, order must overcome confusion or no clear truth emerges from the story. If a life event is not resolved with closure, both parties will be discouraged, and neither will have the clarity required to collect the episode as worthy of remembering.

Consider, for example, what happens when partners feel ambiguous about what is usually a significant life event, the birth of a first child. Perhaps they were not married at the time the child was born. Perhaps they were not even in love. Perhaps they married later, out of guilt, and only gradually and with difficulty built a relationship. If they never agree on the significance of the birth of the child, they will be unable to weave the story into the meaningful myths they tell about their relationship.

A third aspect that determines whether an event will become art is *the kind of outcome that characterizes the event*. Successful outcomes bond people together. Failures often drive them apart.[5]

This does not mean that a relationship cannot work to overcome one failure or a string of bad outcomes. In fact, we should view overcoming adversity to achieve a goal as a success. Many partnership myths are woven out of the struggle against adversity. But failure never relieved by success seldom leads to art. Partners who never achieve the goals they set out to achieve seldom remain together. If they do remain together, their stories are often bitter stories about their individual suffering, not about their collective sharing. Such history does not make ennobling art.

It's important to stress that partners should not make their goal the complete elimination of uncertainty. No one can predict the future. Partners cannot completely guarantee an outcome no matter how much they invest in an event. Instead, partners should focus on approaching the future as a team. The best way for partners to guarantee success is to put forth their best effort and accept a number of potential outcomes as successes. Understood in this way, success characterizes the approach partners take toward their goal. It is not merely a matter of whether or not they achieve the goal. Goals approached by partners in this way are best remembered for the burden the partners carried together, the upward road they traveled, the encouragement they offered each other, and all the other details that go into a good adventure story. In this way partners can make the history of their successes into art.

What Is Truth in Relationship Art?

Truth in relationship art is not about the accurate depiction of reality. It is not really important that partners remember events with factual correctness. The truth that partners focus on in their art is transcendent truth.

The dramatic events we use to make art are those that we can make into a meaningful myth. In relationship myths, faith battles with fear. Stories and symbols that create fear protect a relationship. Stories and symbols that create hope encourage risk-taking. These are much more important than the photographic remembering of actual events.

Often the story of how a couple met becomes a symbol for the birth of the relationship: a hard birth, an easy birth, a painful birth, an unplanned birth, an almost-didn't-make-it birth. Frequently the story of the birth of a real child carries symbolic weight representing a couple's fertility or celebrating their ancestral line. A dangerous event retold in laughter may symbolize the couple's prevailing worldview: *Life is risky, and you must make the best of it.*

Don't blame each other if you sometimes distort reality to make a good story. A good story is the truth, a truth more important than cold facts. It is the transcendent meaning of mythological proportions that transforms an event into the relationship's treasure chest of art. Stories are collected, saved, told, and retold. In each retelling of these stories, the fish get bigger, and Paul Bunyan, a man, becomes a giant. If a story is a product of exaggerated history, the exaggeration represents a desire for the love symbolized in the story to be as deep and rich as the exaggeration. And that is the truth.

What Events Are (and Are Not) Art?

Partners can use an event as an ego defense against blame and shame. They do this by pushing blame onto the other partner. Such events are very unlikely to become parts of the relationship's treasured art. When partners cope with failure by blaming each other, they are engaging in "negative myth-making."[6]

Blame, shame, and humiliation are relationship demons.[7] Though these demons might protect one partner for a time, they will inevitably exhaust and wound the other. In self-defense the attacked partner is likely to push the blame right back, hurting and exhausting the previous blamer — and so forth and so on until both parties are full of shame and humiliation, and the relationship dies. When we blame our partner, we are really exposing the fact that we are so weak that we need to build ourselves up at our partner's expense. Thus blaming someone shames us as much or more than it shames the person being blamed.

Sometimes we can reverse the effects of negative myth-making. One useful tool is confession. It is necessary for only one partner to confess, tell the truth, and take responsibility for what he or she did that helped create the failure. This confession stops the blaming cycle in its tracks, ending the couple's downward slide.

Another way to move the couple out of the blame cycle and into a positive frame of mind is for one or preferably both parties to apologize. A sincere, well-constructed apology is a powerful tool and can change a couple's spiritual atmosphere. It can break up power struggles. It can change a myth from a story that dishonors both the person blamed and the person doing the blaming into a story of integrity, courage, and honor. An example of this is the story of the child who shoplifts and has the courage to take back the stolen item, confess the sin, say "I'm sorry," and promise not to do that anymore. While at the time this may be difficult, as time passes such a story can become a source of pride. The shopkeeper may respect and trust the child who grows toward becoming an adult because of this apology. It works the same way for couples.

Humor can also transform negative myths into art. This requires two partners able to be self-critical and laugh at themselves as they reflect on their roles in events that once seemed so serious and important. A shared sense of humor is a wonderful relationship asset.

Myths, Symbols, Rituals, and Traditions

Some partners easily and naturally go about the practice of creating rituals, collecting keepsakes, and telling stories. Other partners more gradually come to a place where they can begin to make their history into art. Still other partners are afraid of intimacy and resist all attempts to create relationship art. This kind of resistance leads inevitably to feelings of alienation and loss. If a couple overcomes this resistance, they can begin their relationship's art collection.

A relationship's art is more than a collection of apocryphal stories. Partners also collect keepsakes, make photo albums, have special songs and meals, and develop anniversary rituals. The pictures of the family in various developmental stages in the executive's office and the jumble of photographs parents carry in their wallets are as representative of a collective myth as are the paintings on the Sistine Chapel. The special days recognized by families — the wedding anniversaries, the birthdays, the various holidays such as Christmas or Hanukkah — are all days on which the family relationship is honored and celebrated. Gifts are given, decorations made, special foods prepared, special clothing worn—all as a canvas on which the couple's story is painted.

Partners also create relationship art through rituals. A ritual is some behavior we repeat regularly—daily, weekly—as a part of ordinary life. In its repetition this behavior gains mythological power. For some couples it can be the daily good-bye kiss of a couple as they leave for work. It can be a greeting hello kiss and a shared drink at 6 P.M. For some couples it is Saturday morning in bed while the children watch cartoons and eat Sugar Pops. My parents made a family ritual of lunch. Every day my mother prepared lunch so that it was ready when my father arrived home promptly at noon to eat the midday meal with his wife and children.

Rituals are important threads in the fabric of a relationship. If they vanished, we would miss them. The more rituals partners create, enjoy, and maintain together, the more intricate their relationship art grows. In all of these ways—photographs, traditional celebrations, special meals, music, clothing, daily rituals, and countless others—partners develop the art that expresses their bond and symbolizes their history together.

Just as blame, shame, and humiliation are relationship demons, *honor*, *respect*, and *appreciation* are relationship angels. We feel naturally close to persons who witness us as we are honored. If our mate observes us receiving an award, the fact that they witnessed it makes us feel closer. Every time we build a myth honoring our partner we are building his or her strength and faith in us and the relationship. At the same time we are saying that we are wonderful and that we are worthy of this great partner. Just as blaming our partner shames both us and our partner, praising and appreciating our partner in our mythmaking and storytelling brings honor to both our partner and ourselves.

Stories, pictures, celebrations, traditions, and rituals are the art forms that couples use to transcend the humdrum duties of daily existence. These become symbols of their intimate bonds. If shared history isn't symbolized, collected, told, and retold, the partners will lose the joy of their joint activity.[8] If history does become art, the partners become artists together. Their creativity becomes lovemaking in all that they share.

Stories

Time Together

♦ Abe and Sarah

I told Abe and Sarah's story at the beginning of this book to help show what is meant by the *spirit* of love. Early in their relationship they faced together a challenge that enabled them to share sacred secrets—their feelings about Sarah's pregnancy—and to prove their commitment to each other.

They later consulted me about their son, Isaac, a child they had overindulged. In their fourth session with me, I drew their attention back to their own relationship. In its history, it seemed to me, was a clue to what was lacking in Isaac. "How is it that you seem so happily married?" I asked them.

> "We are," Sarah agreed.
> "It hasn't been easy," Abe chimed in. "We began our life together in a one-room apartment a block from Vanderbilt."
> "Abe got a job in the medical library and studied while he manned the front desk," Sarah said. "Our parents helped with tuition expenses, but if Abe hadn't worked that library job, we never would have made it through the first two years of medical school."
> "That was nothing compared to what Sarah went through," Abe said. "Isaac was a hard pregnancy. Her stomach was upset all the time. Her mother came to help for a week after delivery, but then Sarah had to go back to work just a few weeks later. We couldn't make it on my salary alone. She was a secretary in the chemistry department at Vanderbilt. They gave her three extra weeks off with pay when the baby was born. Of course, it was

during the summer and it wasn't that hard on them. Sarah was good to them, too. She ran that department for eight years. At the same time she was the primary parent for Isaac, and she went to school."

"Abe helped a lot with Isaac," Sarah added.

"Looking back," he continued, "I don't know how we did it. We were so happy when I got out of med school. Isaac was six then and starting first grade. My internship was hard, but at least it paid enough money for us to get a two-bedroom apartment. We wanted to have another baby, but then came the miscarriages. I don't believe people understand how much grief there is with a miscarriage. There were three in a row for us. One was stillborn at eight and a half months. After each one we would both go back to work and pretend nothing had happened. Then we would come home and take care of Isaac.

"When he was in bed, we would sit on the couch in front of the TV. Sometimes Sarah would cry first, and sometimes I would, but for months we would sit in front of the TV, hold each other, and cry. I was sad, but Sarah was also filled with the hormonal sadness of her body's grief for the loss of the baby it had been carrying, in addition to her psychic loss. I knew then, when Sarah didn't go crazy with that grief, that she was some strong woman, much stronger than me."

"Not really," said Sarah. "I was lucky that he understood. We were lucky we could comfort each other."

"After the third miscarriage, we got back on birth control," Abe continued. "Our sex life had really suffered through all of this. I began to withdraw, and I became attracted to one of the nurses in my residency. Finally, I told Sarah. She was wonderful. She said she had known about it before I did. She was glad that I had told her, and I found myself relieved from all the guilt and shame I was carrying. You know, I think a lot of my guilt and shame were left over from the loss of those three babies.

Somehow Sarah's forgiveness relieved me and brought us back together again."

"That's when we conceived Sarah Jr.," Sarah said. "When we found out she was a Down's syndrome child, I told Abe I wanted her to have my name so people would know I was proud of her and would protect her. Abe was finished with his residency then, and money was no longer our primary problem, so I was able to stay home and take care of Isaac and Sarah Jr.

"The next few years were relatively good years. But when Isaac was fourteen, all hell broke loose. He began to steal tapes from record stores. He would go to the men's restroom in one of the stores and throw the tapes out the window. Of course it didn't occur to him that there were videocameras monitoring the restrooms. The owner of the store was a high-school friend of Abe's. He called us and told us what Isaac had done. We paid for what Isaac stole. When we confronted Isaac, he said he would keep it up unless we gave him enough money to get what he wanted. We felt so sorry for him. He was born out of wedlock — even though he didn't know it."

"On top of that he had a retarded sister," Abe said. "That really seemed to embarrass him. The trials with Isaac continued through several car wrecks, drug and alcohol treatment, and college failures until here we are today."

"But how did you keep your marriage going through all this?" I asked.

"I think it was all this that kept us together," Abe said.

"We've been through so much together," Sarah said. "We're a part of each other's story."

"And you both seem so proud of that story," I said. "I think if you look again, you might see that the suffering which is a part of your story is what's missing for Isaac. You are both heroes in each other's eyes. You each have transformed tragedy into honor. Perhaps your tragedies have been gifts."

"You may be right," said Sarah.

"That never occurred to me," Abe said.

"Your son has been protected from tragedy," I pointed out. "You've never let him fall flat on his face and find a way to get back up again. He has no stories in which he can find honor. As I listen to the stories you have both shared together, they seem to be works of art to you, great personal treasures."

"Indeed they are," Abe said.

In telling their story to me, Abe and Sarah saw that they had nothing to be ashamed of except giving too much to their son and protecting him from the tragedies that he might have redeemed into honor. They were able to see clearly in contrast to their own history how Isaac had not experienced the risks and challenges and losses that help shape a person's character.

Sharing one's life with another creates a common story. The collecting and telling of that story contributes to love. Abe and Sarah's story is a symbolic reflection of their deep love for each other, and it is a part of their relationship art.

With Abe and Sarah we have traveled a full circle. Sharing *sacred secrets* is the first step in loving. The last is the development of a *shared story* that then becomes a part of the sacred secret. Thus the cycle deepens, broadens, and continues into a self-reinforcing circle of love. This is all made possible by spending time together.

▼

▼ How to Spend Time Together

Make a life commitment. Marriage vows say primarily that you promise to spend time together. Take your time together seriously. Protect it. Do not allow other people, other interests, or other commitments to infringe on that time.

1. Set aside regular times for each other. For example, promise to protect Friday nights so that no matter what demands life pushes on you, Friday night is the time you will have alone together. Make a ritual of these times.

2. Make sure that some of the time you have alone together is physically intimate time. Touching and looking into one another's eyes heals and renews. Sharing sexual passion while nurturing each other's pleasure is a bonding event like no other.

3. Be sure to remember birthdays, anniversaries, and the other days that our culture sets aside as family days. On these days the world expects us to be with our mates. Don't miss these occasions. You have no excuse.

4. If the time you spend together begins to feel ordinary, boring, or obligatory, look for new ways to share time together that stimulate and please both partners. For example, if dinner out and a movie every Friday night no longer seems special and intimate, consider doing something else together for a change: a Wednesday-night dance class, a Saturday-morning bike ride, a Sunday afternoon devoted to yard work.

5. Have many conversations with your partner. Talk to each other about events you believe are important. Anticipate them together, and say why you think they will be important. Discuss them afterwards. Be sure your partner knows how you feel about the purchase of your first home, the birth of your child, the death of your parent, an upcoming surgery, a professional success or failure, and any of the other dramatic experiences you share.

▲

• Exercises

Visualizing

Sit in a quiet place and close your eyes. Think about the quality of the time you spend with your partner. Does it feel as if you are "sharing" when you are together, or do you feel distracted by external events or lack of interest? Do you wish you could spend more time together?

Journal Writing

Think of a time when you felt as if you were spending high-quality time with your mate. Write about this time. Can you identify what it was that made this time special, that made you feel as if your bond was being strengthened?

Talking with Yourself

Before you talk with your partner, ask yourself some questions such as the following:

1. What are some of the obstacles in the way of spending high-quality time with my partner?
2. Do I have the desire to find a way around these obstacles?

Talking with Your Partner

Pick a safe moment and talk to your partner about how you feel about the time that you spend together. It is important that this not be a time of complaining or accusing. Exchange ideas about ways that you can have more time together or improve the quality of your time together.

A Shared Dramatic Event

♦ Will and Maria

Will and Maria came to see me about marital difficulties they were experiencing after the birth of their second child. They were both in their mid-thirties and had been married nearly ten years. Will, a tall, athletic-looking, fair-haired man, worked in a downtown law firm. Maria, petite, slim, and dark-haired, taught history to high-school students.

During that first session I listened to each of them tell "their side." Will said that he loved the new baby, but he hadn't wanted to have a second child so soon after the first. He said Maria had persuaded him that they should start trying since there was no guarantee she would get pregnant right away. And now all the problems he had anticipated were coming true. Now there were two children crying for attention, two children waking them up in the middle of the night, two children's futures to worry over.

Maria admitted that it had been more difficult to get their lives to a place where things ran smoothly than it had been after their first child was born, but she didn't think things were as bad as Will painted them. She expressed her feelings that their conflicts ran deeper.

"Will and I come from very different backgrounds," Maria said. "Our new stresses are making us think a lot about those differences. Will is from a small town and a small family, only two children. His parents have money. Don't get me wrong. I'm not criticizing them. They're generous and very lovely people. I just mean Will grew up pretty well-to-do. I've got six brothers and sisters back in Chicago, a regular big old Catholic Italian-American family. My dad was a fireman, and my mom worked in a bakery after she got all of us in school at the same time.

"Our parents weren't eager for us to get married. My parents wanted me to marry a Catholic, and Will's parents had a Southern belle picked out for him. We were so in love they gave up arguing with us and gave us their blessing. But I keep remembering how my mother told me, 'They just don't think the same way we do.' Will and I used to laugh about that expression, but lately I think it's more and more true. Life isn't as easy as it was with one child, but it's not that bad. You should see what goes on in a house where there are seven children under the age of eighteen! This is nothing. We have so much more than my folks did. And it won't always be as hard as it is now. I don't know why Will can't just get over it."

The story continued as a testament to their differences and growing alienation. Finally I asked Will to say what he thought had first drawn him to Maria.

"Well, look at her," he said, "she's so beautiful. And I guess she seemed exotic to me when we first met. I loved her family, too—so warm and full of opinions, always getting in your business. And we both love to read and talk history—but most of all, we both love the great outdoors."

This caught my interest. It seemed surprising that a big-city girl and a small-town boy would have been attracted by a common interest in nature. "Tell me about that," I encouraged Will.

"We haven't been able to do much canoeing or camping in the last few years, but Maria and I both used to prefer that to any other kind of vacation. We met in college, hiking the Appalachian Trail."

"Yeah," said Maria. "We've had some pretty big adventures together. And one time—on a canoe trip—well, we were having a few problems when we went on this trip, but it seemed to bring us closer together again!"

"We were traveling out West a few years ago, in Utah, when we decided to go on a river-rafting trip," said Will. "We called, made reservations, and showed up at what appeared to be an abandoned filling station on what was once a highway but now was a country road full of potholes. This was not a big rafting operation, just one raft and a guy named Chuck. As soon as he began to load us on the raft, it was clear that there wasn't enough room on it for all of us. 'The raft will only hold eight,' he announced. 'Anyone want to follow in the canoe?'

"Maria held up her hand. I looked at her, then I said, 'We will!'

"'OK, you two can have the canoe,' Chuck said. 'Have you ever canoed before?' he asked us.

"'We've been a lot,' I said with some confidence. It was true that we had been down some level-two, maybe two and a half, rivers—but this was a level-three or four river.

"'It's not that hard, really,' Chuck said as we began to maneuver the canoe into the water. 'I don't think it should be rated a three myself, but there are a couple of large swells. If you just head into them straight, you'll be all right. Just stay behind me. I'll show you the way. Let me get out in front. If by some chance you get ahead of me, stop where you see the blue van.'

"We gave the raft a chance to get a good start. Maria got in the front, sat down, and grabbed a paddle. I pushed us off and jumped in the back. Before long we were right behind the raft.

"'This isn't hard at all!' Maria shouted to me above the river noise as we floated behind the raft with me back-paddling so we would stay behind it.

"'Let's go ahead of them!' I shouted back. 'They're going too slow!'

"Maria nodded in agreement, and we blithely stroked our way around the raft. Some of the people in the raft yelled at us to stay back, but we ignored them.

"Just as we paddled around the raft the river curved to the left, and we heard the stronger roar of rapids. Maria glanced back at me and made the sign of the cross. Pretty soon we were in the rapids. They were much bigger than we'd canoed before, but Maria paddled as hard as she could and that helped me maneuver the canoe away from the rocks. We shot through the rapids and turned the canoe so we could watch the raft come down behind us.

"While we were watching it bounce over the rapids, the river took another curve. A still-green tree with a top that was a mass of limbs and branches stuck out from the bank, right in our path. Maria poked her paddle at one of the large limbs to shove us away from it.

"As the limb shook from the punch, a huge water moccasin that had been sunning on a branch above the water was dislodged and fell in the canoe right at my feet. Maria turned, saw what had happened, and began to try to shovel the snake onto the wide end of her paddle. I held my paddle forward for her to push against. She managed to pick up the snake on the paddle like a pancake on a spatula and flipped it out of the canoe. The passengers in the raft had seen us struggling with the snake and some of them were screaming as the raft passed by us. Maria quickly resumed her seat and took up paddling.

"The river curved again and we heard a roar of rapids that was stronger than before. I looked for the V's in the water that pointed toward us, telling us that there were rocks just beneath the surface waiting to snag our canoe. The V's pointing away from us showed us where the deepest, safest part of the river was. Maria's paddling gave me enough maneuverability to avoid the dangerous V's and find the safe ones. We shot through the rapids easily. As we got through, I turned the canoe sideways, perpendicular to the current, to watch the raft coming down the rapids. The river in front seemed straight, so I felt it was safe to watch. I was wrong.

"Just as the raft came into view, our canoe hit a big boiling wave. The water poured into the side of the boat, and it flipped. The water sucked us under, but the life jackets popped us up, and the water was shallow enough for us to stand. The two kids sitting on the edge of the raft saw us capsize and began to guffaw when they saw us standing in the water holding on to a capsized canoe. They were laughing so hard that when they hit the big wave, they forgot to hold on to the raft. The wave flipped them out of the raft and into the river ten feet away from us in waist-deep water. Now it was our turn to laugh as they clambered back into the raft.

"We followed the raft the rest of the way to the van. The water was cold, and we were wet, but it was an experience that Maria and I would never forget. We told Chuck that the snake hazard alone made the Weber a level-four river!"

"It was great," Maria agreed.

When people believe that they share a common fate, that they are equal partners in an important event, then they are likely to become closer. I called this the "Shared Valent Event Hypothesis" in my first article about sense of community. Shared danger, fear, and risk enhances love.[9] You may have gone on a date to a scary movie and after the date found yourself petting heavier than the relationship warranted. The reason is that you were scared *together*. You were excited by the movie, and your physical contact created enough safety to channel that excitement into physical intimacy.

Will and Maria had literally and figuratively "been in the same boat." They shared the same danger. They experienced the same fate. Their canoe trip was a shared "valent" event. Certainly it was a dramatic moment. Such a shared event can create a bond.

Will and Maria had already begun to create a mythology together out of this and other wilderness adventure tales. Their stories symbolized their shared sense of adventure, respect for each other's courage, and ability to struggle and overcome challenges together.

It took them several months of talking with me to reach a place where they felt they could comfortably shoulder the challenge of raising two children together. It became easier for them to do this when they reevaluated their expectations of this challenge and of each other and grew to understand the true nature of the challenge: that its outcome affected both of them in equal measure and depended on both being invested in the task. They began to feel that they were "in it together." The experience must have given them both new courage, for within a few years they had a third child.

▼ How to Get in the Same Boat

There are things you can do to increase the feeling of sharing in your relationship.

1. As you approach an event or challenge, ask your partner what he or she is risking and hoping will happen. Compare your risks and desires with each other.

2. See yourselves as a team. Make it a fact that because you love your partner, what your partner wants is what you want.

3. Realize that putting two people's lives together is a frustrating experience. Indeed, we are attracted to people who frustrate us! See the frustration of not being in sync with each other as a shared frustration, not as someone's fault. Laugh at your shared absurd predicament when you can. The good-hearted couple who is aware of their personal differences and who is determined to "make it work" with laughter and compassion, who see even their differences as a worthy challenge that they can take on together, will find their love bond grow stronger.

• Exercises

Visualizing

Sit in a quiet place and close your eyes, breathing quietly. Empty your mind of distracting thoughts. Create a mental image of you and your partner paddling (or rowing or sailing) the same boat. Does this image "feel" right to you? Do you think that you and your partner really are "in the same boat" and that you are both conscious of this?

Journal Writing

Write about the "team" aspect of your relationship, or write about an event during which you and your partner were working together as a team.

Talking with Yourself

Before you talk with your partner, ask yourself some questions:

1. Am I able to explain to my partner why I thought an event was significant even if my partner did not feel the same way?
2. Am I ready to listen with empathy to my partner's ideas of what makes an event significant?
3. Am I ready to listen to my partner's personal goals?
4. Can we make the personal goals of each of us something we work on together?

Talking with Your Partner

Talk to your partner about your feelings about whether or not you two are a "team." Tell each other about your personal goals. Now discuss how some of these goals can be seen as challenges to both of you. Discuss how you can meet these challenges together.

Contact Is Not Enough

◆ The Walton Brothers

There is a concept in the social science literature called the "Contact Hypothesis."[10] The idea is that if people spend enough time together in close proximity, they will become friends. Since the 1950s a number of studies have examined whether people who spend enough time in close proximity will become intimate. Many of these studies support the idea that people who interact frequently are more likely to become friends. Other studies cast doubt on the Contact Hypothesis. These studies suggest what common sense, history, and many family therapists know to be true—that time together is not enough to create love. In families and in love relationships, if the time people spend together consists of events that humiliate or shame them, their "contact" will eventually drive them apart. Consider the Walton brothers, two middle-aged men who came to see me after their mother died.

One fall day I got a strange phone call from Doug Walton. He asked if I would see him with his brother, Jeff. I rarely get a request to see two brothers and was intrigued by what they would want to discuss.

Later that week I went down to the waiting room to meet the Walton brothers.

"I'm Doug," said a man sitting on the couch. He wore a black business suit and tie, and a *New Yorker* was spread across his lap. The other man was standing by the water cooler, drinking a cup of water, his back to Doug. He wore chinos, a cashmere sweater, and penny loafers. "I'm Jeff," he said. Neither offered any more information as we shook hands, and I suggested that we go upstairs to my office.

They followed me in silence. I could feel tension, but I wasn't sure why.

Jeff sat on one side of the room in the swivel armchair, and Doug took the blue overstuffed chair on the opposite side of the room.

"Jeff, I don't usually mind where anyone sits," I said, "but with the two of you at opposite ends of the room, my head will be going back and forth like I'm watching a tennis match."

"OK," Jeff said accommodatingly, and he moved to the center of the couch. "Why don't you go ahead and read him Mother's letter, Doug?"

"All right, I will." He pulled a letter from his inside breast pocket and began to read. "'Dear boys, I am proud of both of you. You have become such good men. But there is one thing that saddens me. And that is that while I was on this earth, I couldn't help you get along. It has pained me for years that the two people I loved more than anyone else, other than your father, did not like each other. My mother's two brothers didn't like each other either. I talked with our minister about it, and he said it was sibling rivalry. But giving it a name doesn't make it right.

"'You spent your childhood together. You have nieces and nephews that you are both kind to. You have always come dutifully together to our long schedule of family events and birthdays. Your wives get along, but you don't.

"'I'm gone now, and you are the only blood family of your generation or older that you have left. Now I'm asking that before you spend a cent of my money, you see a therapist that our minister recommends. I want you to find things you can like in each other. There are many things about you both that I found to love. I just have to believe that you can see these things in each other, too.

"'I wanted our minister to do this, but I suppose he didn't want to get into the middle of it. Well, old ladies do ramble on. If you have this letter, I'm dead. And I will haunt you both if you don't at least try it. Love, Mother.'"

"What do you think has made your relationship so difficult?" I asked.

"Memories," Doug said.

"Yes, memories," Jeff asserted.

"What is one of your earliest memories of difficulty between you?" I asked.

"Well," Jeff said, "there was the time Doug shot me with a pellet gun."

"Oh, yeah. I did it on purpose," Doug said sarcastically.

"You pumped air into the gun," Jeff said, "pointed it at me, and pulled the trigger, and you say you didn't mean to do it?"

"I didn't," Doug retorted. "I was ten years old, for God's sake. They left us home alone and told me to take care of you. I was mad because I couldn't go to the ravine and shoot at squirrels. I didn't know what to do with you or how to take care of you. I looked at the chamber. I swear it was empty. I pointed it at you because I wanted to scare you. I was mad at you, but I didn't want to shoot you.

"And do you know what happened to me when Dad got home? He took me outside with my pellet gun, my BB gun, and an old single-shot .22 that he had said he was going to give me the following year, and he bashed their butts into a tree, smashing them. I'll never forget what he said to me: 'Maybe this will teach you to take care of your brother.' I hated you even more for that. It was an accident. I didn't mean to do it. I was just a boy left to take care of a six-year-old that I was mad at. I didn't know what to do with you. I was just ten years old."

"And I got shot and had to watch a doctor cut the lead out of me, and I'm supposed to feel sorry for you?" Jeff said. "I've still got the scar. Do you want me to show you?"

"I've got one, too," Doug said.

"I think," I said, "you both would have compassion for your children or your nieces and nephews if this happened to them."

"I'll tell you one thing," Doug said, "I've never left my ten-year-old alone to take care of his sister. It's too much for a child to handle. I proved that."

"Perhaps this was your parents' mistake," I suggested. "Neither of you was old enough or competent enough to be in charge, and you, Doug, acted like the child you were. What else could you be expected to do? You were both lucky that no permanent damage was done to make the psychological scars even worse."

Both brothers fell silent and looked away from each other and me. After a few moments, I asked, "Are there any other memories that make your relationship difficult?"

"What about our neighborhood football championship that we played a month after I shot you?" Doug asked. "I'll bet you don't even remember that, do you?"

"No, I don't," Jeff admitted.

"Well, I do," Doug said. "I was the quarterback. We played in Aunt Juanita's vacant lot. We played Pine Street and beat them. We played Sixth Street and beat them. We played Henderson Street and beat them. That day we were going to play Sweethill for the championship. For us this was the Super Bowl. Everybody was talking about it at school. Even the girls knew. As I was going out the door to go play, Mother stopped me. 'Take Jeff along with you,' she said. 'You know what you did to him. I know he's only six years old, but let him play. He wants to play with you so badly. Maybe this is your chance to make up to him for shooting him in the leg.'

"I tried to argue with her, but it was useless. Mother didn't understand. So I took you to the game. I told my teammates that we had to let you play some. I would go out when we were on defense, and you would take my place. Well, every time they got the ball, they ran at you. You tried, but they beat us, and it was your fault. I was so disappointed. You have no idea."

"No," Jeff said, "I guess I don't. I'm sorry."

"But once again," I said, "this was not the fault of either of you. This was set up by your mother. You loved your mother, Doug, and you couldn't be mad at her, so you blamed Jeff."

"Yes, I did," Doug admitted. "It seemed to me that every time I was linked with Jeff, I failed."

"Remember," Jeff said, "the time Grandmother had all the cousins sleep over? It was summer and so hot that we slept on the porches. She laid sleeping bags out on the floor of the front and side porches and turned on the fans full blast. She put the girl cousins on the front porch and the boy cousins on the side porch. You were the oldest. David and Donny and Lee and Tommy were there, too.

We all lay there in our underwear, soaking up the wind from the fan. I dozed off for a moment, and the next thing I knew you had jerked off my underwear, and you were running out in front of the house with all my clothes.

"There was a street lamp about twenty yards down the street, and you laid my clothes right under it for all our girl cousins to see. I walked outside naked, hiding in the shadows as you ran back laughing. I looked around the corner of the house at the white, yellowish spot of light on the pavement made by the street lamp and at the dark, small pile of clothes in the middle of that spot. I was mortified. I didn't know what else to do but to run out there under the light, pick up my clothes, and run back. And that's what I did, as fast as my little legs would go. The pea gravel stuck into my feet, but I didn't care. The shame hurt worse than the rocks. I can still hear the girls giggling and the boys whooping and laughing."

The Walton brothers worked hard with me to honor their mother's request. They recalled many other situations in their shared past that had contributed to their long-standing feelings of resentment, jealousy, anger, and hurt, and they tried to understand how to let go of those feelings. But the negative mythmaking siblings produce is sometimes more difficult to undo than the kind created by married couples because many of the experiences remembered are childhood experiences. When siblings recall unhappy childhood experiences, all the fear, helplessness, cruelty, and ignorance of childhood comes rushing back to deepen their reaction against each other.

Ambiguity, failure, and cruelty are barriers to love.[11] Again and again family patterns that result in hostile relations show that people must have more than time together to have shared experiences that they will later transform into art. Their contact must be the kind that makes them feel they are in the same place together, meeting the same challenges, sharing the same unhappy and happy outcomes. They cannot feel, as the Walton brothers often did, that one's loss always works to the other's advantage. No idea of a shared story can emerge from this kind of experience.

▼ How to Stage Your Own Dramatic Moments

Because you are human, there will be drama in your life. Use dramatic moments to enhance your relationship.

Here is what not to do in dramatic moments:

1. Don't use an event to humiliate or shame your partner.

2. Don't use an event as a way to demonstrate that you are better than your partner.

3. Don't accept failure as an outcome. Find ways to "make lemonade out of lemons"—to see good in an outcome that you didn't want to happen but that did happen. This can help you find success and pride in your relationship and in the way you and your partner face a shared challenge.

4. Don't allow chaos and ambiguity to dominate your relationship. Ambiguity exhausts a relationship. Take an action or make a decision and don't second-guess yourself (and each other).

• Exercises

Visualizing

Sit down in your visualizing posture. Think about how you feel when a difficult challenge confronts you and your partner. Do you feel OK about it because you know you and your partner will face it together and support each other? Or do you dread it? Think about how it would feel (or how it feels) to be part of a supportive, loving team.

Journal Writing

Write about a dramatic moment in the history of your relationship. Did it strengthen or weaken the relationship?

Talking with Yourself

Ask yourself some questions:

1. Do I ever try to diminish my partner by blaming him or her when "bad" things happen?
2. Am I willing to learn a different way of responding to events?

Talking with Your Partner

It is more important that you learn how to constructively respond to dramatic events yourself than it is to discuss this topic with your partner. In all your conversations with your partner about life events, avoid using blaming or humiliating words. Remember to "find the silver lining" in the dark clouds.

A Suspicion Confirmed

♦ Sam and Donna

Sam and Donna had been married for seventeen years and had four children, the oldest of whom was fourteen. They both had municipal government jobs. Sam was a court administrator who helped judges balance their caseloads, and Donna worked as a court officer in one of the circuit courts. Sam was easy to get along with, eager to please, a diplomat. Donna was slight and tense and had short blonde hair. She had been through surgery, radiation, and chemotherapy for ovarian cancer, and it had been in remission for three years.

They came to see me because Donna believed Sam was having an affair.

"I saw how you looked at that woman attorney when she came into your staff office," said Donna. "I know you are having an affair with her. I just know it."

"I am not," replied Sam. "All right, I do like her. I think she is attractive, and she is kind to me. She has been sweet to me since you have been sick. She understands. You know her husband died of cancer. She knows all the feelings a person has when a spouse is threatened with a terminal illness. She has been a good friend to me. That's all."

"I know I haven't been able to be there for you during my recovery," apologized Donna, "and you have needed someone to talk to. I also know that one natural feeling you have toward me and the cancer is anger, anger that you won't express to me, but you do express to her."

"I don't talk to her about my anger toward you," Sam responded defensively.

"No, you just act it out by having sex with her," Donna shot back.

"There you go again. Dr. McMillan, how can I convince her?"

"You know how I am so sure? You stopped kissing me in the hall when you went to your office and I went to my courtroom. We have kissed in the hall every day since even before we were married, for seventeen years, and then one day you stopped. I will never forget that day. We were walking down the hall, my running shoes squishing and your wingtips clomping on the marble floor in rhythm with one another. I stopped where we usually kissed and parted, and you kept on walking.

"Every day since then it is as if I am out of my body watching us as we walk to work on that marble floor. I listen to my shoes squishing and yours clomping. My squishing stops when I stop and wait for you to kiss me, but your shoes just keep on clomping as you continue down the hall to your office. It makes a terrible echo in the marble hallway. That's how I know, Sam. When that kiss was gone, I discovered it meant a lot to me. As we started our day, it had been something that reminded us that we had someone in our corner, someone who loved us. I still looked to you for that, but you didn't need it from me anymore."

"Dr. McMillan, what do we do here?"

"Well, Sam, I don't know what the truth is, but I've watched married couples for a long time. Often mates, especially those of the female variety, have good instincts about such things. You have an opportunity that doesn't always happen in a relationship. If the truth is that you are having an affair, it will be a relief to Donna for you to admit it so that she doesn't feel crazy for suspecting that you are. If the truth is that you are not having an affair, then if you stick with the truth, Donna will eventually see it. You know, the truth has a smell to it, just as a lie does. The truth is often risky, but I find it is the only basis for a sound relationship and usually worth the risk."

"I don't want a divorce."

"I don't either," Donna said.

Sam sighed. "Well, I am having an affair. You are right."

"I knew it." Donna closed her eyes with relief and sadness.

Rituals are often subtle daily activities that we don't miss until they are gone. Sometimes they seem empty; at other times they are filled with depth and significance.

The repeated ritual creates opportunities for the unexpected inspiration to surprise us inside the ritual. For Donna this surprise and depth came with the powerful feelings she experienced when Sam stopped and kissed her again the way he had done for seventeen years.

▼ How to Create Rituals

Here is how to use habits and patterns:

1. Create enjoyable relationship habits, and consider it your duty, like a religious duty, to repeat your part of the habit.

2. Find habits that seem to meet needs that can become a natural part of your daily or weekly life.

3. Look at patterns created in other relationships that you think would be good for you to do in your way.

4. Goings and comings offer excellent opportunities for creating rituals.

▲

The Dangers of Mythmaking

Sam did end the affair, but that was only one part of their work with me. Divorce became the subject of a later session.

"I'm tired of this," Donna began. "I can't go on with this anymore. I am angry. He cancels our policy for cancer insurance, and he doesn't even talk to me about it. Do you know how much our medical bills have been because of cancer?"

"But darling, I only canceled the cancer policy for me and the children. The children and I have no medical bills to speak of. We don't really need that insurance."

"See what he does? He always makes it my fault. I know the $250,000 we have spent on medical bills have been mine. He doesn't have to remind me. But to not even consult me before he makes a decision that affects my children—it's like I don't exist anymore. Like I'm dead already. It's over."

"What's over?" I asked.

"The marriage," Donna said. "I should have left last summer when I found out he was having an affair."

"But you didn't, and now it's over because of a dispute about insurance coverage?" I asked.

"No, it's not just that. It's years of his passive-aggressive crap. I'm always the bad guy, and he's the saint. Poor him, he had the affair because I was not there for him during my treatment. That's the kind of thing I can't take anymore. I knew it was finally over when we found our cat dead last month. I was driving home one day, and when I was about two blocks from the house I heard a thump under the car. When I got home I mentioned that I heard this strange noise. It sounded like I hit something, but I didn't see anything. The cat didn't come home that night. The next day Sam assumed that I had run over the cat."

"I didn't assume. I wondered if it was a possibility."

"Well, it was a very good possibility, wasn't it? So then he went to the place where I'd heard the noise and yes, Spanky our cat was dead in the ditch next to the road. That was a sign for me. The cat had died, and I killed it."

"So that means the marriage is over?" I asked, confused and unable to connect the dots.

"To her it does," Sam said. "We got the cat fifteen years ago. Donna thinks its death symbolizes the death of our marriage."

"When we got Spanky as a baby, we were happy," Donna said. "We had no bills, no children, no disease. We loved each other then. Spanky was so full of life then. Now he's dead, and so is our love."

"So let me see if I understand. You didn't leave when Sam had an affair or canceled the insurance without consulting you, and you've been coping with his passive-aggressive tendencies for years. But now your cat has died, and you have invested this event with the symbolic meaning of your marriage. So it is more than just the death of your cat. This death gives you permission to get a divorce."

"Well," Donna said. "I would say that it instructs me to get a divorce. Poor Spanky."

"Well, before you go talk to the lawyers," I said, "let me suggest something to you both. You do have problems relating to each other, but you have even more serious problems coping with the demands fate has given you, such as four parochial-school tuition payments, recovery from cancer, and big medical bills. Soon you will be adding the children to your car insurance bills, and we haven't even mentioned college.

"It seems to me that you are attacking each other rather than the sources of your stress. Sam fights indirectly with an affair, and Donna attacks outright with hostile words and threats of divorce. But you are really allies in the battle against the demands life has given you both. To turn against each other now would injure you both and create a whole new set of problems.

"You have used the cat's death as a mythological moment invested with symbolic meaning. The death of a family pet is a sad event. It is a loss worth grieving. But it becomes a symbol of something more than that only when you decide that it is. You are giving this dramatic moment the meaning that transcends what happened. You can do that if you want to and declare this the death of your relationship, but you are doing this, not the cat. If this is your decision, so be it, but please be aware that it is your choice to make."

All couples have dramatic moments that can become part of the fabric of the art of the relationship. Fortunately for Sam and Donna the dramatic moment of the death of their cat did not define their future.

It is important to realize that it is within a couple's power to shape the meaning of a dramatic moment. It sometimes requires much discussion, apology, reflection, and imagination for partners to shape the meaning in a direction that will allow them to endure as partners. But their shared effort often will strengthen and renew their relationship.

Sam and Donna faced many pressures to remain married. Religious prohibitions, financial worries, and the desire to spare their children the unhappiness of a divorce all combined to make them feel they couldn't "afford" to get divorced. All of these factors slowed the momentum of their dramatic "it's over" moment and encouraged them to give the possibility of repairing their relationship more thought. Despite Donna's depression over her illness and her anger toward Sam for his affair, she decided to give her best to the challenge. She began by transforming the meaning of Spanky's death. Shortly after this session she brought home a new kitten. She named it Spanky II and told Sam it represented the second chapter of their marriage.

▼ How to Use Dramatic Moments

Some dangers may occur in giving meaning to events.

1. Investing an event with mythological meaning can be dangerous. Be careful. Determine whether a moment has the same meaning for your partner.

2. Be sure that when you put a meaning onto an event you understand that you are doing this. Fate may have participated in giving you the moment, but the meaning comes from you and your partner. If you believe differently—if you believe you have no control over what a given moment might mean for you and your relationship—you may be indulging in "magical thinking."

3. Consider the type of meaning you apply to a given event. Is it a transcendent meaning that represents eternal values such as honor, courage, truth, sacrifice, and compassion? Or are you making the event a symbol of how you and your partner are better than other people (or how you are better than your partner)? "Better than" myths are false and will collapse.

4. Before you decide that a moment symbolizes the collapse of your relationship, consider whether it might in any way represent a manageable challenge.

Blaming Myths

♦ Frank and Connie

We could accuse most couples of using poetic license when they tell stories of their relationships. They exaggerate events and enlarge heroic and villainous qualities, sometimes for the sake of a good story but more often because the teller's feelings are deeply invested in the story. In a happy relationship heroic stories about both partners will outnumber and outweigh stories in which either is seen as a villain. A sure sign that a relationship is in trouble is when stories that cast one partner as the villain dominate the relationship's myth-making. Blaming myths of this kind undermine the trust between partners and their sense of a shared experience. This was the direction in which Frank and Connie were headed when they first came to see me a number of years ago.

"Thursday night was a prime example," Frank said. "I had cousins coming through town and staying with us. The next day we were all going to go to the North Carolina mountains where another branch of the family lives to spend some time together and to enjoy the fall color.

"We had planned dinner for 7 P.M. when my cousin and her husband arrived Thursday night. Dinner was cooked, and my cousin and her husband were there, but no Connie. 'The Star' was not home yet from her charity gig. This happens to me all the time, but that night was particularly important to me. I kept dinner warm for a while, but then I didn't feel right about waiting anymore, and the kids were starving. So we ate, and Connie got home at 9:30 in time for dessert. She doesn't care about what's important to me. Pleasing fans is more important. Her fans are what matter most to her."

"I really appreciated what you had done, Frank," Connie said. "I'm sorry I wasn't there to help you cook and entertain your cousins. You did it so well. You made a wonderful evening for them even though it didn't go as we had planned. Frank has a great family, and he really loves them. I know he felt insulted because I wasn't there to be with them."

"Why weren't you there?" I asked.

"This was Fan Fair Week. Frank wanted me to leave in the middle of it so I could go with him and his family to the mountains at noon on Friday. In order to do that, I had to double up on my activities. I had been working extra hard also because Frank and I are going on vacation for two weeks in August. I have people who are raising families working for me. If I don't work, they can't earn money to feed their families."

"You are the star," Frank said. "They are lucky to work at all. You have no one to be accountable to. What about the person who backed you? I would have thought the forty thousand dollars I invested in studio time and session musicians would get me some consideration. The plan was that you would become a star, and we would have more time for each other and our family. No star works the way you do. And you make good money, but it feels as if I have become the wife. I don't work anymore. I grocery shop and cook and take care of the kids. This is not what I invested in. This was not the plan."

"Frank," Connie responded, "you are wrong about the other artists. They work hard too. Some do 340 dates a year. Some work sixteen-hour days signing autographs, doing interviews, practicing, writing. I know you are disappointed that I don't have more time for you. So am I."

"This incident ruined the whole weekend," Frank said. "I was humiliated that you were not there to be with my cousins for dinner on Thursday. I think they felt insulted and rejected as well. The whole weekend I could see pity in their eyes. Poor Frank invested all his money in his wife's career so she could be a performer and now she has abandoned him for stardom."

"I know it hurts you that sometimes my work comes before you, Frank, but to defend myself, the money you spent to help me become an artist was not wasted. I make more money now than we both did before, and what about the money we lost in those stocks? We will be paying that debt for years. It's a good thing that I do so well. And I am glad to contribute. When we invest, we win some and lose some. I think the investment in me was one that we won, even if I must spend more time working than either of us imagined."

"Yeah, well, what about the ruined weekend? I know my family wonders about our marriage. They could tell something was wrong, and everyone was uncomfortable. It was miserable. Things didn't get any better until Saturday when I cooked my famous rack of lamb with crème brulée for dessert. Then finally the pall lifted."

"I don't have the same feeling you do about the weekend," Connie said. "I thought it went very well. I enjoyed your cousins. You seemed to have a good time playing golf. Your family seemed very glad to have us stay with them. I don't think they pity you for being married to me. They seemed to enjoy talking to me about my act and songs. You're right, your rack of lamb and crème brulée were a great success. I'm sorry you didn't enjoy the weekend."

"Well, I didn't."

"Let me try to help," I said.

"Please," Frank invited.

"This will require that you step outside yourselves and look at how you are interpreting your experience. Can you do that?"

"Sure," Frank said.

"I'll try," Connie said.

"The two of you see the same facts very differently. Connie sees the story of the Thursday dinner as an event where Frank was the hero in the story, and he saved the day. She sees herself as a casualty of fate, not as a person with bad intentions. Frank too sees himself as the hero, but a hero who suffered the ordeal of embarrassment and overcame the adversity brought on by Connie, the villain of the story.

"Then there is the story of how and why Connie became a performer. Frank sees himself as the victim/hero who gave the money and the behind-the-scenes support for his wife's career. He sees Connie as the unappreciative wife who has reaped the benefits of his generosity and is not living by the bargain they made.

"Connie sees the story in a different way. She is disappointed along with Frank about the work that she is required to do, but she takes her role as an artist seriously and feels trapped by fate and by Frank. She does not blame Frank nor does she see herself as a victim. She sees this difficulty as a part of life, a challenge to be overcome.

"Now let's look at the weekend in North Carolina. Once again Frank sees himself as a victim of Connie's inattention and neglect. He sees his relatives as witnesses to the humiliation he endures because he has been abandoned and shamed by Connie. Frank becomes the hero in this story by preparing a wonderful meal and rescuing the weekend.

"Connie sees the relatives not as witnesses but as co-players who have their own agendas and for whom she serves a purpose as they have enjoyable conversations with her about her work. She sees the weekend as a success. She recognizes and appreciates Frank's presentation of dinner. She refuses to see herself as the villain or Frank as the victim."

"Frank didn't always make me into the monster in his stories," Connie said. "For a long time I was a beautiful princess. The transformation occurred after my career took off."

"That's right," Frank said. "I could understand how she had to work so hard at her job before her success. She had a boss and clients who needed her. But performers don't have to work that hard. We agreed. She would become a star, and when she wasn't working, she would be home with her family, enjoying making our house a home. She would spend a lot more time with our children. We would have friends over more often. Our house would become a welcoming place with interesting friends dropping by and sharing in our hospitality and conversations."

"This dream did not come true," I observed.

"No," Frank said. "Didn't even come close. Connie's time at home is basically no different than before. I think she doesn't want it to be different. This is what I'm angry about. We both thought our lives would change, but only *her* life changed. She became a star, and I was left at home with the kids or alone offstage standing in the wings."

In these and other stories Frank told me about their relationship, Connie was always the villain. He built these blaming myths about their relationship because he felt betrayed when she became a performer. Not only had their dream of a rich home life not been realized after her success, but Frank also felt that Connie's life had changed for the better while his own life had worsened. Connie "the star" had grown in value in the world's eyes, while people saw him as "poor Frank." His negative myths about Connie took her down a peg and compensated for his feelings of inferiority. In them, "the star" was seen as a selfish and inconsiderate wife who cared more about her career than about her family.

But relationships will not hold up long under the weight of blaming myths. Consider how Frank's negative myth-making burdened Connie. Not only did Connie have to work harder than ever to meet her professional responsibilities, she also had to do what she could to overcome Frank's continual portrayal of her as the selfish, inconsiderate, and betraying partner while she tried to prop up his declining self-esteem. Connie would be unable to carry the responsibility for Frank's well-being forever. She might try to reassure him or confront him with her own version of their story until she was exhausted. But if he couldn't learn to take responsibility for his own well-being and continued to blame her for his unhappiness, she would very likely begin to ignore him and distance herself or possibly even divorce him. Or perhaps Frank would persuade himself that "the star" really was a "wicked witch" and he must divorce her. A relationship burdened with myths that shame and blame one or both partners usually self-destructs. But if partners can learn to reframe their hurt and fear with respect and honor, they will have a strong enduring bond. In our next two stories Frank and Connie learn this skill.

The Confession

We were in the middle of a therapy session largely devoted to Frank's irritation over Connie's late arrival at a restaurant the previous week. I had begun to wonder why Connie tolerated this endless litany of blame. I asked her.

"Why do I put up with this blaming?" Connie repeated. "Partly because I do feel that I've let Frank down. And I feel guilty sometimes because I love my work, even though it steals from my time with Frank.

"But mostly it's because I'm grateful to Frank. He was there for me when I was very unhappy. A few years ago I made my first attempt to become an artist. I was considered for a record contract but didn't get it. It was humiliating for me. But Frank didn't let me give up. He invested money in my own production of a record. He came to the studio to encourage me. When I performed at the Bluebird Café for my first showcase, Frank began the standing ovation. Then the people clapped for what seemed like forever.

"Trying to be an artist is sort of like a political campaign, and I campaigned hard. I was out meeting deejays and radio station program directors. I was traveling, doing showcases in industry towns like L.A. and New York. Frank stayed at home with the kids and wrote the checks. He rarely saw me. I wasn't much of a wife to him and not much of a mother either. Frank wrote me one letter a day while I was on the road, just like I was a little girl away at camp. At the end of each letter he told me he missed me and loved me.

"I will never forget the day I won my first award. Along with my children, there were Frank and my father, the two men who have meant the most to me, watching me at the proudest moment of my life. That night I wore the gold heart necklace Frank gave me before we were married. Later Frank took the heart and had it surrounded with diamonds, and then he gave it back to me. I wear that heart every day. I touch it and think of Frank. It means as much to me as my wedding ring."

The stories of Connie's career struggles, Frank's letters, and his gift of the gold heart had created a myth that captured Connie's heart. The stories honored Connie's courage and strength in adversity and Frank's steadfast commitment and support.

Connie confessed that she had been unable to keep her bargain with Frank. She acknowledged his support and sacrifice. Connie's confession, her expression of her true feelings about the recent past—that she felt badly about Frank's disappointment and acknowledged it as legitimate—was an important first step in emptying the meaning of Frank's blaming myth. It signaled to Frank that she cared about his feelings and that she shared them. When she honored him by remembering his unwavering support during the ups and downs of her career journey, she was making him a part of the memories she cherished and in which she took deep personal pride. Frank's blaming myth began to fall apart in the face of her story. It seemed that Frank and Connie might have a hopeful future that could begin with a simple reframing of the past.

As we will see in the story that follows, Connie's confession changed the atmosphere surrounding their relationship.

The Apology

During the next therapy session Frank again brought up the early struggles in Connie's career. This time, however, he was not bitter about how it had changed his life.

"Hearing Connie remember those wonderful moments made me feel guilty," Frank said.

"How so?" I asked.

"She worked very hard to become a star, harder than I worked, and I was making it sound as if I was the only one who suffered. But what I did was nothing compared to how hard she worked. There was a time when she had to hold down a job, go to the studio and work until midnight, perform showcases, and worry about there being something in the refrigerator for the family to eat. She did a great job.

"I admit that life on its terms is sometimes hard for me to face. I always had a dream of how life could be. I thought we would work hard, Connie would become a star, and we would live happily ever after. I never thought about how difficult it must be to be a symbol of people's dreams and hopes, to share a part of yourself with millions of strangers and pretend to be what people dream you are. And I never realistically understood how much time it would all take. Connie had no idea what she was going into. Neither did I. I am disappointed, but it's not Connie's fault.

"I've been blaming Connie for a long time. I'm sorry, Connie. I know it has been hard to try to love someone who has treated you like an enemy. When I realize what you have been putting up with, I'm ashamed. Please forgive me. I can do better than this, and I will."

After Connie's confession, it was impossible to think of her simply as a selfish, inconsiderate, ungrateful wife—a villain. Frank saw that Connie valued him, and he began to rethink his antagonism in that light. If his wife valued him so, then her current struggle to meet her work demands was perhaps a challenge they could struggle to manage together.

When Frank began to take responsibility for his behavior and to stop blaming Connie, he was able to say he was sorry and to promise to do better. This apology had to come from Frank. A therapist can help a couple find their way to an apology. A therapist can even model an apology for the couple. But a therapist cannot create a genuine apology for the couple. This must come from one of the partners. The partner making the apology must have the courage to acknowledge how the other partner has experienced his or her behavior, the courage to agree to be held accountable, and the courage to accept the challenge to do better. Such courage is often rewarded by the transformation of a negative myth surrounding the couple into a positive myth symbolizing love and growth and commitment.

▼

▼ How to Say "I'm Sorry"

It is important to admit when you are wrong. But be careful to say this in a way that heals rather than injures. Saying "I'm sorry" is a special art form.

1. Never say, "I'm sorry you feel hurt." That can mean to the listener, "You stupid idiot, I'm sorry you haven't got any more sense than to feel hurt." Never say, "I'm sorry you feel that way." That might mean to the listener, "You stubborn fool, I can't stop you from feeling that way." And never lie and say that you are sorry when you are not.

2. Say, "I can see how you would feel that way. I might very well feel the same way you feel if I were in your position. You thought (*state what you think your partner is telling you*). Is that right? Well, I didn't mean to (*step on your toe*), but I see that I did. I'm sorry. I will pay more attention next time."

3. The elements of an apology are as follows:
   (a) I now see the world from your point of view, and that is _____.
   (b) You are not crazy for seeing the world that way.
   (c) From that point of view I can see what I did that hurt you.
   (d) I don't have to do what I was trying to accomplish that way.
   (e) Your hurt matters so much to me that I will try to find a way to accomplish my purpose while being sure not to hurt you.

4. It is important that you not overpromise. You can never do anything perfectly. All you can promise is that you can improve to some degree because you felt your partner's feelings for a moment, and the pain you felt with your partner mattered to you. That is the best most of us can promise.

5. Finally, forgive. Don't forgive someone who doesn't know or care what he or she did. No learning takes place with an accepted and forgiven false apology. But when your partner truly apologizes, forgive and let it go. Do not prosecute this case further. Don't bring up this event again.

▼ How to Build Myths That Honor Your Relationship

First take a look at the myths you are creating about your marriage.

1. Think of ordeals your relationship has survived and obstacles you have overcome together. What are your feelings about how you and your partner handled these challenges?

2. Remember your last few fights. Who was the hero in these conflicts? Who was the victim? Who was the villain? Do you see a pattern?

3. In a remembered conflict, what did you do to create the problem? When you can hold yourself responsible, you acquire some control. When you blame your partner, you no longer have control. Find ways that you can have some responsibility in the story you tell about your conflict.

4. To reframe a myth you have created, find a way to tell the story so that the hero/victim role (which is usually yours) and the villain/perpetrator role (which is usually your partner's) are reversed. This will help you see your partner's version of the story, and if you can stop blaming your partner, you will be able to begin retelling your story as a shared myth that brings honor to you both.

5. Keep plugging. Don't give up. Tell your stories without making your partner a villain or yourself a victim. Don't use your story to blame your partner or defend yourself. Commit yourself to the relationship first when telling your story.

• Exercises

Visualizing

Go off by yourself, sit down, and close your eyes. Be still and call up a past event in your mind. Use your imagination, reflection, empathy, and compassion to see in this story how your partner was indeed a hero.

Journal Writing

Remember a story about your relationship that honors your mate. Write it down. As time passes, continue to make a conscious effort to remember events and moments that impress you with your partner's best qualities. Write down these stories. Tell them often to your partner, your children, and your friends.

Talking with Yourself

Ask yourself what it is that you would like to communicate to your partner:

1. Is there something I would like to confess to my partner? Are there feelings I have that I assume my partner knows about but I have never really expressed?
2. Is there something for which I need to apologize?
3. Is there a "story" I would like to tell my partner? Can I tell it in a way that does not blame him or her?

Talking with Your Partner

With your new awareness of the myths that have been created in your own relationship, sit down with your partner for an empathetic discussion. Confess what you know you are responsible for. Acknowledge your partner's sacrifices, especially those that seem to have gone unrewarded. If you need to apologize to your partner, speak honestly and with compassion.

Challenge Makes a Myth

♦ Ernest and Cynthia

We first met Ernest and Cynthia in Chapter I. The exchange that occurred during their first session with me illustrated the power of truth-telling in relationships. During that session I confronted Ernest with the need to set aside his anger at Cynthia in order to discover and express his own feelings about his impotence. I stressed to Ernest and Cynthia that truth-telling is never about blaming someone but is always about one person taking a risk to tell another how he or she truly feels. When they returned for a second therapy session the following week, I opened with a question to them both: "Where are you now?"

"The last session really helped me," Cynthia began. "I think I understood what Ernest was going through and what had happened to us for the first time. I'm not taking our lack of sexual intimacy so personally now."

"Yeah, I think it helped to clear the air," Ernest said. "We're more understanding and considerate of each other. But we haven't had sex yet."

"When it doesn't work for the first time, that can be very frightening," I said. "And after avoiding sex for a long time, sex can become frightening."

"So we have a sex phobia?" Cynthia said.

"Yes, especially Ernest has one. It has to do with sex and his depression from the severe loss he felt when he lost a trial he thought he should have won, and it has to do with his fear that he may not be attracted to you."

"So, could he have sex with another woman? Is that what he needs to do? Trade me in?" she exclaimed.

"It is a natural thing to want to end a relationship when the relationship fails in some way. You can blame the failure on your partner or on the bad fit between the two of you and go on to someone else. This is what was in the process of happening when Ernest blamed your figure for his lack of interest."

"Or lack thereof," Cynthia said. "So a new woman might fix Ernest?"

"For a time, perhaps, but the real problem is that Ernest is not eighteen. He is over fifty. This will happen again to Ernest and whatever woman he is with. So a new woman is only a temporary fix."

"Well, I want a permanent fix," Ernest said. "I've done a lot of thinking this week. I love Cynthia. I don't want to lose her. But I may not be who she wants. She should have a younger man who can give her the attention she deserves. I am afraid of her, of failing her again. And you say that I *will* fail again and again? Oh boy, that's what having more candles on my birthday cake means, huh?"

"Impotence is a problem you will face again," I said. "It is a problem all relationships face at some time. But you really have several different problems. There's Ernest's anger at himself for losing the trial and the loss of power it symbolizes. There's your age difference and the potential differences in your individual libido. And then there's how your relationship began, as an extramarital affair."

"How is the fact that we began as an affair a problem?" Ernest asked.

"Well, extramarital affairs often set up expectations for a relationship that are impossible to sustain," I said. "Let's think for a minute about the first time you had sex. Can you tell me about that?"

"It was at one of those political fund-raisers," Cynthia began. "Ernest and I always went to the same ones. I represented the bar association as a lobbyist with the state legislature. Ernest was chairman of the legislative committee for the bar. We often had a drink together and debriefed after a legislative lobbying assault.

"Eventually I told him about how unhappily married I was. Ernest told me how attracted to me he was. I told him it was too dangerous, but he said he didn't care. Then one night my husband and I were at a fund-raiser and Ernest was there, too. He followed me into the women's restroom and pasted an OUT OF ORDER sign on the door. And Ernest, you have to finish. I'm too embarrassed."

"I don't need to know more about that time," I said. "But was your courtship like that?"

"Like what?" Ernest said.

"Did it usually involve risk and danger? Did you take chances on being discovered by Cynthia's husband?"

"I'll say," Ernest said. "We were nearly caught once in a closet in the Legislative Plaza. One night I used the keys Cynthia left in my apartment to sneak into her house and be with her in her bedroom while her husband was asleep in his."

"I admit it was exciting," Cynthia said, "but it was nerve-racking, too. After the divorce I felt relieved."

"And after the divorce, how was your sex life then?" I wondered.

"Well, I'm glad to say we didn't do it in the closets of the Legislative Plaza anymore," Cynthia said. "I guess because we could be together when we wanted, we weren't as desperate for sex as when we began."

"So what do you mean about there being a problem with how we began our relationship?" Ernest said. "Are you a priest? Do you think we are immoral?"

"No," I said quickly. "I don't. I don't want to sit in judgment of you. I simply want to point out that risk, danger, and adventure add excitement to a relationship. Before the divorce, you were like teenagers whose parents had forbidden them to be together. The fact that it was so risky made your sex more exciting. But think about what happens when a couple who was forbidden by their parents to have sex gets married and then it is OK for them to have sex. Their parents may even pressure them to produce grandchildren."

"I imagine sex becomes less exciting," Cynthia said. "Are you saying that my ex-husband made our sex life more passionate?"

"Well, he certainly made it more of a challenge. But the kind of challenge he gave you was temporary and false — temporary because it vanished with the divorce, and false because forbidden love is not a challenge to mature lovers, especially when their relationship becomes publicly acceptable. So now that you don't have the ex-husband to create the temporary challenge, can you think of a real challenge you have to overcome to be together?"

"Well, we have the challenge to stay together at all," Ernest said.

"Yes, you do. That is the challenge all couples must face. When there is nothing to fight against, no common enemy, will you still have a basis for intimacy? That is the real challenge, isn't it? And if you solve that problem you will have your permanent solution, Ernest."

"You mean I will have an erection at will?"

"No, I mean it won't matter. You will have each other, and as your impotence comes and goes, it won't matter."

"But how do we solve the problem of being afraid of intimacy with each other?" Cynthia asked.

"You need to embark on a plan for restoring physical intimacy," I said. "I'm going to help you learn how to follow a step-by-step process that begins with backrubs and proceeds slowly."

Ernest and Cynthia learned that the real challenge of restoring physical intimacy, like most real challenges, calls for discipline and practice. It was work for a time, but eventually they relaxed with each other. Intercourse became a part of their physical time together, but it was no longer the focus. Sharing physical caresses was their shared joy.

A challenge is important to a relationship. If a couple overcomes a challenge and has nothing left to do, their relationship may die. How many couples do you know who have made it, built their dream house on a hill overlooking the city, and soon after they move into it file for divorce? To continue to discover a shared, just-manageable challenge is a great achievement for a relationship. To do this a couple must be willing to practice, work together, and learn what to expect of each other. Then they will be ready to face their target challenge as a team.

Ernest and Cynthia learned how to tell their problems in a way that represented all of our ideal selves. When their story became invested with myth and became art for the couple, I became a "genius-therapist-priest," Cynthia a patient and generous woman, and Ernest a courageous man. They invested their history with transcendent meaning. The truths it spoke were, among others, that a relationship which began in secret and dangerous passion could grow into one of exciting truth-telling, mutual understanding, and trust.

▼ How to Choose Your Challenges

Choosing the appropriate challenge is a challenge itself.

1. Sometimes challenges will seem to choose you. But you always have a choice of some kind. If fate puts an impediment in your way, you can choose to walk around it, turn around and go back, or choose a different path. Remember, you always have a choice.

2. Nourish your ambition. If you feel positive about your desire to achieve, you will recognize new challenges. Don't let failure destroy your ambition. You will fail to reach some goals, but see the failure as a challenge to adjust your expectations and try again. Give yourself credit for having the courage to set new goals.

3. Talk to your partner about his or her goals. Talking will increase the understanding each of you has of the other's goals. Join your partner in support of his or her goals. Evaluate each other in terms of challenges embraced, not just in terms of achievements.

4. All just-manageable difficulties become manageable if you can remain flexible enough to change your goals when you face the reality of what can be achieved and what cannot.

5. Choose challenges for which you and your partner have practiced and prepared.

Shared Symbols in Relationship Art

♦ My Mother

One day after my mother and I had returned home after her regular visit to the oncologist, she asked me to walk through the house with her. She wanted to talk to me about some of her things and what she wanted done with them.

> We started in the den. She pointed to an old Civil War musket mounted on the wall. "Your father said," she began in a tone meant to convey distrust of my father's memory, "that this was your great-grandfather's gun. I want whoever wants it and takes it to know what your father said and to keep it in the family."
>
> She pointed to the sword under it. "Now, I'm pretty sure this is the sword your great-grandfather had in the Civil War. You boys found it in your grandmother's attic, remember? If someone wants both the gun and the sword, I think that is OK."
>
> She walked me over to the old grandfather clock standing in the corner. "Now, this clock we got in Sebastopol, Mississippi. Your father loved going to a certain antique store there. After a big case we often went to visit your aunt Jane in Sebastopol. Every mile on the road from town would melt a little more tension out of his body. The day after we got to Jane's house, we'd go down to that store and bargain with the antique dealer there. Every time it was the same. Your father would say the price was too high. He would pretend he was going to leave, and the dealer would call him back and offer a lower price.
>
> "This clock was bought after he won the Ashland Oil Company case. The rotating bookcase was the Hill Concrete case." She led me into the dining room. "The china cabinet was the Strong murder case." She picked up the sugar bowl from a silver tea set that sat on the table. "Your father gave me this tea set right after you were born. He knew I was angry because he hadn't gotten back

from visiting his mother in time to be there when I was in the hospital having you. He brought home the tea set. I thought it was beautiful, but I don't think I ever let him know how much I loved it. You all can decide who wants what, but make sure whoever takes these pieces knows how we came by them."

In the upstairs hallway, she paused in front of a framed photograph of my brother and his girlfriend that sat on a mahogany table. "I talked your father into buying this old mahogany table just after we were married, even though we really couldn't afford it. I just fell in love with it. And I want you to give that picture of your brother Bill and his girlfriend Jo Carol to Bill's best friend Robert. You know, Robert still grieves their death after more than thirty years."

In my parents' bedroom, Mother picked up an antique perfume bottle on her dresser. "David, I shouldn't be telling you this, but we used this bottle as a signal. On the nights I wanted to make love, I left the stopper off the bottle. When I didn't, I put the stopper back in. That way I never had to reject your father. Maybe people don't do things that way anymore, but we kind of liked having a secret signal."

And on she went through every room of the house, telling me the story behind each of her possessions.

Love has a multitude of symbols, both common and unique ones, that define its living spirit and grow in meaning over time. Mother's house was full of her relationship symbols. She wanted me to treasure them as much as she did. They did mean something to me, but to represent my own marriage, my wife and I wanted to collect our own symbols in our lifetime.

Symbols serve many functions. Wedding rings, for example, help establish and maintain boundaries. Some symbols are special words that have private meaning to the couple. Other symbols, like the picture of my deceased brother and his girlfriend, are unique to a couple and represent the survival of a shared profound tragedy. Others, like the furniture from the Sebastopol antique store, represent shared rewards for hard work. Still other symbols, like the antique perfume bottle, are secret and symbolize a couple's most intimate bonds. Love has many symbols that identify and define its spirit and commitment.

Common symbols serve several important functions in creating and maintaining love relationships. One is to establish and maintain boundaries. And another is to symbolize the relationship in art, so that the spirit of this love has a symbol of its own that identifies and defines that spirit and commitment.[12]

▼ How to Develop Common Symbols

Developing symbols of significance to both partners requires thought.

1. Look around. Listen. Remember. There are special words that have unique meaning to you and your partner. This is the language that only the two of you understand. A rock picked up on a hike from the first time you hiked together and camped out can become a symbol.

2. Give presents in recognition of special moments. These presents become symbols.

3. Buy furniture together when you have had a financial success. The furniture becomes a symbol of the shared success.

4. Take pictures. Make scrapbooks.

5. Tell stories. Tell them over and over, whenever you have a willing audience. Collect stories you can tell.

6. Build your own traditions and celebrations. Commemorate your special times. Have your own special way to celebrate holidays.

Summary

The Elements of Relationship Art

Spending time together is the first requirement of the development of relationship art. But the time partners spend together, their history, must have certain qualities or they will not be able to transform it into art.

First, their time must be shared so that they see the consequences of the events they experience in a similar way. Think of the stories that Abe and Sarah told about their long history together, stories about partners who had almost never wavered in seeing themselves as facing the same challenges, running the same risks, enjoying the same rewards. A couple's myths—stories that speak to shared truths—can only come from this kind of shared experience.

Second, the time that partners share must involve dramatic moments when partners believe something important is happening to them. Abe and Sarah's unplanned pregnancy, Will and Maria's triumph over danger on the Weber River, and Frank and Connie's shared struggle to support Connie's career were all moments of significance to both partners. They were experiences that revealed something important: Abe's strength and Sarah's truthfulness, Will and Maria's competence and courage, Frank's devotion and Connie's gratitude.

Third, dramatic moments that become art must have resolution and closure of a kind that honor both partners. Partners must be able to interpret positively the outcomes of shared events in ways that bring honor and respect to each other, never humiliation or shame. The Walton brothers' continuing animosity toward each other was a result of the repeated humiliating outcomes of their shared experiences. With a therapist's help, Sam and Donna, Frank and Connie, and Ernest and Cynthia were able to begin finding their way together toward this third requirement of relationship art. They learned to salvage experiences that threatened their relationships and to turn these experiences into challenges that would eventually be retold in positive, honoring relationship myths.

Relationship art is multifaceted. It includes stories that are told and retold until they achieve legendary status. It also includes various symbolic possessions that partners collect over time. Donna's cat Spanky, Connie's diamond-encrusted gold heart, my parents' mahogany table — all were invested with meaning that symbolized the partners' relationships. Relationship art is also shaped in the traditions partners invent or borrow and in the rituals they practice over the years. Their relationship art grows richer with time as they collect more stories, acquire more symbolic possessions, observe more traditions, and repeat small and large relationship rituals.

This last principle of the McMillan Relationship Theory reveals how love relationships take partners on a winding and eventually circular path through life. When partners transform their history into art, they transcend their experiences to illuminate truths about passion, joy, grief, commitment, courage, or honor. These truths that partners have discovered together are new sacred secrets they share. In this way lovers come full circle, from the first risky and fearful telling of sacred secrets that ignites love's spirit to the final telling of tales, fond sharing of symbolic possessions, and faithful honoring of personal traditions and rituals that commemorate their time together and speak of their shared sacred secrets.

As we conclude the explanation of this theory, we can see that every part relates and overlaps with every other part.[13] Some of the lines drawn between parts are arbitrary. These lines help us understand the distinct elements of the theory so that we can use the theory to make love work in our relationships.

The Paradoxes of Art

1. The building blocks of beauty are often ugly. We must be willing to endure pain and hurt if we are to reach joy.

2. Our greatest relationship treasures come from moments that might have been disastrously humiliating. We can transform these events from tragedy into glory.

3. In relationship art, truth is of overwhelming importance, but this kind of truth has little to do with actual facts.

4. When one partner is willing to go into his or her own "dirt" and confess, this individual becomes clean. When a partner has the courage to face him or herself, take responsibility for his or her behavior, and change (i.e., offer an apology), this self-humiliation becomes a basis for honor.

5. The opposite is also true. When one partner tries to lift him or herself up at the expense of the other, this actually shames the shamer as well as the partner.

6. Time together is necessary to create art, but it is not enough by itself.

7. When we get what we want, we don't want it anymore. Challenge, not satisfaction, is a source of excitement and happiness.

8. A great achievement held possessively by one person is small when compared with any shared accomplishment. Having it all alone is empty.

Epilogue

Shortly after we were married, Marietta and I moved into a new house. I was determined to find the accomplishment I could achieve to endear me to Marietta forever. After moving into our new home, Marietta said, "Oh, how I would love a flower bed near the house."

So I dug her one.

"You know," she said, looking at the new bed, "soil near a house is usually foundation dirt. That means it's bad dirt, full of old clay that came from below the topsoil when the basement was dug. It won't grow pretty flowers."

"OK," I said.

I bought three hundred cubic feet of peat moss and a half-ton of manure and blended this with the soil in the garden. When I was finished, I presented Marietta with this rich, newly tilled soil. "Done," I said, "it's all yours. Are you happy now?"

"Well," she said, "not exactly. Help me decide what to plant."

"OK," I said. For several days we looked through plant and flower catalogues, making a list of perennial flowers and drawing a garden map. Then we shopped at several garden stores until finally we had found all the plants on the list. "Done," I said to Marietta as we unloaded the last plants from the car.

"Well," she said, "not yet. Will you help me plant them?"

With a sigh, I agreed. I dug, while she put starter fertilizer in the holes and planted the flowers. After a weekend of planting and mulching, we were finished. We were now the proud owners of a planted perennial flower bed.

"It looks great," I said. "I hope you're happy now."

"I've still got to water the garden," she said. "Would you please hook up the hose for me?"

I got the hose from the garage, hooked it up, and sat down to watch Marietta water the garden. "How often will you have to water it?" I asked, still sitting there a quarter of an hour later.

"Every day or two in the summer," she said.

"How will you find the time?" I asked. I was thinking about how we often didn't have time to cook a good dinner, or get the oil changed on the car, or answer a letter.

"I will."

I rolled my eyes.

"The plants need water. We'll manage it together."

"I thought I was finished," I said. "I dug the garden. I put in the manure and peat moss. I helped decide what to plant and shopped for the plants. I helped plant and mulch, and now you want me to help you water the garden?"

Marietta gave me a look.

"OK. I'll buy a sprinkler system."

"You don't have to do that."

"Well, I don't want to spend my life watering flowers."

The day the sprinkler system was installed I took Marietta outside to inspect it. "Oh, it works beautifully," she said as we walked the length of the bed. "It gets to all the plants. Thank you, David." I surveyed the garden and heaved a sigh of relief.

One Saturday a few weeks later, Marietta and I were in the yard studying a place on the roof where I thought the shingles needed to be replaced. "You're right," she said. "I'll call a roofer on Monday." We headed back toward the house. "Can you help me weed the garden?" I heard my wife ask.

"I thought you said the mulch would keep out the weeds. How much more do I have to do?"

Marietta stopped. "You're never finished working on a garden, David," she said, as though anyone with any sense knew that much. I went on inside and shut the door, *force-fully*. After a while I looked out the window. Marietta had gotten a foam garden-kneeling pillow, gardening hat and gloves, and a hand-spade from the garage and was on her knees in the flower bed pulling weeds and dumping them into a large bucket at her side. After a while, I decided to pour her a glass of iced tea.

"Thank you," she said. She removed a glove and took a long drink of the cold tea, watching me over the top of the glass. Then she set the glass beside the bucket, put on her glove, and picked up her hand-spade. "I guess it takes a while to learn that the joy of having a garden is the joy of attending to it," she said, digging around a clump of weeds. "It's a labor of love. The pleasure comes from doing everything you can to keep it healthy and beautiful." She glanced at me again. Apparently, I still looked unconvinced. "It's kind of like marriage," she said smiling, "don't you think?"

Yes, of course, I do. Creating your own love story is not something you do once and then walk away from, as you may when writing a book. It is an ongoing process. Entropy is as constant a force in relationships as it is in gardens and in the rest of the universe. Weeds, or whatever form chaos takes, are always tearing at order. We humans are happiest when we have someone to love who loves us and someone who will let us love him or her. Happy relationships require continual attention, and the joy of a relationship comes from the work of carefully maintaining it. This happiness is not something you earn once and own. It is not a product, perfectly packaged with preservatives that enhance its shelf life, but a living process that requires skill and devotion to keep flowering season after season.

All human systems work by the same rules. Governments, communities, churches, families, and couples are systems. If we apply the theory of community to couples, as we have in this book, we will see that it works. The rules are the same.

I believe we can create intimacy by using and enjoying our differences, but we must realize that our relationship conflicts are thousands of years old. They are part of our cultural and genetic programming. Nature selects for diversity. If you married someone genetically similar to yourself—your sister or brother, for instance—you'd damage the gene pool. We are programmed to be attracted to someone who is different. The relationship battles we experience are conflicts between all men and all women, or conflicts between classes, or conflicts between cultures. They are the consequences of the systems in our culture, in our families, and from our history.

We may easily miss the fact that we play roles in our particular systems and that conflicts are natural to any system. We forget this and take conflicts personally. We defend ourselves with blame. We try to protect ourselves from a character or spiritual challenge by building a myth that he or she is our problem. If he or she would think or feel as we do, then everything would be fine. This misses the point of the spiritual challenge that a relationship provides. To grow we must ask the questions *Why am I with my mate?* and *What do I have to learn from this relationship?* A monogamous relationship offers each partner the opportunity to learn and relearn our character and spiritual lessons. In a committed relationship we always have the potential for grace and forgiveness and an opportunity for redemption.

The appropriate practical question for each partner in a relationship is not *Am I getting enough?* or *Is my partner loving me the way I want to be loved?* but *How well am I loving my partner?* Too often we want to make relationship contracts on a "my-needs-first" basis that simply doesn't work. Partners must be willing to push their needs aside and listen to each other before they can truly begin to receive the fruits of their relationship.

The skills we are required to have are enormous. Learning them takes a lifetime. The good news is that, using a foundation of self-awareness, we can learn these skills. We can learn to speak our truth with passion and without blame. When we do, we bring excitement and adventure to our relationship. We can make our relationship a safe place to tell the truth with empathy. We can make healthy contracts and create norms that allow us to know what to expect. We can make fair trades and share in the grace that can come from a history of fairness. We can build myths of shared meaning together. Confessions can cleanse our relationship. Apologies can transform shame into honor.

Being in a committed relationship provides us with the artist's challenge. We don't know what to expect from our medium. We can't really control what happens. We must have the strength to make a mistake and keep on with our work, not knowing if we will succeed. We must be able to tolerate the anxiety that is part of the creative process.

This hard work needs support. We need the support of friends, family, and a community. We need to share our struggles with others. A couple needs each other. But a couple who is trying to love needs all of us.

Even with help from friends, family, ministers, and therapists, we won't always live up to the standards put forth here. We won't always tell the truth or really listen or live by our contracts or make fair trades or avoid blaming as a defense. These are standards of perfection that we can strive for but reach only occasionally.

The greatest gift we as partners can give each other is commitment, the promise not to run away, not to give up, but to remain present, to stay in place, to be there for each other. You who keep this promise will discover in marriage's shadowed valleys the truths about yourself that will set you free—free to love as best you can and to be loved as much as you will allow.

Appendix A

Know Thyself

To be a partner we must first be prepared to know how we feel and then we must find the courage to say it. We stunt love's development when both partners do not bring to the relationship the capacity to know and represent themselves. Without the skill of self-awareness, all our efforts to build intimacy will fail.

The basic building block of self-awareness is the ability to recognize and experience how our body feels, how we feel emotionally and spiritually. Most of us do not know much about ourselves before becoming intimately involved with others. But this early lack of knowledge doesn't limit us unless we refuse to learn from our experience. Fear of self-discovery can prevent us from learning the truths that would help us avoid relationship crises. Another problem when we refuse to know ourselves is that our partner's version of our self-knowledge may replace our version. The story of Laura and Gil illustrates this possibility.

Developing Self-Awareness

♦ Laura and Gil

Laura was a person of strong feelings who had trouble containing her powerful emotional reactions. When I saw that her name was on my appointment schedule once again I was not surprised, but when I went to the waiting room to meet her I *was* surprised to see her with her husband—"Mr. Engineer," she had always called him, "a man without feelings." She had often told me he would never consider coming to see a therapist.

229

Yet there he was. I must have appeared startled, because Laura quickly said, "Gil agreed to come here with me if it would help me." Laura looked at Gil. He nodded, looked down, and silently followed us upstairs to my office.

We found seats and I asked, "How can I help you?"

Laura wasted no time. "I am upset with Gil. He says he loves me, but he spends all his time with his computer. He says he has to work, that he is working on the computer because he has to, not because he wants to. Isn't that what you say, Gil?"

Gil nodded.

"I went into the study Wednesday night. He was so absorbed he didn't hear me and there he was, playing a computer game. I stood by the door for ten or fifteen minutes just watching him. He was absolutely fascinated by the game. He was playing with a little knob on the keyboard, and every time he moved it the game made noises in response. As I stood watching him, I felt sick to my stomach, as if I had walked in on Gil and his lover. We haven't had sex in three months and there he was, playing with the computer instead of with me. I feel as if our marriage is over. I can't even compete with a computer for his attention."

"And how do you feel about that?"

"I'm furious. But more than just furious, I'm hurt. I'm ashamed that I don't seem to be worthy of his attention. I want to have children and Gil says he does, too, don't you, Gil?"

Gil nodded.

"Yet he won't have anything to do with me. He stays up till past midnight playing computer games to avoid me. How am I supposed to feel? I feel inadequate, powerless, rejected, discouraged. That's how I feel."

She paused. Hastily, I interjected, "How do you feel about this, Gil?" and I focused on Gil for the first time.

He was silent for a while. He shifted uncomfortably under my gaze. I asked him again, as gently as I could, "Gil, how do you feel about all this?"

"I don't know," he said finally.

"I will tell you how he feels," Laura said.

"Well, I would like to hear that from Gil."

Gil was slow to answer. He squirmed in his seat. Then he said, "But Doctor, I'm not sure I know how I feel."

"Is Laura's story an accurate version of what happened?"

"Well, yes, I guess. I was playing a computer game and she saw me. Sometimes I do play computer games. I guess that's true. We haven't had sex for a while, but I don't think it has been three months."

"It has been." She began fumbling in her purse. "I've got it right here. I mark it on my calendar because I want to know when we might have conceived."

"That's all right—" I began.

"Well it's not all right with me. Here it is, April 28. Let's see, that's two months and seventeen days, almost three months."

"Well, what about the rest of what she said? Do you see things the same way, Gil?"

"Not exactly, but I don't know what to say differently."

"Well, tell me how you see it."

"I would, but I don't know what to say," Gil said. "Any time I disagree with her she gets upset."

"Have you always had trouble expressing your feelings?"

"Yes, he has," Laura said.

"I want Gil to speak for himself, Laura," I said. "Gil, has expressing how you feel always been difficult for you?"

"I guess so," Gil replied.

"Do you know why that is?" I asked.

Laura almost jumped out of her seat to answer, but I glared her down in order to give Gil a chance.

"Do you know why that is?" I repeated.

"No. I can't say that I do. It's just that it's always been hard for me. That's all I know."

"OK, Laura," I said, a little frustrated that I could not get more out of Gil. I gave into Laura's intrusion with the hope that she would say something that Gil might take exception to and speak out at last.

"Well, which question do you want me to answer?"

"What do you mean?" I asked.

"Well, do you want me to first tell you how he feels or why he doesn't express his feelings?"

"Start with number two," I said.

"OK. Gil's parents were always fighting. They fought before they divorced when he was six, and they fought over him all the time after they were divorced. Each one would come to him and ask him, 'Gil, how do you feel— don't you want to spend Christmas with me?' Every day one of them would put him on the spot. If Gil expressed a feeling to one parent, it became a betrayal to the other. Gil's mother keeps it up even today. Even though his father is dead, she will ask Gil to remember one of their family fights and ask him to agree: 'Wasn't that dumb of your father?' Now that his father is dead, Gil will answer, 'I guess so; I don't know,' as a way of placating her without siding against his father.

"Males play football to learn repression. They throw a ball to a fifteen-year-old boy and say, 'Catch this and run toward those eleven boys who want to bury you into the ground!' That's what happened to Gil, the halfback. He had his parents and football to teach him and now he's a man a lot like all the rest, except worse. Oh, I don't mean he's worse. Gil is a good man. He just doesn't know how he feels."

"Gil, do you have anything you would like to comment on? You are the subject of this inquiry, and you are the expert on this subject."

"No, not really."

"Is Laura right that you don't know how you feel?"

"I don't know; I guess so."

"I want him to answer another question," Laura said.

"What is that?"

"How does he feel about me? I want you to ask him how he feels about me. I know that he either doesn't know or won't say."

"Do you want to answer the question of how you feel about Laura, Gil?"

"Well, I love her."

"Well, if you love me, why do you play computer games instead of coming to bed with me?" Laura asked. She had begun to cry. "I'll tell you why," she said to me loudly when Gil did not respond. "It's because my body is disgusting to him. I've gained ten pounds. My breasts used to stand out from my chest; now they sag. I'm almost forty years old, and I've lost it. That's it. Besides that, he's afraid that I won't work if I have children. I do want to stay home for a while, and I'm not sure when I would go back to work. He doesn't say anything about it, but I know the idea bothers him. At first I thought our problem was another woman. But it's not another woman—he's fallen in love with the computer. That's how he feels."

"Is that right, Gil?" I asked.

"No," he answered curtly. His jaw was clenched and his left hand was balled in a tight fist.

"What don't you agree with?" I asked.

"I don't want to talk about it."

"That's what he says when he does feel," Laura explained. "He says, 'I don't want to talk about it,' and stomps off to his computer."

"Well, let me take a stab at describing how you might feel. May I, Gil?" I asked.

"OK," he said. He unclenched his fist.

"I think Gil feels as if he married his mother," I suggested. "He is afraid to tell you how he might feel for fear that you will explode emotionally and he won't be able to handle your feelings. If he lets himself know how he feels, he'll have the problem of dealing with those feelings, and then he also has to deal with yours in response to his. He believes he can't do both. Am I right so far, Gil?"

"Yep," Gil said, almost smiling. I must have been on the right track. He leaned back into the couch.

"But—" Laura said.

"I'm not through. Laura, you were right about Gil's parents training him as a child not to feel. Wasn't she, Gil?"

"Yep." When I got this affirmation I knew I had Gil's support to go even further. "But you weren't at all correct about how he feels about you. I think Gil still finds you attractive. Am I right, Gil?"

"Yep."

"I'm not sure how he feels about your going back to work. How do you feel about that, Gil?"

"I don't care when she goes back to work. She doesn't know it, but I have a savings plan. We have over one year's income saved. I have a college program that is completely funded for one child. We have a retirement plan that is fully funded. I've been paying ahead on our house note. Our mortgage will be paid in five years. I expect to get a promotion soon that will mean a raise that is more than Laura makes. If we have a baby, I don't care if Laura ever goes back to work."

There was a long silence. "I'm stunned," Laura finally said. "That's more than I've gotten out of him in years. How did that happen?"

"I think he feels safe here and knew that I would understand him, so he was able to tell you how he feels. Is that right, Gil?"

"Yep."

"Do you want to tell us how you feel about the computer?"

"No, you are doing fine. You go ahead."

"Well, I'm not sure I can, but I will try. Gil is not in love with his computer. Sometimes he needs a break from the intensity of his engineering work, and he takes a break with a computer game."

"Is that right, Gil?" Laura asked him.

"Yep."

"Then why do I feel so rejected?"

"I think there are two reasons for this," I said. "The first has to do with what you, Laura, are doing to yourself. You are using Gil's silence about his feelings as a blank screen. You use this screen as something on which to project your fears. Do you think you are too fat?"

"Yes."

"Do you think she is too fat, Gil?"

"Nope."

"Do you worry about the appearance of your figure as you age?"

"Yes."

"Do you, Gil, think her figure is less appealing than when you met her?"

"No," Gil said sharply.

"Laura, do you feel inferior sometimes, whether it's about Gil or work or your family?"

"Yes."

"Do you love the computer more than you love your wife, Gil?"

"No."

"Laura, these are your own fears you are projecting onto Gil. Then you fight him, blame him, and accuse him, when the person you are really fighting is yourself."

"I see. You could be right," Laura said.

"He *is* right," Gil said.

"You said there were two reasons why I feel rejected. What is the second one?"

"It is because you *are* being rejected. Gil is avoiding you."

"I don't know about that," Gil said.

"Well, Gil, what happens when you tell her with words that you are not avoiding her but your behavior tells her that you *are*? What do you think she is likely to feel and think?"

"Oh, I see," Gil said thoughtfully. "If I act this way and don't say anything about it, she believes the worst. She believes the things her fears tell her, and then she attacks me with them."

"You get the prize," I replied. "Is that what you want?"

"No."

"Well, Gil, if you are not willing to know and say how you feel, then someone else will. And when that person, Laura, does represent your feelings, she will represent them to her advantage."

"What do you mean?" Gil asked.

"Remember what happened when Laura described your feelings for her? She completely skewed what you really feel in order to indict you and your relationship and to reflect how she is used to treating herself, which is to target herself and abuse herself. In a sad way, it worked to her advantage because it confirmed what she feels to be true about herself."

"I see," Gil said. "When I don't tell her how I feel, I get hurt and she gets hurt."

"Yes. If you refuse to know what you feel and to say it, both of you get hurt."

"I get it," Laura chimed in. "I always know something is wrong when he stays with the computer night after night. But when he won't admit something is wrong, I fill in the blanks with my imagination. And my imagination can be brutal to him and to me."

"That's how I see it," I concurred.

"So, Laura," Gil explained, "I was avoiding you because I didn't want to upset you. You get upset so easily. You cry or get mad. I can't handle that. It's better for me if I avoid you. I get so afraid of that scene that I just keep working and stay away from you." Gil seemed much more relaxed, as if he now felt he could speak the truth about feelings without fear of an emotional explosion.

"How do you feel about being with Laura now?" I asked him.

"Fine."

"What I mean is, do you feel more sexually interested in Laura now that you have told her how you feel?"

"Yes, now that you mention it, I do."

"I do too," Laura said.

"Well, then, I think this session is over."

In order to be a love partner, you must know how you feel. If you don't, you can't participate in the truth-telling that is the centerpiece of love's spirit. If you refuse to be aware of what you feel, then you are at the mercy of your mate who will devise his or her own version of what you are unwilling to know about yourself. How can your mate get it right? How can your mate read your feelings accurately when his or her own feelings color this perception?

If you leave the task of self-awareness to your partner, he or she will take control of the pulpit you have abandoned. He or she will stand up and speak for you about how you feel. Some of what your partner says will be true, but your partner will bend this portrayal somehow to meet his or her needs. As you listen to your partner, you'll know something is wrong with what he or she is saying about how you feel. But if you don't recognize and express your true feelings, you won't know what is wrong.

Each of us is a unique package of intuition, reason, wisdom, and creativity. Each of us has strengths and weaknesses of character. To be effective as a person and as a partner we must know our instincts, tendencies, and character flaws, work on them, forgive them, and build on them in order to grow into our best unique self.

Fortunately, if you want to become self-aware, you can nurture and develop this skill.

▼ How to Become More Self-Aware

This "how-to" exercise does not require our usual fourth step, a conversation with your partner. This is a time for you to focus on yourself, to become more aware of your own thoughts, feelings, and habits. There will be time for talking with your partner later.

These questions are but a few of the issues you should consider if you intend to bring self-awareness as a strength to a relationship. You may not know all these answers at first, but the answers will come if you are willing to know how you feel and to carry on an internal dialogue of discovery.

1. Our bodies always reflect our emotions, and our bodies disclose our feelings to others. It is foolish for us to clench our fist and jaw and then say to others and ourselves that we aren't feeling anything. This reaction gives the observer a great advantage. He or she can see in our clenched fist and jaw how we feel. Our denial forces us to defend a lie, we abandon the playing field of reality, and we surrender.

2. Our behavior can also tell us how we feel. When we find that we are avoiding something or someone, we may be angry or frightened. We may watch our own behavior in response to a situation and ask, *Why did I do that? What does this behavior say about me?*

3. Our private thoughts can also tell us how we feel. We can listen to things we think about our mate, such as, *Why did he/she do that? That makes no sense.* This mind conversation tells us something about how we are feeling.

4. Often our first response to a situation is anger. But anger is never the base emotional experience. The base is a vulnerable feeling such as fear, sadness,

weakness, or inadequacy. *Anger is always a defense against hurt or against something that we believe will cause hurt.* If we can trust our mate and if we have the courage to talk about our vulnerable feelings, we can communicate effectively and intimately. Before we can do this, however, we must be aware of what we are feeling beneath the anger. The vulnerable feeling for a woman is often one of feeling *disregarded, unimportant, unworthy, or unlovable.* For a man, the underlying vulnerable feeling is often one of feeling *rejected, unlovable, inadequate, or powerless.*

▲

• Exercises

Visualizing

Sit in a quiet place and close your eyes. Breathe quietly for a few moments, experiencing the rise and fall of your belly, and allow your body to relax. Think of an incident or situation in your life that upset you in some way. What do you feel when you think about this situation? Reach inside yourself and try to bring your feelings to your consciousness.

Journal Writing

Writing in a journal can help stimulate the development of self-awareness. Record your thoughts when you reflect on one or more of these questions:

1. What does my body feel like when I am angry? What vulnerable feeling do I most often protect with my anger?

2. What does my body feel like when I am depressed? What unfulfilled desire is being covered up by my depression?

3. What does my body feel like when I am afraid? Can I learn something about myself from my fear?

Talking with Yourself

Self-awareness involves more than the awareness of feelings. It is the awareness of your instincts, your personal tendencies, your behavioral habits, your core values, and your typical thought patterns. These personal qualities may emerge as you carry on a conversation with yourself that should last throughout your life. Here are some questions that you may wish to ask:

1. Am I risk-aversive and cautious, or am I impulsive and excited about taking risks?

2. Do I value privacy and tend to respect others' boundaries, sometimes risking isolation?

3. Do I value personal connectedness and tend to merge easily with others, thus sometimes pushing myself into places where I find I am not wanted?

4. Am I politically conservative or liberal?

5. How do I think about God and death?

Appendix B

The Development of a Theory

I grew up in Arkadelphia, Arkansas, on a street sheltered by arching, magnificent pin oak trees and lined with the houses of countless aunts, uncles, grandparents, cousins, and friends. We children played in the cool, dark shadows of the stately pin oak trees all through the long, hot summer days, and at night twelve of my cousins and nearly as many neighborhood children gathered for a game of kick-the-can in Aunt Juanita's vacant lot a block from my house. During the afternoons, cousins and aunts sat on the front porch with my mother, shelling lima beans and drinking iced tea. If I was sick, Uncle Doc Barnett or Dr. Reid dropped by to check on me, and Aunt Selma was likely to send over an angel food cake.

There was always someone to talk to, someone to play with, someone to offer care and nurturing. And there were wonderful places to play—creeks to wade, trees to climb, ravines to explore, hedges to hide in, fields to roam, and vacant lots where we played ball for hours. It was a fine way to spend a boyhood.

By the time I was in graduate school I knew that my loving childhood sanctuary was gone forever. There was no place for a psychologist in Arkadelphia, Arkansas, or so I believed. My future was in a big city with strangers for neighbors. There was pain in this realization, and in retrospect it is no surprise to me that I devoted my graduate research and training to trying to figure out just what it was that had created my childhood refuge of safety and delight. Was the experience of a community like Arkadelphia possible only in a small town, living among blood relatives? Was there something special about the South in the 1950s that afforded just the right conditions for the growth of a powerful sense of community? Was it possible to re-create the elements of safety, bonding, nurturing, and excitement in another time and place? Could such a community be a part of my future in a large city, far from the roots of my boyhood?

My yearning for something valuable I had lost provided the kernel around which my research and scholarship clustered. I turned my attention to answering these questions about what creates a safe and nurturing community. Over the next few years I developed a comprehensive theory of love and community called the Sense of Community Theory.

This theory identified four elements to measure a group's sense of community: its shared spirit, the degree of trust that exists among its members, the degree to which trade goes on between its members, and the existence of art through which the group shares experience. My colleague David Chavis and I developed a questionnaire to study "sense of community" in neighborhoods and other groups, and later research with this instrument confirmed the four elements of my theory and demonstrated its efficacy in the field of community psychology.

After graduate school I started a private practice in clinical psychology. Immersed in my practice, for many years I scarcely gave my graduate school theory of love and community another thought. After fifteen years, however, I decided to take another look at the theory I had developed so many years before. I wanted to see if it could be applied to my clinical and personal experience. I wondered if there was something more wide-ranging I could learn by examining that experience within a theoretical framework.

The job of shepherding the Sense of Community Theory had fallen to Bob Newbrough and David Chavis, two of my colleagues who saw to it that the theory was published in a journal and mentioned in several academic conference papers. Bob Newbrough said the theory had taken on a life of its own in the field of psychology. It had been published in several community psychology textbooks and used as the theory base of many social science and community psychology studies. It was now one of the leading theories in the field of community psychology. Its acceptance and proven usefulness in that field encouraged me to examine what further significance it might have in my practice with couples.

I began by reviewing the extensive social science literature on community psychology to learn how the theory had been adapted and what permutations it had undergone. I discovered considerable support for the principles of the theory and materials that stimulated and expanded my thinking on the subject of human attachment. A number of studies confirmed that, using the Sense of Community Theory, one can predict a group's behavior based on what is known about the presence or absence in the group of the theory's four basic components: Spirit, Trust, Trade, and Art.

Perhaps more important, researchers can use the theory to develop a working community, one that provides safety and adventure, tranquillity and excitement, social nurturance and respect, and, for each individual, a feeling that he or she is a part of something larger than himself or herself.

Sense of community, attachment, bonding, personal attraction, and group cohesiveness are all different elements of the glue connecting human beings. As I examined my work it became clear that the strongest bonds between couples had been built, whether unconsciously or not, on foundations including the same four elements in the Sense of Community Theory. In my practice I began to see that partners could nurture and maintain a strong relationship if they learned how to keep these necessary elements of Spirit, Trust, Trade, and Art alive in their marital bond. I began to think of marriage as an *intimate community*.

There are many books about love, some strong in "human interest" and others long on scholarship. *Create Your Own Love Story* offers a "human interest" approach and a solid base in scholarship that makes these ideas accessible to laypeople and professionals. In this book I have presented my theory of love in part through stories about ordinary people. I hope these stories will interest the student of therapy who wants to have a look at what goes on in the therapy room as well as the layperson who wants to investigate the topic of love and may be looking for help in building a love relationship. All stories except for those about me and my wife, Marietta, are composite case studies. None is about a specific real person, but many insights and topics come from my clinical practice and from what I believe to be the universality of much of human experience. In this sense, they are real.

Though men and women are different, the work of marriage and relationships is the same for both. Our differences create opportunities, and our differences are worth exploring and acknowledging. That men and women are different cannot excuse us from the work we have to do in a relationship. It is ultimately the same work for a man and for a woman: that work is to become a whole and complete person.

I have provided an annotated list of some of the studies I used in development of the theory. Some of these altered my thinking, as did my own discoveries, my conversations with colleagues, my clinical practice, and my personal life. But for the most part, my research and exploration confirm the body of the theory I first developed as the Sense of Community Theory. In its application to couples' relationships, I have called it the McMillan Relationship Theory.

Our culture trivializes love. Television and movies suggest married life is a romantic comedy. Romantic novels my wife reads and affectionately calls "trash" depict love as an irresistible impulse that will lead us all to "happily-ever-after" lives. The theory in this book and the stories told to illustrate it make the point that love is not just an impulse but a complex spiritual and emotional experience. It is the spirit in a relationship that creates an exciting transfer of energy and builds on the sheer pleasure of being part of a supportive, affectionate team. The focus in such a relationship is on the fit between the parties and the joy of possessing something valued by the other partner. As the relationship matures, trading scores are no longer kept, and giving for its own sake becomes a spiritual state which can be called Grace. I offer the following definition of love:

Love is the spirit that comes from telling the truth, the trust that comes from sharing power, the faith that comes from mutual rewards, and the creativity that comes from making shared history into shared art.

Appendix C

The Role of the Therapist

What Are the Characteristics of a Good Therapist?

Psychotherapists may be viewed as the direct descendants of the nineteenth-century Catholic priests who heard their parishioners' confessions. Though modern therapists may have more sophistication and training, our task is essentially the same: to help our parishioners proceed with their lives in the face of tragedy.

Our parishioners (we call them *clients*) have lost hope, and we must remind them that their lives are precious works of art. It is a therapist's job to help our clients find their unique style of redeeming pain and transforming it into beauty. We serve the role of consultant to our clients' spirits.

Our clients have lost something very special, something that once belonged to them: their faith in their own essential worth as humans. Their pain comes to them because they had the courage to care. By showing them to themselves, by pointing out the validity of their emotions, by identifying healing information about themselves, we help them reclaim (or create) a core belief in themselves as worthy human beings.

The therapist's job is to tell our clients the truth. The therapist must try to understand the origins of our clients' defenses and self-destructive traits, to discover the pain beneath them, and to tell our clients what we have discovered. Becoming aware of how defenses cause pain empowers the client with choice.

Therapists can tell our clients the truth only after we first create a safe place for them by embracing them with heart and soul, with all the empathy we have to give them. In other words, we must love our clients.

Therapists with a distant manner who listen with no change of expression or body language and who offer only an occasional nod or intellectual comment will be profoundly limited in effectiveness. Personal growth cannot take place when clients display their lives before therapists who give no indication that they care. When a client tells me her story, my eyes may water when she cries and smile when she smiles and feel a little frightened when she is afraid. With these responses I am saying to her that her pain matters to me. She can see by her effect on me that her drama is a universal drama which draws even me, her therapist, into it.

Therapists must allow access to our own pain. This distinguishes empathy from sympathy. With empathy, we feel our own pain along with other people as they feel theirs. The therapist's empathy shows a client that we are a part of the universal exploring of the human condition. I must be willing to be moved by the client's struggle, or the client will feel that he or she is alone.

I don't believe therapists should have secrets from their clients. Therapists should delay telling clients what they have learned only when the truth is a provocative, potentially harmful truth that the client is not yet ready to hear.

When providing treatment for a couple, the therapist must be careful to love two people. If I have been seeing a client who wants to bring her partner to see me, I warn my longtime client that I may begin our session by listening to her partner at her expense. Even if he says bad things about my longtime client, I will not contradict him, because I must earn his trust. I will listen and understand his pain. When he begins to be comfortable and feels that I know how to hear him, then I can become an "honest broker" third party who both partners can trust and who provides good support to both.

How Does a Therapist Know?

Sometimes I try to help a client who has low self-awareness by "telling her how she feels." In reality I am making educated guesses that often resonate truthfully with the client. Sometimes the client will say in amazement, "Yes, that's me! How did you know I felt that way?"

The answer to this question is that most of what I know as a therapist did not come from earning a Ph.D. My knowledge came from having a brother who died when I was fourteen and a sister with Down's syndrome and from experiencing my share of personal failures as well as the deaths of two parents. In other words, I know about pain, and this knowledge is the most valuable thing I own when I need to understand somebody. As I put myself in the other person's place, I am aware of what my own wounds feel like, and I can be fairly certain that the other person's wounds feel similar.

We have different life experiences and different genes, but we are all emotionally wired in the same way. We all hurt or feel shame or guilt as we are battered by life. When I talk about these universal feelings with a client who has difficulty knowing what she feels, I am confident that something will resonate with her and she will respond. I won't get everything right as I make my educated guesses, but I will be right enough so the pump will be primed, and eventually the client will recognize and claim her own feelings. She might begin to correct me: "You're right about this and this, but you're not right about that." When she starts correcting me, I know that she is becoming engaged in exploring herself. My role was simply to start the process by "pretending to know."

I don't believe that some people (say, experienced therapists) knows things that other people can't know. I believe an observant third-grader can diagnose a person who is in pain and can tell if that person is *hurt* or *mad* or *difficult* or a *predator* or a *victim*. The diagnosis is easy if a person knows the categories. The real skill in therapy is knowing how to listen to and care about and make room for people, and then to help them reframe their own experiences so that they can accept themselves more easily.

If a therapist does have a special talent, it is probably a talent for reframing a client's experience so the client can recognize his or her own value and courage. Therapists may help clients look at a trait they consider a weakness and then help them turn it over so they can see it is also a strength. This reframing is often accomplished by the use of metaphors and myths, communicating to clients that they are not alone, that all of us have experienced the kinds of things they find disturbing, and that we all have to find a way to get through it somehow.

It is useful to look at the therapist/client relationship in the context of the McMillan Relationship Theory. The tasks of therapist and client are the same as the tasks of individuals in a love relationship as described in this book. The theory describes what goes on in a strong therapeutic relationship (even if therapist and client would not view their behavior in the context of this particular theory).

Spirit

Therapists must tell our clients the truth; we must give the client the sense that he belongs with us; we must make sure the client sees that he is known and accepted and loved.

All of this is done within the boundaries of the therapeutic relationship. The session begins and ends at the therapist's discretion; it takes place in the therapist's space, a space that is bounded and made sacred by the lock on the door and the absence of interruptions. The therapist avoids having a dual relationship with the client: we do not have sex with the client, and we do not exploit the client. We keep our therapeutic relationship within its bounds so the therapeutic process can be protected.

Trust

To develop trust the therapist must make some sacrifices. We must give up our ego completely to the client and sacrifice our time, greed, lust, and narcissistic needs and wants to the role of therapist. The client sacrifices money.

The authority structure in this relationship is clear: the authority is the client, for he is the one who ultimately knows the truth about himself. He is in charge of his reality and of what goes on during the therapy hour. The therapist retains the power to set boundaries of time and space as described.

Relationship norms are flexible within limits. Therapists must keep confidential what we learn in the therapy room, and we must not consume our clients. In other words, the client should never be an object from whom the therapist benefits (except monetarily). The client must not tear up the therapist's office or inflict physical harm on the therapist. Other than that, the client may have a great deal of freedom, including the freedom to scream or yell or say whatever he wants to say.

Trade

There are a lot of subtle trades between client and therapist; a big one is the trading of money for empathy. In return for money the therapist gives the client empathy and love.

Effective therapists love their clients, and often this love does not go away. The client, however, never has to feel guilty about leaving the relationship. After she leaves therapy, she need not stay in contact with the therapist. She never has to write a note or make a phone call to let us know how things are going. The client can take the therapist's love and walk away, for she has already given the therapist what the therapist deserves.

For some therapists, this is a hard sacrifice. Some therapists miss their clients when they leave—even though they do want them to leave, for that is the outcome which is best for the clients. The therapist's job is to love and let go, over and over again. It's a difficult job, and that is one reason a therapist is paid money.

The most important medium of exchange in therapy, however, is not money for empathy. It is the expression of "how each feels about the other in the present moment." This is a powerful exchange. Every therapist tries to help a client talk about the immediate moment and how she feels about the relationship with the therapist. If a therapist can get the client to come alive in the moment and process how she feels about the relationship—a task that requires courage and is difficult—the client can begin to know what intimacy is. She can begin to experience telling the truth about a relationship in the moment.

The therapist must be careful not to make demands on our clients to expose themselves before they are ready. The therapist must respect the client's rhythms about how she moves into her pain and her reality. As is true of any form of intimacy, we cannot force therapeutic intimacy; we must allow it to happen.

Art

The therapist can help the client find art in his life. We can help him form his experience into a redeeming story of overcoming adversity with the client as the main character and hero, performing difficult tasks, suffering and retreating, fighting the odds and overcoming them. This is a story that belongs to all of us, for life is a tragedy, and we must have the courage to live in spite of the fact that we're going to die. Living in the face of all this takes a great amount of courage—and everyone who comes into my office has at least that amount of courage.

The therapist can help the client create art forms with his stories, help him find honor in his stories, and help him find his symbols. In this way, the therapist uses art to reframe experience.

The Couple in Therapy

There is an added dimension when a therapist treats a couple. Not only must we be careful to love both partners with equal strength and to honor the therapeutic contract with both, but we must also work to help the partners develop and strengthen the bonds and interactions within their relationship.

The therapist encourages the partners to speak their truths to each other, and we help them find ways to show each other that they belong together and that each can be known, accepted, and loved.

The therapist helps the couple—sometimes as a "referee," sometimes as a teacher—as the two struggle to learn the skill of listening with empathy.

The therapist can help the couple develop and bring into consciousness important elements of their relationship such as boundaries, the balance of power, and fair trading. Through encouraging development of stories and symbols, the therapist uses art to help a couple see and remember that what they are working on *together* is important and honorable.

How to Find a Therapist

Meet with a therapist for a session to see if you feel comfortable with that person. If you feel the therapist understands you and has the capacity to care about you—if you make a connection that makes you want to go back and talk some more—then go back. If you find yourself talking to a therapist who does not seem really there for you, don't go back. Look for a new therapist.

Notes

Chapter I

1. Love requires safety for the truth. Several studies suggest that people feel safer in expressing angry feelings to people they know rather than to strangers (Wright, 1943; Gage and Suci, 1951; Pepitone and Reichling, 1955; Bugental and Lehner, 1958). Several more recent studies indicate that people disclose more if they feel safe (Canary and Spitzberg, 1989; Brandt, 1989; Canary and Cupach, 1988; Prager, 1989; Roscoe, Kennedy, and Pope, 1987). A study that is closer to the point is one by Wood (1971). He found that subjects who made an effort to make those around them emotionally safe (i.e., subjects who were sensitive to others' feelings) were seen as more attractive. Antonuccio et al. (1987) confirmed this finding. Fitzgerald (1962) found that women were more likely to self-disclose to women they liked than to women with whom they felt no affinity. Ehrlich and Graveson (1971) extended this finding by demonstrating that the amount of self-disclosure one is willing to make is dependent on how safe (as expressed in knowing and liking) one is with the listener.

2. Boundaries define who is "in" and who is "out," who belongs and who doesn't. Most social-science studies on the subject of boundaries focus on the role of the deviant and the group process of scapegoating. In *Wayward Puritans*, Kyle Erikson (1966) demonstrated that deviants are used to establish boundaries. He recounted the banishment of Anne Hutchinson as a heretic in 1637, the persecution of the Quakers from 1656 to 1665, and the Salem witch trials in 1692. For each of these incidents, Erikson showed how the sense of order and authority was deteriorating among the Puritans. To remedy this, the Puritans found an enemy around which they could unite. The discovery of an enemy who was not like them served to shore up their boundaries and define who the Puritans were and who they were not.

Among the many social-science experiments on this point, one clearly demonstrates the effect of boundaries on the strength of the social bond. Buss and Portnoy (1967) created two experimental conditions. In one, they told their subjects (all Americans) that they were testing the pain tolerance of Americans as compared to that of Russians. After this explanation the experimenters administered electric shock. Of course there was really no comparable test for Russians. In the second condition the same procedure was followed, but subjects were told that they were being compared to Canadians. As you might guess, the subjects' pain tolerance was greater when the comparison group was the Russians — at that time, the cold-war enemy of the United States. This study demonstrated that the clearer the boundaries between "us" and "them," the more strongly people feel their common bond.

More recently Forsyth (1988) replicated this phenomenon of scapegoating to define group boundaries in a social-science experiment. Other recent studies confirm this principle (Alexander, 1986; Stein, 1989; Ng, 1989). Kalma and Ellinger (1985) found that groups created boundaries defining the *us vs. them* in circumstances of scarcity and lack of resources. Vernberg (1990) found that newcomers to seventh and eighth grades had difficulty penetrating the boundaries of social peer groups. Several studies suggest that spatial boundaries create privacy, and with this distance in place, people find intimacy easier (Keller, 1986; Kaplan, 1988; Weenig, 1990; Weiss, 1987). Simon and Pettigrew (1990) and Karasawa (1988) found that the more cohesive the group, the more clearly defined were group boundaries.

Social-science literature, as it explores the social use of boundaries, is out of balance in its sympathy for the deviant. Deviants often use groups to get special attention by testing limits, just as groups use deviants in the definition of group boundaries. The literature does little to investigate this phenomenon. More and more in the 1990s, the popular literature and social science are beginning to recognize that boundaries serve as protection against threat. As boundaries separate "us" from "them," they allay our fears by identifying whom we can trust as "one of us."

3. Backman and Secord (1959), in a classic study, gave all subjects a psychological test — then they ignored the results. They deceived the subjects by reading a mock list of names of persons among the subject group who were likely to be fond of one another, according to the test. The remaining subjects' names were not mentioned. Following a meeting introducing this group of strangers to one another, the subjects responded to sociometric questioning, ranking the people they liked best. The persons on the list of "likely to be fond of one another" ranked significantly higher on their sociometric ladder than those whose names were not mentioned. This experimental treatment created the impression that they were likely to be welcome. The manipulation of expectation of belonging or being welcome created a bond between the subjects. This study makes the point that we are most fond of those whom we believe will make us welcome.

A study of high-school football teams demonstrated that acceptance creates group cohesion (Westre and Weiss, 1991). This was demonstrated again in study of psychotherapy groups (Rugel, 1987).

4. In one set of studies (Kelley and Shapiro, 1954; Dittes and Kelley, 1959), experimenters focused on acceptance. They manipulated the subjects to believe that they would be accepted and liked by the group (just as Jack did with Jan and Phil). They exposed the subjects and controls to the group. Then they asked the subjects to rate how attracted they were to the group. As predicted, those who believed themselves to be accepted found the group more attractive.

In a second set of studies (Pepitone and Wilpizeski, 1960; Pepinsky, Hemphill, and Shevitz, 1958) rejection was the manipulated variable. The experimenters led one group of subjects to believe they were accepted by the group and another to believe they were rejected. Obviously the rejected ones were significantly less attracted to the group than the accepted ones. These experiments and the story of Jan and Phil make the same point: When you believe you are welcome and wanted, you are more likely to share your sacred secrets.

5. See note 2 above.

6. See note 1 above.

7. See note 3 above.

8. See note 4 above.

Chapter II

1. Festinger (1950) conducted the classic study of paying dues. Festinger joined a religious cult that believed the world was coming to an end in a cataclysmic explosion. To prepare for this the members of the cult sold everything they owned, gave the proceeds to the poor, and prayed together daily "until the end time." Festinger hypothesized that when the world didn't end, the cult members would not change their beliefs because they had sacrificed so much that they couldn't give up their faith. The "end time" came and passed. The cult members prayed and waited for their leader to explain what had happened. After much silent prayer and meditation, the leader announced that God had spoken to him in a vision. He said that their faith and prayer had so impressed God that God had decided to save all humankind because of them.

The studies examining personal attraction (Schopler and Bateson, 1962; Berkowitz and McCaulay, 1961; Zander and Cohen, 1955) followed the same design as Jackson (1959), with basically the same correlational results. Jackson studied office workers in a welfare agency. He asked the subjects to indicate the persons who had given the most (i.e., paid the most dues) to the agency. Then he asked the subjects to indicate how attracted to that group they were. Those who were judged as contributing the most to the group found the group most attractive.

Ingram (1986) defined paying dues as a personal testimony in front of a church congregation. He found that such dues-paying increases a person's status in the group. Rugel's (1987) study of therapy groups indicated that the more one invests in a group, the more one is accepted by the group. Recently these studies have investigated the limits of this concept (Swann, 1992). Seta, Seta, and Erber (1993) found that there is a limit to the amount of sacrifice that creates closeness. If the sacrifice is too much, the person will be repelled by the group because the group will have violated a basic sense of justice.

2. Social scientists have demonstrated that these forces operate concurrently (Grossack, 1954; Thrasher, 1954; Taguiri and Kogan, 1960; Carron, Widmeyer, and Brawley, 1988; Newmann et al., 1989; Miller, 1990; Steel, Shane, and Kennedy, 1990). Grossack's experimental paradigm perhaps makes the point best. He gave one set of subjects the instruction to work together cooperatively. He gave the other group of subjects the instruction to compete against one another as they worked. He assumed that these instructions would create high-cohesive or low-cohesive groups. He found that in the "cooperative" group, members made more attempts at influencing their fellows and accepted more pressure to conform than did subjects in the competing groups. The forces of love, intimacy, and cohesiveness operate from individual participant to the relationship (or group) and from the relationship (or group) to the person concurrently, all together, all at the same time. Order, authority, and justice create the atmosphere for the exchange of power.

3. Power is dangerous. Lawler (1992) found that the more unequal the distribution of power, the meaner and more ruthless are all parties in the group. Fung (1991) found that people exerted greater personal force when they were in a strong position in relation to people who were in a weaker position. People exerted less personal force when they were in a weaker position relative to others who were in a stronger position. And finally he found that people used greater personal force when they believed they were in the right. The point here is that power is dangerous, but when people believe they are following a transcendent principle they are inspired to passion. Thus a principle that is set above personalities can be used effectively as an authority. Seta, Seta, and Erber (1993) found that when groups expected more from their members than was considered fair, those groups lost the allegiance of their members. Chin

(1990) also observed the principle of justice as a cohesive force in a study of Hong Kong Chinese College students.

Cottrell, Eisenberger, and Speicher (1992) studied wary, suspicious college students. They found that when these students interacted with peers, their distrust was contagious. Probably the obverse is that trust is contagious. Roark and Sharah (1989) compared factors of empathy, self-disclosure, acceptance, and trust to see which of these were more effective in producing intimacy. They found trust to be the most important of these factors.

4. Hamblin (1958) subjected some experimental groups to unresolvable tasks through arbitrary game rule changes. They were treated with ambiguity and offered unclear expectations; the control groups were not. After the tasks were over, the experimental groups exhibited less helpfulness, less praise for co-participants, and greater antagonism than the controls. We can conclude that a clear decision-making strategy for a relationship is required for love to grow.

Several studies suggest that for members of a group to be attracted to a group, an authority structure must exist that enforces group norms and makes group decisions (Bettenhausen and Murighan, 1991; Griffith, 1988; Hazani, 1987; Littlepage, Cowart, and Kerr, 1989).

5. Several studies of group cohesiveness make the point that people become more cohesive when they know what to expect from one another (Bettenhausen and Murighan, 1991; Dobbins and Zaccaro, 1986; Fucher and Keys, 1988; Keller, 1986; Zahrly and Tosi, 1989).

6. Several studies show that the concept of members conforming to group norms is associated with group cohesiveness (Festinger, 1950; Kelley and Woodruff, 1956; Berkowitz, 1954).

Thibaut and Strickland (1956) used an experimental design that created a contrast in subject identification with a group. They used two subject populations: a group of strangers and a group of "positively associated individuals" (i.e., fraternity pledges). They exposed subjects in both populations to two types of experimental treatment. The experimenter gave the subjects either a *group orientation* suggesting that they would be working together as a team or a *task orientation* suggesting that those present were working to complete the task as individuals. The second treatment manipulated the subject's belief that he/she was in the minority of the group with regard to judgments. The result was that those subjects who (a) perceived themselves to be in the minority, (b) were among strangers, and (c) received a task orientation were the least conforming. Those subjects who were positively identified with the group and who were given a group orientation were more conforming.

Thus, the more association with the group (i.e., the more cohesiveness), the more pressure to conform.

In a study of coaching strategies of high-school football teams, Westre and Weiss (1991) found that teams were more cohesive when the coach appealed to the principle of serving the team rather than the coach.

7. See note 1 above.

8. See note 3 above.

Chapter III

1. Tantum (1990) studied shame in groups. He contended that shame is a primitive response to the breakdown of one's social presentation. When such a breakdown in pride, self-esteem, and dignity occurs, one is likely to become self-destructive, appear shame-faced, become resentful and brazen, and compulsively self-disclose.

2. Several studies in the social-science literature demonstrate that status is part of the bargain you can get from relationships (Hurwitz, Zander, and Hymovitch, 1960). Kelley's (1951) study taken together with Cohen's (1958) study graphically make this point. Kelley studied the exhibition of friendly behavior. He found that low-status but potentially mobile subjects exhibited friendly behavior to high-status subjects. This was not true for low-status nonmobile individuals. Cohen (1958) replicated Kelley's study and found nonmobile, low-status individuals to be friendlier to those within their own subgroup than to low-status mobile subjects. Brawley, Carron, and Widmeyer (1988) confirmed the relationship between status and cohesion. These two studies suggest that when people believe they cannot get any reward from those outside their group, they are not motivated to try to create friendships with those outside their group. But when people consider themselves to be mobile (in terms of social status), they will establish friendships with those outside their group who are in positions to which they aspire. Status seems to be something that is part of love's bargain.

3. Several studies demonstrate that people choose to associate with persons who have a valued skill or resource more readily than they do with those who do not (Burnstein, Stotland, and Zander, 1961; Baron, 1969; Zander and Havelin, 1960).

Spink (1990) found that competence and success in volleyball teams was attractive.

The point is clearer in a number of studies of groups in difficulty or under pressure to perform (Ziller and Behringer, 1960). Kleiner (1960) used two subjects and one stooge to form experimental groups who were asked to work on a puzzle. In each group the stooge was clearly helpful.

The groups were ostensibly compared with business executives on their ability to solve puzzles. The experimenters varied the degree of threat of failure. Participants liked the stooge most when the threat of failure was highest and the stooge's aid seemed to help reduce the threat.

The point of these studies is that we love people who can help us.

4. A relationship must be rewarding to both parties in order to survive. This is called *reinforcement*. Lott and Lott (1965) in their excellent review of the group-cohesiveness literature stated: "It is taken for granted that individuals are attracted to groups as a direct function of the satisfaction they are able to derive within them" (p. 284). Since this is taken for granted, we have little empirical evidence to clarify exactly what is reinforcing in a relationship or group membership. Rather, most theory and research in this area only underscore the contention that if people associate, it must be reinforcing to do so. Since individuals and the groups that they compose are so varied, we cannot define precisely what reinforcements bind people together into a cohesive group. In this book I contend that love is partially a product of a bargain between two people. The intimacy will be as strong as the bargain was effective at meeting the needs of both parties to the bargain. In addition to a relationship meeting the needs of its parties, a love will be more enduring if the relationship can continually find ways to juxtapose and integrate the parties' needs and resources into a bargaining process that is continuous.

Most group researchers do not attempt to distinguish among the types of interdependencies that bind people together. Conclusions are rather general. For example, Newcomb (1956) stated that the amount of reinforcement one experiences while interacting with another is the major independent variable determining attraction to the other. Heider (1946) observed that a person tends to like another whom he/she has benefited and who also has benefited him/her. Lazarsfeld and Merton (1954) agreed that reward is the primary factor in friendship formation. Thibaut and Kelley (1959) used more elaborate language to make the same point: "A person's attraction to a dyad depends upon his/her evaluation of his/her outcome in relation to his/her comparison level" (p. 24). In plain English, people evaluate the possibilities and choose the best deal — whatever benefits them most.

Several other studies make the point that people are attracted to relationships that benefit them (Cline, 1989; Cline and Musolf, 1985; Donovan and Jackson, 1990; Lashley et al., 1987; Prager, Fuller, and Gonzalig, 1989). Homans (1961) defines cohesiveness in specific terms of its rewards to the person: "Cohesiveness refers to the value of different kinds of rewards available to members of the group; the more valuable to a group's members are the activities they receive from other members or from the environment, the more cohesive it is" (p. 88).

Even if these social scientists don't know how to talk simply, I expect you can tell that they agree with Machiavelli and are basically capitalists in their ideas of love. People will love whatever rewards them.

5. We label most of the research on humans trading to protect themselves from emotional pain as *consensual validation*. This means that we humans need to know that others understand in the same way the things we see, feel, and understand. The force of this comes from pressure on the individual to conform and to become part of a consensus, to not be separate from the group. Several experimenters have made this point (Solomon, 1960; Kipnis, 1961; Fiedler, 1954; Backman and Secord, 1962; Preston et al., 1952; Davitz, 1955; Rasmussen and Zander, 1954; Stotland, Zander, and Natsoulas, 1961; Taguiri, 1958; Taguiri, Blake, and Bruner, 1953; Taguiri, Bruner, and Blake, 1958).

Howard and Berkowitz (1958) used what, I think, was the best experimental paradigm to demonstrate this. Researchers gave the subjects a task. Four observers evaluated their performance. In each circumstance, three judges agreed in their positive or negative evaluation. However, in every circumstance, one judge's evaluation deviated from the consensus. Subjects reliably chose the evaluator who deviated from the consensus as the one with whom they would least like to work. They made this choice regardless of whether the deviant's evaluation was positive or negative. Their study indicates that a person appreciates consensual validation more than positive feedback.

The organizational-development literature uses the term *groupthink* to represent the power of the search for similarity among groups. This literature is basically a complaint about this force. Most contend that consensus provides security for group members and inhibits creativity and individuality. Though there may be debate about whether or not the press toward conformity is positive, most of these groupthink studies confirm that it exists (McCauley, 1989; Posner-Weber, 1987; Turner et al., 1992).

Greene (1989) in his study of cohesion and productivity in work groups found that group consensus is associated with productivity and cohesion in groups. In a study of psychotherapist/patient relationships, Klein and Friedlander (1987) found that when the patients perceive themselves to be similar to the therapist, they are more attracted to the therapist. In a study of the effect of perceived homogeneity on interpersonal communication in groups, Storey (1991) found the perceived homogeneity made group interaction easier. Bernard et al. (1992) found that group consensus increased group cohesion and created room for dissent and disagreement in groups without hurting the cohesion of the group.

6. Social science hasn't produced many studies about the complementarity of resources and needs. There is, however, a great deal of research about people being attracted to success (Chapman and Campbell, 1957; Goodacre, 1951; Berkowitz, 1956; Sacks, 1952; Peterson and Martens, 1972; Deutsch, 1959; Klein and Christiansen, 1960; Myers, 1962; Thibaut, 1950; Wilson and Miller, 1961; Stendler, Damrin, and Haines, 1951; Phillips and D'Amico, 1956; Deutsch, 1959; Gottheil, 1955; Jennings, 1950; Bandura and Huston, 1961; Solomon, 1960).

Riley produced the study that makes this point specifically (1970). He matched groups for compatibility on the Firo-B scale. This scale measures the need for affection and other qualities and the tendency to express affection and other qualities. The study matched a group of persons expressing a need for affection with those who were likely to express affection. Riley found that groups matched in this way for compatibility were more cohesive than those who were less compatibly matched.

Dyce and O'Connor (1992) studied bar bands and found it important that the band members' personalities complemented one another. He found that if the groups were successful in integrating the different personality styles, they were more cohesive as a group and more successful professionally.

In general, the social-science literature supports the notion of the song "You Get a Line and I'll Get a Pole"—a great bargain. Love is expressed in the joy of having a resource that satisfies the need of the partner. A good team continually makes good bargains together.

7. Polzer, Neale, and Glenn (1993) found that intimacy makes people more generous to their intimates (perhaps without calculating).

Chapter IV

1. The research literature provides resounding support of the Contact Hypothesis (Gullahorn, 1952; Stotland, Cottrell, and Laing, 1960; Stotland and Cottrell, 1962; Norfleet, 1948; Maissonneuve, Palmade, and Fourment, 1952; Byrne and Buehler, 1955; Gullahorn, 1952; Kipnis, 1957; Jackson, 1950; Sherif, White, and Harvey, 1955; Heber and Heber, 1953; Wilson and Miller, 1961; Palmore, 1955; Deutsch and Collins, 1958; Mann, 1959; Allan and Allen, 1971; Griffith, 1989; Schectrman, Vurembrand, and Malajah, 1993; Sampson, 1991; Sharabany and Weisman, 1993).

Gullahorn's (1952) is a good example of these studies. In his study of clerical workers, he found that the distance between desks was the single most important factor in determining workers' rate of interaction. In addition there was a tendency for those who "interacted" most frequently to develop "sentiments of friendship."

Many of these studies were conducted to find a cure for our nation's racial prejudice. The hope of these studies was that if people of different colors could spend time together, prejudice would evaporate.

Gundlach's (1956) study cast some doubt on this theory. He studied a leftist labor organization that supported the ideal of equal employment opportunity for all, regardless of race. From his sample of this group, Gundlach found prejudice where the contact hypothesis would least predict to find it. The labor union members who had the highest frequency of contact with blacks of similar education and social aims were the most hostile and derogatory toward blacks.

Cook (1970) suggested that it took conditions in which racial expectations were broken before the contact hypothesis might work to mitigate prejudice.

Rainey and Sweickert (1988) conducted an exploratory study of an athletic team after a ten-day road trip. The question they posed was *Would the ten days of uninterrupted contact bring team members closer?* The answer was no.

Gundlach (1964), Cook (1970), Rainey and Sweickert (1988), the Walton brothers, the Protestants and Catholics in Northern Ireland, the Jews and Germans in pre–World War II Germany, whites and African Americans in the South, prison guards and prisoners, and common sense all suggest that *contact is not enough to produce love.*

2. A few studies help demonstrate the value of the dramatic element in an event (Berkowitz, Levy, and Harvey, 1957; Wilson and Miller, 1961; Wright, 1943; Lanzetta et al., 1954; Lanzetta, 1955). These studies follow the same experimental paradigm, more or less, as Wright (1943). Wright created a shared "valent" (important) event by subjecting pairs of children to a frustrating experimental task (like canoeing a level-three river). As a result of this common frustration the pairs increased their cooperative behavior and decreased time spent in conflict. Lanzetta (1955) used a similar design and found that the groups subjected to a common threat (i.e., a shared valent event) were more sociable, cooperative, and friendly than groups who were not under such a threat.

Clark, Goering, and Tomlinson (1991) studied groups that went on a canoe trip together. They found that the canoe trip event increased the group's sense of belonging and the ability of the members to talk with one another.

Schneider (1993) studied eleven patients in a psychiatric unit in a Jerusalem hospital during the Gulf War crisis of 1991. He found that the crisis bonded patients and helped them develop trust.

Gal and Manning (1987) and Grant (1993) demonstrated that threatening events make groups more cohesive.

3. See Chapter II, note 1 above.

4. Several research studies confirmed that ambiguity is likely to make a relationship difficult (Hamblin, 1958; Mann and Mann, 1959; Kalma and Ellinger, 1985; Simon, 1990; Sodentani and Gudylennst, 1987).

In a study of classroom behavior Mann and Mann created task study groups. They gave some groups a list of books to read and discuss. They gave others no reading list and no structure for meetings. All groups met four hours a week for three weeks. The sociometric ratings among group members increased in the groups with structure. In the group with ambiguity and no structure, sociometric ratings among members decreased.

5. The research literature confirms the importance of success in bonding (Wilson and Miller, 1961; Shelley, 1954; Heber and Heber, 1953; Hoffman, 1958; Zander and Havelin, 1960; Myers, 1962; Granito and Rainey, 1988; Wright and Duncan, 1986). Shelley set the basic design of these studies (1954). He manipulated success or failure in talk groups. Success groups reported higher cohesiveness and more favorable attitude toward the group.

So nothing succeeds in bringing people closer than success, and nothing pushes them apart like failure.

6. See Chapter III, note 1 above.

7. Several studies make the same point on the topic of humiliation (Festinger, 1953; Pepitone and Kleiner, 1957; Stotland, 1959; Spector, 1956; Lott and Lott, 1960; James and Lott, 1964). Several experimental paradigms have tested both sides of the honor/humiliation hypothesis. One psychologist, for example, had high-school students rank words and phrases according to their expectations of which words and phrases would be most familiar to their fellow students. Initially they did this ranking privately; then they did it openly after group discussion of what others thought; then privately again. They followed this by giving the correct ranking to the subjects assembled in the group. In this last feedback session they told the group which members were the least successful in the task. Each person's success or failure in the task was the most significant determiner of his/her attraction to people in the group. Experiments like this one make the point that cruelty is the enemy of love. And kindness is love's friend.

8. Schlorshere (1989), writing about sense of community among college students, suggested that symbolic rituals create a sense of belonging and of being a part of something important. Gregory (1986) studied a group of Air Force personnel who developed and used their own language. This code signified membership and sense of belonging. When symbols emerge from intimacy, this is evidence of an enriching and deepening phase of relationship development.

9. See note 2 above.

10. See note 1 above.

11. See note 7 above.

12. See note 8 above.

13. As a serious student of this theory can see, much of my theory (especially in Chapter IV) exceeds its social-scientific base. There are two reasons for that. One is my laziness for not looking hard enough. The second is that theory is almost always ahead of research. The job of research is to test ideas. I hope that these ideas might be further tested in future social-science literature.

References

Alexander, Richard D. "Ostracism and Indirect Reciprocity. The Reproductive Significance of Humor." *Ethology and Sociology* 7 (1986): 253–70.

Allan, T. H., and K. H. Allen. "Sensitivity Training for Community Leaders." *Proceeding of the Annual Convention of the APA* 6 (1971): 557–58.

Antonuccio, David O., Cheryl L. Davis, Peter M. Lewinsohn, and Julia S. Breckenridge. "Therapist Variables Related to Cohesiveness in a Group Treatment of Depression." *Small Group Behavior* 18 (1987): 557–64.

Backman, C., and P. Secord. "The Effect of Perceived Liking on Interpersonal Attraction." *Human Relations* 12 (1959): 379–84.

———. "Liking, Selective Interaction, and Misperception in Congruent Interpersonal Relations." *Sociometry* 25 (1962): 321–25.

Bagby, R. Michael, James D. Parker, and Alison S. Bury. "A Comparative Citation Analysis of Attribution Theory and the Theory of Cognitive Dissonance." *Personality and Social Psychology Bulletin* 16 (1990): 274–83.

Bandura, A., and A. C. Huston. "Identification as a Process of Incidental Learning." *Journal of Abnormal and Social Psychology* 63 (1961): 311–18.

Baron, R. M. "Cognitive Dissonance and Projected Hostility toward Outgroups." *Journal of Social Psychology* 79 (1969): 171–82.

Berkowitz, L. "Group Standards, Cohesiveness, and Productivity." *Human Relations* 7 (1954): 509–19.

———. "Group Norms under Bomber Crews: Patterns of Perceived Crew Attitudes, and Crew Liking Related to Air Crew Effectiveness in Far Eastern Combat." *Sociometry* 19 (1956): 141–53.

Berkowitz, L., B. Levy, and A. R. Harvey. "Effects of Performance Evaluations on Group Integration and Motivation." *Human Relations* 10 (1957): 195–208.

Berkowitz, L., and J. McCaulay. "Some Effects of Differences in Status Level and Status Stability." *Human Relations* 14 (1961): 135–48.

Bernard, J. S. *The Sociology of Community.* Glenview, Ill.: Scott, Foresman, 1973.

Bernard, William A., Carol Baird, Marilyn Greenwalt, and Ray Karl. "Intragroup Cohesiveness and Reciprocal Social Influence in Male and Female Discussion Groups." *Journal of Social Psychology* 132 (1992): 179–88.

Bettenhausen, Kenneth L., and J. Keith Murighan. "The Development of an Intragroup Norm and the Effects of Interpersonal and Structural Challenges." *Administrative Science Quarterly* 36 (1991): 20–35.

Brandt, Laurie, M. "A Short Term Group Therapy Model for Treatment of Adult Female Survivors of Childhood Incest." *Group* 13 (1989): 74–82.

Brawley, Lawrence R., Albert V. Carron, and W. Neil Widmeyer. "Exploring the Relationship between Cohesion and Group Resistance to Disruption." *Journal of Sport and Exercise Psychology* 10 (1988): 199–213.

Bugental, D., and G. F. Lehner. "Accuracy of Self-Perception and Group Perception as Related to Two Leadership Roles." *Journal of Abnormal and Social Psychology* 56 (1958): 396–98.

Burnstein, E., E. Stotland, and A. Zander. "Similarity to a Model and Self-Evaluation." *Journal of Abnormal and Social Psychology* 62 (1961): 257–64.

Buss, A. H., and N. W. Portnoy. "Pain Tolerance and Group Identification." *Journal of Personality and Social Psychology* 6 (1967): 106–8.

Byrne, D., and J. A. Buehler. "A Note on the Influence of Propinquity upon Acquaintanceships." *Journal of Abnormal and Social Psychology* 51 (1955): 147–48.

Canary, Daniel J., and William R. Cupach. "Relational and Episodic Characteristics Associated with Conflict Tactics." *Journal of Social and Personal Relationships* 5 (1988): 305–25.

Canary, Daniel J., and Brian H. Spitzberg. "A Model of the Perceived Competence of Conflict Strategies." *Human Communication Research* 15 (1989): 630–49.

Carron, Albert V., W. Neil Widmeyer, and Lawrence R. Brawley. "Group Cohesion and Individual Adherence to Physical Activity." *Journal of Sport and Exercise Psychology* 10 (1988): 127–38.

Chapman, L. J., and D. T. Campbell. "An Attempt to Predict the Performance of Three-Man Teams from Attitude Measurements." *Journal of Social Psychology* 46 (1957): 277–86.

Chin, Chi Yue. "Distributive Justice Among Hong Kong Chinese College Students." *Journal of Social Psychology* 130 (1990): 649–56.

Clark, Carrie, Paula Goering, and Grant Tomlinson. "Client Perceptions of White Water Canoeing." *Psycho-Social Rehabilitation Journal* 14 (1991): 71–76.

Cline, Rebecca. "The Politics of Intimacy: Costs and Benefits Determining Disclosure Intimacy in Male-Female Dyads." *Journal of Social and Personal Relationships* 6 (1989): 5–20.

Cline, Rebecca J., and Karen E. Musolf. "Disclosure as Social Exchange: Anticipated Length of Relationship, Sex Roles and Disclosure Intimacy." *Western Journal of Speech Communication* 49 (1985): 43–56.

Cohen, A. R. "Upward Communication in Experimentally Created Hierarchies." *Human Relations* 11 (1958): 410–54.

Cook, S. W. "Motives in Conceptual Analysis of Attitude Related Behavior." In *Nebraska Symposium on Motivation,* edited by W. J. Arnold and D. Levine. Lincoln: University of Nebraska Press, 1970.

Cottrell, Norman, Robert Eisenberger, and Hilda Speicher. "Inhibiting Effects of Reciprocation Wariness on Interpersonal Relationships." *Journal of Personality and Social Psychology* 62 (1992): 658–68.

Davitz, J. "Social Perception and Sociometric Choice of Children." *Journal of Abnormal and Social Psychology* 50 (1955): 173–76.

Deutsch, M. "Some Factors Affecting Membership Motivation and Achievement Motivation in Group." *Human Relations* 12 (1959): 81–95.

Deutsch, M., and M. Collins. "The Effect of Public Policy in Housing Projects upon Interracial Attitudes." In *Readings of Social Psychology,* edited by Eleanor Maccoby, T. M. Newcomb, and E. L. Hartley. 3d ed. New York: Holt, 1958.

Dittes, J. W., and H. H. Kelley. "Effects of Different Conditions of Acceptance upon Conformity to Group Norms." *Journal of Abnormal and Social Psychology* 53 (1959): 100–107.

Dobbins, Gregory H., and Stephen Zaccaro Jr. "The Effects of Group Cohesion and Leader Behavior on Subordinate Satisfaction." *Group and Organization Studies* 11 (1986): 203–19.

Donovan, Regina L., and Barry L. Jackson. "Deciding to Divorce: A Process Guided by Social Exchange, Attachment and Cognitive Dissonance." *Journal of Divorce* 13 (1990): 23–25.

Dyce, Jamie, and Brian P. O'Connor. "Personality Complementarity as a Determinant of Group Cohesion in Bar Bands." *Small Group Research* 23 (1992): 185–98.

Ehrlich, J. J., and D. B. Graveson. "Reciprocal Self-Disclosure in a Dyad." *Journal of Experimental Social Psychology* 7 (1971): 389–400.

Erikson, K. *Wayward Puritans.* New York: John Wiley and Sons, 1966.

Ettin, Mark F. "Within the Group's View: Clarifying Dynamics Through Malpractice and Symbolic Imagery." *Small Group Behavior* 17 (1986): 407–26.

Festinger, L. "Informal Social Communication." *Psychological Review* 57 (1950): 271–82.

———. "Laboratory Experiments: The Role of Group Belongingness." In *Experiments in Social Process,* edited by J. G. Miller. New York: McGraw-Hill, 1950.

———. "Group Attraction and Membership." In *Group Dynamics: Research and Theory,* edited by D. Cartwright and A. Zander. Evanston, Ill.: Row, Peterson, 1953.

Fiedler, F. E. "Assumed Similarity Measures as Predictors of Team Effectiveness." *Journal of Abnormal and Social Psychology* 49 (1954): 381–88.

Fitzgerald, M. P. "Relationship between Expressed Self-Esteem Similarity and Self-Disclosure." *Dissertation Abstracts* 22 (1962): 4402.

Forsyth, Dan. "Tolerated Deviance and Small Group Solidarity." *Ethos* 16 (1988): 398–420.

Fucher, Ann, and Christopher Keys. "Group Development in Self-Help Groups for College Students." *Small Group Behavior* 19 (1988): 325–41.

Fung, Samuel S. "The Effects of Power, Relationship and Purpose in Gaining Compliance." *Contemporary Social Psychology* 15 (1991): 44–52.

Gage, N. L., and G. Suci. "Social Perception and Teacher-Pupil Relations." *Journal of Educational Psychology* 42U (1951): 144–52.

Gal, Reuven, and Frederick J. Manning. "Morale and Its Components: A Cross-National Comparison." *Journal of Applied Social Psychology* 17 (1987): 369–91.

Goodacre, D. M. "The Use of a Sociometric Test as a Predictor of Combat Unit Effectiveness." *Sociometry* 14 (1951): 148–52.

Gottheil, E. "Changes in Social Perceptions Contingent upon Competing or Cooperating." *Sociometry* 18 (1955): 132–37.

Granito, Vincent J., and David W. Rainey. "Differences in Cohesion between High School and College Football Teams and Starters and Non-Starters." *Perceptual and Motor Skills* 66 (1988): 471–77.

Grant, Peter R. "Ethnocentrism in Response to a Threat to Social Identity." *Journal of Social Behavior and Personality* 8 (1993): 143–54.

Greene, Charles N. "Cohesion and Productivity in Work Groups." *Small Group Behavior* 20 (1989): 70–86.

Gregory, Stanford W. "A Sociolinguistic Indicator of Group Membership." *Journal of Psycholinguistic Research* 15 (1986): 189–207.

Griffith, James. "Measurement of Group Cohesion in U.S. Army Units." *Basic and Applied Social Psychology* 9 (1988): 149–71.

———. "The Army's New Unit Personnel Replacement and Its Relationship to Unit Cohesion and Social Support." *Military Psychology* 1 (1989): 17–34.

Grossack, M. M. " Some Effects of Cooperation and Competition." *Journal of Abnormal and Social Psychology* 59 (1954): 341–48.

Gullahorn, J. "Distance and Friendship as Factors in the Gross Interaction Matrix." *Sociometry* 15 (1952): 123–34.

Gundlach, R. H. "Effects of On-the-Job Experience with Negroes upon Racial Attitudes of White Workers in Union Shops." *Psychological Reports* 2 (1956): 67–77.

Hamblin, R. L. "Group Integration During a Crisis." *Human Relations* 2 (1958): 67–76.

Hazani, Moshe. "Prevention of Delinquency through Repentance: An Ethnographic Study in a Jerusalem Slum." *Small Group Behavior* 18 (1987): 82–89.

Heber, R. F., and M. E. Heber. "The Effect of Group Failure and Success on Social Status." *Journal of Educational Psychology* 48 (1953): 276–84.

Heider, F. "Attitudes and Cognitive Organization." *Journal of Psychology* 21 (1946): 107–12.

Hoffman, L. R. "Similarity of Personality: A Basis for Interpersonal Attraction." *Sociometry* 21 (1958): 300–308.

Homans, G. C. *Social Behavior: Its Elementary Form.* New York: Harcourt, Brace, 1961.

Howard, R. C., and L. Berkowitz. "Reactions to the Evaluators of One's Performance." *Journal of Personality* 26 (1958): 494–507.

Hudgins, Katherine, and Donald J. Kiesler. "Individual Experimental Psychotherapy: An Analogue Validation of the Intervention Module of Psychodramatic Doubling." *Psychotherapy* 24 (1987): 245–55.

Hurwitz, J. E., A. F. Zander, and B. Hymovitch. "Some Effects of Power on the Relations among Group Members." In *Group Dynamics: Research and Theory,* edited by D. Cartwright and A. Zander. 2d ed. Evanston, Ill.: Row, Peterson, 1960.

Ingram, Larry C. "Testimony and Religious Cohesion." *Religious Education* 81 (1986): 295–309.

Jackson, J. M. "Reference Group Processes in a Formal Organization." *Sociometry* 22 (1959): 307–27.

James, A., and A. J. Lott. "Reward Frequency and the Formation of Positive Attitudes toward Group Members." *Journal of Social Psychology* 62 (1964): 111–15.

Jennings, H. H. *Leadership and Isolation.* 2d ed. New York: Longmans, Green, 1950.

Kalma, A. P., and E. Ellinger. "The Impact of Uncertainty and Insufficient Resources in Intergroup Bias." *Psychologic* 13 (1985): 29–43.

Kaplan, Kalma J. "Teaching Individuals to Live Together." *Transactional Analysis Journal* 18 (1988): 220–30.

Karasawa, Minoru. "The Effects of Cohesiveness and Inferiority upon Ingroup Favoritism." *Japanese Psychological Research* 30 (1988): 49–59.

Keller, Robert T. "Predictors of the Performance of Project Groups in R & D Organizations." *Academy of Management Journal* 29 (1986): 715–26.

Kelley, H. H. "Communication in Experimentally Created Hierarchies." *Human Relations* 4 (1951): 39–56.

Kelley, H. H., and M. M. Shapiro. "An Experiment on Conformity to Group Norms Where Conformity Is Detrimental to Group Achievement." *American Sociology Review* 19 (1954): 667–77.

Kelley, H. H., and C. L. Woodruff. "Members' Reactions to Apparent Group Approval of a Counternorm Communication." *Journal of Abnormal and Social Psychology* 52 (1956): 67–74.

Kipnis, D. M. "Interaction between Members of Bomber Crews as a Determinant of Sociometric Choice." *Human Relations* 10 (1957): 263–70.

———. "Changes in Self-Concepts in Relation to Perceptions of Others." *Journal of Personality* 29 (1961): 449–65.

Klein, Jill G., and Myrna L. Friedlander. "A Test of Two Competing Explanations for the Attractiveness Enhancing Effects of Counselor Self-Disclosure." *Journal of Counseling and Development* 66 (1987): 82–85.

Klein, M., and G. Christiansen. "Group Composition, Group Structure, and Group Effectiveness of Basketball Teams." In *Sport Culture and Society*, edited by J. W. Loy and C. D. Kenyon. London: Macmillan, 1969.

Kleiner, R. J. "The Effects of Threat Reduction upon Interpersonal Attraction." *Journal of Personality* 28 (1960): 145–55.

Kotler, Tamara. "Patterns of Change in Marital Partners." *Human Relations* 42 (1989): 829–56.

Lanzetta, J. T. "Group Behavior under Stress." *Human Relations* 8 (1955): 29–52.

Lanzetta, J. T., D. Haefner, P. Langham, and H. Axelrod. "Some Effects of Situational Threat on Group Behavior." *Journal of Abnormal and Social Psychology* 3 (1954): 445–53.

Lashley, Joyce K., Eric H. Gamble, Charles E. Grenier, George A. Roundtree et al. "An Empirical Account of Temperature Biofeedback Applied in Groups." *Psychological Reports* 60 (1987): 379–88.

Lawler, Edward J. "Power Processes in Bargaining." *Sociological Quarterly* 33 (1992): 17–34.

Lazarsfeld, P. J., and R. K. Merton. "Friendship as Social Process: A Substantive and Methodological Analysis." In *Freedom and Control in Modern Society*, edited by M. Berger, T. Abel, and S. H. Page. New York: Van Nostrand, 1954.

Littlepage, Glenn E., Louis Cowart, and Bernalette Kerr. "Relationships between Group Environment Scales and Group Performance and Cohesion." *Small Group Behavior* 20 (1989): 50–61.

Lott, A. J., and B. Lott. "Group Cohesiveness as Interpersonal Attraction: A Review of Relationships with Antecedent and Variables." *Psychological Bulletin* 64 (1965): 259–309.

Lott, B., and A. J. Lott. "The Formation of Positive Attitudes toward Group Members." *Journal of Abnormal and Social Psychology* 61 (1960): 284–300.

Maissonneuve, J., G. Palmade, and C. Fourment. "Selective Choices and Propinquity." *Sociometry* 15 (1952): 135–40.

Mann, J. H. "The Effect of Inter-Racial Contact on Sociometric Choices and Perceptions." *Journal of Social Psychology* 50 (1959): 143–52.

Mann, J. H., and C. H. Mann. "The Importance of a Group Task in Producing Group Member Personality and Behavior Changes." *Human Relations* 12 (1959): 75–80.

McCauley, Clark. "The Nature of Social Influence in Group Think: Compliance and Internalization." *Journal of Personality and Social Psychology* 57 (1989): 250–60.

McClure, Bud H., and Constance D. Foster. "Group Work as a Method of Promoting Cohesiveness Within." *Perceptual and Motor Skills* 73 (1991): 307–13.

Miller, Danny. "Organizational Configurations, Cohesion, Change and Prediction." *Human Relations* 43 (1990): 771–89.

Myers, A. "Team Competition, Success and the Adjustment of Group Members." *Journal of Abnormal and Social Psychology* 65 (1962): 325–32.

Newcomb, T. M. "The Prediction of Interpersonal Attraction." *American Psychologist* 11 (1956): 575–86.

Newmann, Fred M., Robert A. Rutter, and Marshall S. Smith. "Organizational Factors That Affect School Sense of Efficacy, Community and Expectations." *Sociology of Education* 62 (1989): 221–38.

Ng, Sik Hung, and Shelley Wilson. "Self Categorization Theory and Belief Polarization among Christian Believers and Atheists." *British Journal of Social Psychology* 28 (1989): 47–56.

Norfleet, B. "Interpersonal Relations and Group Productivity." *Journal of Social Issues* 4 (1948): 66–69.

Palmore, E. B. "The Introduction of Negroes into White Departments." *Human Organization* 14 (1955): 27–28.

Pepinsky, P. N., J. K. Hemphill, and R. N. Shevitz. "Attempts to Lead, Group Productivity and Morale under Conditions of Acceptance and Rejection." *Journal of Abnormal and Social Psychology* 57 (1958): 47–54.

Pepitone, A., and R. Kleiner. "The Effects of Threat and Frustration on Group Cohesiveness." *Journal of Abnormal and Social Psychology* 54 (1957): 192–99.

Pepitone, A., and G. Reichling. "Group Cohesiveness and the Expression of Hostility." *Human Relations* 8 (1955): 327–37.

Pepitone, A., and G. Wilpizeski. "Some Consequences of Experimental Rejection." *Journal of Abnormal and Social Psychology* 60 (1960): 359–64.

Peterson, J. A., and R. Martens. "Success and Residential Affiliation as Determinants of Team Cohesiveness." *Research Quarterly* 43 (1972): 63–76.

Phillips, B. N., and L. A. D'Amico. "Effects of Cooperation and Competition on the Cohesiveness of Small Face-to-Face Groups." *Journal of Educational Psychology* 47 (1956): 65–70.

Polzer, Jeffrey T., Margaret H. Neale, and Patrick O. Glenn. "The Effects of Relationships and Justification in an Interdependent Allocation Task." *Group Decision and Negotiation* 2 (1993): 135–48.

Posner-Weber, Cheryl L. "Update on Group Think." *Small Group Behavior* 18 (1987): 118–25.

Prager, Karen J. "Intimacy Status and Couple Communication." *Journal of Social and Personal Relationships* 6 (1989): 435–49.

Prager, Karen J., Doris O. Fuller, and Antonio S. Gonzalig. "The Function of Self-Disclosure in Social Interaction." *Journal of Social Behavior and Personality* 4 (1989): 563–80.

Preston, M. G., W. L. Peltz, E. H. Mudd, and H. B. Froscher. "Impressions of Personality as a Function of Marital Conflict." *Journal of Abnormal and Social Psychology* 47 (1952): 326–36.

Rainey, David W., and Gerald J. Sweickert. "An Exploratory Study of Team Cohesion Before and After a Sporting Trip." *Sport Psychologist* 2 (1988): 314–17.

Rasmussen, G., and A. Zander. "Group Membership and Self Evaluation." *Human Relations* 7 (1954): 239–51.

Reid, Kenneth E. "The Use of Confrontation in Group Treatment: Attack or Challenge?" *Clinical Social Work Journal* 14 (1986): 224–37.

Riley, R. "An Investigation of the Influence of Group Compatibility of Group Cohesiveness and Change in Self-Concept in a T-Group Setting." Ph.D. diss., University of Rochester, 1970.

Roark, Albert E., and Hussein S. Sharah. "Factors Related to Group Cohesiveness." *Small Group Behavior* 20 (1989): 62–69.

Roscoe, Bruce, Donna Kennedy, and Terry Pope. "Adolescents' Views of Intimacy: Distinguishing Intimate from Non-Intimate Relationships." *Adolescence* 22 (1987): 511–16.

Rugel, Robert P. "Achieving Congruence in Tavistock Groups: Empirical Findings and Implications for Group Therapy." *Small Group Behavior* 18 (1987): 108–17.

Sacks, E. L. "Intelligence Scores as a Function of Experimentally Established Relationships between Child and Examiner." *Journal of Abnormal and Social Psychology* 47 (1952): 354–58.

Sampson, Robert J. "Linking the Micro- and Macrolevel Dimensions of Community Social Organization." *Social Forces* 70 (1991): 43–64.

Schectrman, Zupora, Neoni Vurembrand, and Neli Malajah. "Development of Self-Disclosure in a Counseling and Therapy Group for Children." *Journal for Specialists in Group Work* 4 (1993): 189–99.

Schlorshere, Nancy K. "Marginality and Mattering: Key Issues in Building Community." *New Directions for Student Services* (winter 1989): 5–15.

Schneider, Stanley. "Group Analytical Psychotherapy under Threat of War: The Gulf Crisis, Special Section: In Times of National Crisis." *Group Analysis* 26 (1993): 99–108.

Schopler, J., and N. A. Bateson. "A Dependence Interpretation of the Effects of a Severe Initiation." *Journal of Personality* 30 (1962): 633–49.

Seta, John J., Catherine E. Seta, and Maureen W. Erber. "The Role of Costs in Generating Expectations and Value: A Personal Equity Comparison Theory Analysis." *Basic and Applied Social Psychology* 14 (1993): 103–11.

Sharabany, Ruth, and Hodas Weisman. "Class Relationships in Adolescence: The Case of the Kibbitz." *Journal of Youth and Adolescence* 22 (1993): 671–95.

Shelley, H. P. "Level of Aspiration Phenomena in Small Groups." *Journal of Social Psychology* 40 (1954): 149–64.

Sherif, M., B. J. White, and O. J. Harvey. "Status in Experimentally Produced Groups." *American Journal of Sociology* 60 (1955): 370–79.

Simon, Bernard, and Thomas F. Pettigrew. "Social Identity and Perceived Group Homogeneity: Evidence for the Ingroup Homogeneity Effect." *European Journal of Social Psychology* 20 (1990): 269–86.

Smith, A. J. "Perceived Similarity and the Projection of Similarity: The Influence of Valance." *Journal of Abnormal and Social Psychology* 57 (1958): 376–79.

Sodentani, Lori L., and William B. Gudylennst. "The Effects of Surprising Events on Intercultural Relationships." *Communication Research Reports* 4 (1987): 1–6.

Solomon, L. "The Influence of Some Types of Power Relationships and Game Strategies upon the Development of Interpersonal Trust." *Journal of Abnormal and Social Psychology* 61 (1960): 223–30.

Spector, A. J. "Expectations, Fulfillment and Morale." *Journal of Abnormal and Social Psychology* 52 (1956): 51–56.

Spink, Kevin S. "Group Cohesion and Collective Efficacy of Volleyball Teams." *Journal of Sport and Exercise Psychology* 12 (1990): 301–11.

Steel, Robert P., Guy S. Shane, and Kenneth A. Kennedy. "Effects of Social System Factors on Absenteeism, Turnover and Job Performance." *Journal of Business and Psychology* 4 (1990): 423–30.

Stein, Howard F. "The Indispensable Energy and American-Soviet Relations." *Ethos* 17 (1989): 480–503.

Stendler, C., D. Damrin, and A. Haines. "Studies in Cooperation and Competition: I. The Effects of Working for Group and Individual Rewards on the Social Climate of Children's Groups." *Journal of Genetic Psychology* 79 (1951): 173–97.

Storey, Douglas. "History and Homogeneity: Effects of Perceptions of Membership Groups on Interpersonal Communication." *Communication Research* 18 (1991): 199–221.

Stotland, E. "Determinants of Attraction to Groups." *Journal of Social Psychology* 49 (1959): 71–80.

Stotland, E., and N. B. Cottrell. "Similarity of Performance as Influenced by Interaction, Self-Esteem, and Birth Order." *Journal of Abnormal and Social Psychology* 64 (1962): 183–91.

Stotland, E., N. B. Cottrell, and G. Laing. "Group Interaction and Perceived Similarity of Members." *Journal of Abnormal and Social Psychology* 61 (1960): 335–40.

Stotland, E., A. Zander, and T. Natsoulas. "Generalization of Interpersonal Similarity." *Journal of Abnormal and Social Psychology* 62 (1961): 250–56.

Swann, William B. "Dance with the One Who Bring Ya." *Psychological Inquiry* 3 (1992): 346–47.

Taguiri, R. "Social Preference and Its Perception." In *Person Perception and Interpersonal Behavior*, edited by R. Taguiri and L. Petrullo. Stanford: Stanford University Press, 1958.

Taguiri, R., R. R. Blake, and J. S. Bruner. "Some Determinants of the Perception of Positive and Negative Feelings in Others." *Journal of Abnormal and Social Psychology* 48 (1953): 585–92.

Taguiri, R., J. S. Bruner, and R. R. Blake. "On the Relation between Feelings and Perceptions of Feelings among Members of Small Groups." In *Readings in Social Psychology*, edited by E. Maccoby, T. Newcomb, and E. Hartley. 3d ed. New York: Holt, 1958.

Taguiri, R., and N. Kogan. "Personal Preference and the Attribution of Influence in Small Groups." *Journal of Personality* 28 (1960): 257–65.

Tantum, Digby. "Shame and Groups." *Group Analysis* 23 (1990): 31–43.

Thibaut, J. W. "An Experimental Study of the Cohesiveness of Underprivileged Groups." *Human Relations* 3 (1950): 251–78.

Thibaut, J. W., and H. H. Kelley. *The Social Psychology of Groups.* New York: Wiley, 1959.

Thibaut, J. W., and L. H. Strickland. "Psychological Set and Social Conformity." *Journal of Personality* 25 (1956): 115–29.

Thrasher, J. D. "Interpersonal Relations and Graduations of Stimulus Structure as Factors in Judgmental Variation: An Experimental Approach." *Sociometry* 17 (1954): 228–41.

Turner, Marlene E., Anthony R. Pratkinis, Prestin Probasco, and Craig Leve. "Threat, Cohesion and Group Effectiveness: Testing a Social Identity Maintenance Perspective on Group Think." *Journal of Personality and Social Psychology* 63 (1992): 781–96.

Vernberg, Eric M. "Experiences with Persons following Relocation During Early Adolescence." *American Journal of Orthopsychiatry* 60 (1990): 466–77.

Weenig, Mieneke W., Taco Schmidt, and Cess J. Midden. "Social Dimensions of Neighborhoods and the Effectiveness of Information Programs." *Environment and Behavior* 22 (1990): 27–54.

Weiss, Avrumi G. "Privacy and Intimacy: Apart and a Part." *Journal of Humanistic Psychology* 27 (1987): 118–25.

Westre, Kirk R., and Maureen R. Weiss. "The Relationship between Perceived Coaching Behaviors and Group Cohesion in High School Football Teams." *Sport Psychologist* 5 (1991): 41–54.

Wilson, W., and N. Miller. "Shifts in Evaluations of Participants following Intergroup Competition." *Journal of Abnormal and Social Psychology* 63 (1961): 428–31.

Wood, H. G. "An Analysis of Social Sensitivity." *Dissertation Abstracts International* 32 (1971): 1200.

Wright, M. E. "The Influence of Frustration upon the Social Relations of Young Children." *Character and Personality* 12 (1943): 111–22.

Wright, Thomas L., and Douglas Duncan. "Attraction to Group, Group Cohesiveness and Individual Outcome: A Study of Training Groups." *Small Group Behavior* 17 (1986): 487–92.

Zahrly, Jan, and Henry Tosi. "The Differential Effect of Organizational Induction Process on Early Work Role Adjustment." *Journal of Organizational Behavior* 10 (1989): 59–74.

Zander, A., and A. R. Cohen. "Attributed Social Power and Group Acceptance: A Classroom Experimental Demonstration." *Journal of Abnormal and Social Psychology* 51 (1955): 490–92.

Zander, A., and A. Havelin. "Social Comparison and Interpersonal Attraction." *Human Relations* 13 (1960): 21–32.

Ziller, R. C., and R. D. Behringer. "Assimilation of the Knowledgeable New Comer under Conditions of Group Success and Failure." *Journal of Abnormal and Social Psychology* 60 (1960): 288–91.

Beyond Words Publishing, Inc.

Our corporate mission:

INSPIRE TO INTEGRITY

Our declared values:

We give to all of life as life has given us.
We honor all relationships.
Trust and stewardship are integral to fulfilling dreams.
Collaboration is essential to create miracles.
Creativity and aesthetics nourish the soul.
Unlimited thinking is fundamental.
Living your passion is vital.
Joy and humor open our hearts to growth.
It is important to remind ourselves of love.

Our promise to our customers

We will provide you with the highest quality books
and related products that meet or exceed your
expectations. As our customer, you will be satisfied
with your purchase and will receive your order
promptly, or we will refund your money.

To order or to request a catalog, contact
Beyond Words Publishing, Inc.
20827 N.W. Cornell Road, Suite 500
Hillsboro, OR 97124-9808
503-531-8700 or 1-800-284-9673